SOCIO-HISTORICAL EXAMINATION OF RELIGION AND MINISTRY:
A JOURNAL OF THE GLOBAL CENTER FOR RELIGIOUS RESEARCH

VOL. 3, NO. 1
SUMMER 2021

Copyright © 2021

www.shermjournal.org

ISSN 2637-7519 (print)
ISSN 2637-7500 (online)
ISBN 978-1-7362739-4-4 (print)
ISBN 978-1-7362739-5-1 (eBook)

GCRR Press
1312 17th Street Suite 549
Denver, CO 80202
www.gcrr.org

Printed copies of this issue are available for purchase on the GCRR website at www.gcrr.org/products.

General Editor:
Darren M. Slade, PhD

Editorial Advisory Board:
Abimbola A. Adelakun, PhD
Abbas Aghdassi, PhD
Gbenga Emmanuel Afolayan, MA
Peter Antoci, PhD
Robert Gregory Cavin, PhD
Mike Clawson, PhD
Sandra Cohen, MaHL
Carlos Colombetti, PhD
Jack David Eller, PhD
Evan Fales, PhD
Anthony Gill, PhD
Ken Howard, MDiv, MEd
Charles David Isbell, PhD
Mark A. Moore, PhD
Josh Packard, PhD
Josfin Raj S.B, MDiv, ThM
Elisa Robyn, PhD

Typesetters & Copyeditors:
Kimberly Dell
Christian Farren
Allison Guy
Katie Curlee Hamblen
Holly Lipovits
Kortland Phillips
Hannah Purtymun
Amanda Reser

Socio-Historical Examination of Religion and Ministry (SHERM Journal) is a biannual (not-for-profit) peer-reviewed academic journal that publishes the latest social-scientific, historiographic, and ecclesiastic research on religious institutions and their ministerial practices. SHERM is dedicated to the critical and scholarly inquiry of historical and contemporary religious phenomena, both from within particular religious traditions and across cultural boundaries, so as to inform the broader socio-historical analysis of religion and its related fields of study.

The purpose of SHERM Journal is to provide a scholarly medium for the social-scientific study of religion where specialists can publish advanced studies on religious trends, theologies, rituals, philosophies, socio-political influences, or experimental and applied ministry research in the hopes of generating enthusiasm for the vocational and academic study of religion while fostering collegiality among religion specialists. Its mission is to provide academics, professionals, and nonspecialists with critical reflections and evidence-based insights into the socio-historical study of religion and, where appropriate, its implications for ministry and expressions of religiosity.

Editorial Advisory Board
SHERM journal is a division of the non-profit organization, the FaithX Project, and therefore receives endowments from FaithX to maintain a significant presence within academia and the broader faith community. Nonetheless, the journal is overseen by an independent, religiously unaffiliated Editorial Advisory Board to ensure the content of the published articles meet stringent standards of critical scholarship uninfluenced by theological or ideological allegiances.

Copyright Privileges
When publishing an article through SHERM, authors are able to retain copyright privileges over their research. As part of the rights agreement, however, all authors wishing to publish their research through SHERM must transfer exclusive licensing rights over to SHERM, thereby granting SHERM the right to claim the article as part of its publishing proprietary corpus. Authors retain copyright credit for the article while SHERM becomes the sole publisher of the material. Because SHERM is a non-restrictive licensing publication, authors (as copyright owners of their research) are allowed to share and repost their article on any platform of their choosing.

As partners with SHERM, upon acceptance and publication of an article, authors are automatically granted the right to share, disseminate, use, and repost their article in any way they deem necessary to expand the visibility of their publication. Likewise, authors retain all intellectual property rights, including the specific research content and data employed throughout the article, as well as the right to retain attribution rights as the article's original creator and writer.

Licensing Transfer
As the sole licensee of all the articles, SHERM retains the exclusive right to publish, distribute, or transfer the license of an article to other third parties for private and commercial purposes. SHERM reserves the right to create and authorize the commercial use of all published articles.

In order to make the articles available to as many audiences and researchers as possible, SHERM reserves the right to post (and repost even after initial publication of) all articles in any form or media as allowable by the newest technological developments. Currently, this means SHERM will post all articles to numerous open access websites and social media platforms. SHERM also reserves the right to advertise the publication of any article through various mediums.

By transferring exclusive licensing rights to SHERM, authors agree to the following stipulations:
- Authors cannot republish their article (either in English or in another language) with a different academic journal (without express consent from SHERM).
- Authors who repost their article online must incorporate a citation that indicates SHERM as the publisher of the content (including a link to the original article on the SHERM website, as well as the volume and issue number).
- Authors who wish to use portions of the article for other publications or work must cite the original SHERM publication.
- SHERM is granted authorization to impose copyright infringements laws, as well as combat instances of plagiarism against third parties on behalf of the author(s).

No part of this journal or issue may be used, copied, or reproduced in any manner without written permission from the editors except in the case of brief quotations embodied in critical articles, reviews, and other scholarly publications. In accordance with the "fair use" agreement of Title 17 U.S.C. Section 107 of the US Copyright Act, the following permissions are granted for the express purposes of teaching, research, and scholarship: **Reproduction**—authors and readers can make multiple copies of individual articles without profit. **Distribution**—authors and readers can distribute and publicly display individual articles without profit. Opinions and conclusions expressed in SHERM are those of the individual article authors and do not necessarily reflect those of the Editorial Advisory Board, the FaithX Project, or other affiliated partners. For questions or permissions, contact the SHERM editorial staff: shermeditor@gmail.com.

Table of Contents

Vol. 3, No. 1
Summer 2021

Editorials

Genus Unbelief, Species Atheism: The Case for and Against Unbelief as a Master Concept for Non-Religion
 Jack David Eller 1

Dialogues in Philosophy

Inference to the Best Explanation and Rejecting the Resurrection
 David Kyle Johnson 26

Social-Scientific and Philosophical Research

A Fruitful or Wild French Vineyard? Distinguishing the Religious Roots of Albigenses and Waldensians in the Twelfth Century
 Ottavio Palombaro 54

Bayesian Reasoning's Power to Challenge Religion and Empirically Justify Atheism
 Richard Carrier 75

Epidemics and Religion: From Angry Gods and Offended Ancestors to Hungry Ghosts and Hostile Demons
 Louise Marshall 97

Ministry Research

"Jesus is a Stranger Here": The Healing Jesus Crusade and its Perception by the Muslim Community of Ede (Southwest Nigeria)
 Raheem Oluwafunminiyi, Siyan Oyeweso 119

'Emet: The Paradox of Death and Afterlife
 Zev Garber 143

TABLE OF CONTENTS
-CONTINUED-

Vol. 3, No. 1
Summer 2021

STUDENT HIGHLIGHTS

Crime and Sin in Early Medieval England
    Hannah Purtymun   169

BOOK REVIEWS

Faith After Doubt by Brian D. McLaren
    Deena M. Lin   182

The Date of the Muratorian Fragment by John F. Lingelbach
    Lucy C. Bajjani   194

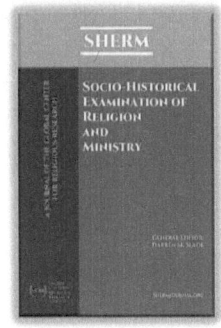

CALL FOR PAPERS!
SOCIAL-SCIENCES
HUMANITIES
PHILOSOPHY
MINISTRY

Submit Proposal

GCRR and SHERM Journal are accepting submission proposals for the following fields of study:

- Religious History
- Historical Theology
- Historical Jesus
- Psychology of Religion
- Sociology of Religion
- Anthropology of Religion
- Philosophy of Religion
- Religious Trends and Demographics
- Issues in Contemporary Theology
- Ancient, Medieval, and Contemporary Christian Literature
- Patristic, Medieval, and Contemporary Exegesis
- Ancient Near Eastern Languages and Writings
- Ancient Israelite Religion and Second Temple Judaism
- History and Literature of Contemporary Judaism
- Hebrew Bible
- New Testament
- Textual Criticism
- Islamic Studies
- Mormon Studies
- Native American Religion
- Hinduism, Buddhism, and Other World Religions
- Historical and Contemporary Religious Revivals and Sects
- New Religious Movements (Cults)
- Religious Violence
- Religious Liberty
- Freedom from Religion
- General Religious Studies

Ministry Research:
- Ancient, Medieval, and Contemporary Ministry Practices
- Experimental Faith Communities
- Ecclesiastical Trends and Issues
- Economic, Political, Social, and Ecological Issues in Ministry
- Ethical, Racial, Sexual, and Gender Issues in Ministry
- Case Studies / Case Reports

Genus Unbelief, Species Atheism: The Case for and Against Unbelief as a Master Concept for Non-Religion

Jack David Eller,
Global Center for Religious Research

<u>Abstract</u>: *Recent initiatives by Stein, Flynn, Conrad, and others have promoted 'unbelief' as a replacement, an 'umbrella term,' for concepts like atheism, secularism, and irreligion. In this essay I show that unbelief as it is currently construed cannot serve this function: it is simultaneously too broad (embracing not only irreligion but heterodox religious belief) and too narrow (focusing on religious belief to the exclusion of other types of belief), and it commits a taxonomic error of equating unbelief with categories above and below its level. However, I also argue that, once reformed and disciplined, unbelief is a valuable and essential tool, and I provide some resources and models for a future Unbelief Studies in the Credition Research Project and the literature on agnotology, as well as ethnographical material questioning the cross-cultural applicability of belief and unbelief. Finally, I charge Unbelief Studies with the mission not only to analyze belief but to criticize and ultimately banish it as a bad mental and linguistic habit that perpetuates mistakes and leaves individuals vulnerable to further faults while eroding social trust and facticity itself.*

<u>Keywords</u>: Atheism, Belief, Credition, Religion, Unbelief

There has recently been a campaign for the term "unbelief" as not only an analytical category but *the* analytical category for the study of "the decline of religion."[1] Like Nickolas Conrad, who most recently advocated the term, Tom Flynn's 2007 *The New Encyclopedia of Unbelief* finds "atheism" too "rigid" and "political" to suffice, and both take inspiration from Gordon Stein's previous incarnation of *The Encyclopedia of Unbelief*, which posited, thus,

> In the English language about the closest synonym for *unbelief*, as it is being used here, is heterodoxy. That word, in turn, can be said to mean

---

[1] Conrad, "An Argument for Unbelief," 7.

'not holding orthodox beliefs or traditional opinions'— on religious matters, in our context....This is the history of heresy, blasphemy, rejection of belief, atheism, agnosticism, humanism, and rationalism. In many respects, it is also the history of the intellectual progress of the human race.[2]

All three, and presumably other proponents of the term, promote it as inclusive and flexible—an umbrella term, Conrad calls it—and as untainted by atheist activism and identity politics. Whether the subjects of study are atheists or agnostics, humanists or deists, or apparently heretics and innovators, Flynn opines, "They're all unbelievers."[3]

There certainly is a lot of terminological confusion and disagreement in the field of secularism and non-religion, and we should welcome all—well, almost all—attempts to clarify and settle the differences and disputes. However, in this article I will position myself against unbelief as it is formulated by the scholars above; that is, unbelief is not a substitute for research on atheism, most assuredly not an equivalent for atheism or even for irreligion, and emphatically not a synonym for heterodoxy. I will, nevertheless, defend the virtue of unbelief as an analytical tool properly conceived, establishing some prolegomena to any future Unbelief Studies. Along the way I will argue that atheism is a type, a subcategory, of unbelief that still merits examination in its own right; that unbelief is not limited to religion; and that unbelief is the correct stance to take in response to all belief, belief being a bankrupt and bankrupting habit of mind to be distrusted if not discarded altogether.

The Case Against Unbelief

The problem with unbelief as construed by Stein, Flynn, and Conrad rests in the very quality that establishes its value for them, namely, its broadness; added to this are the implications that they impute to atheism, which perhaps describe how some atheists understand it, and themselves, but are not inherent in the concept itself. To take the former objection first, Conrad asserts that unbelief "exists on a spectrum" that covers the extensive ground of "the supernatural or intangible beliefs in things like progress, or unverifiable phenomena (spirituality, aliens, ghosts, spirits, ancestors, etc.)."[4]

---

[2] Stein, *The Encyclopedia of Unbelief*, xv.
[3] Flynn, *The New Encyclopedia of Unbelief*, 16.
[4] Conrad, "An Argument for Unbelief," 2.

I submit that this is not a "spectrum" at all (where precisely on the spectrum would you place ghosts and aliens relative to gods and progress—before, after, between?), but rather a congeries of dubious and mostly false ideas.

If we think of the jumble of beliefs as more of a field than a spectrum, the real problem pertains to the breadth of this field, which is at once ironically too wide and too narrow. As we saw, both Stein and Flynn imagine unbelief as synonymous with "heterodoxy"; Conrad joins them when he explicitly restates Stein's definition of unbelief as "the position of not holding orthodox beliefs or traditional opinions—on religious matters—and the rejection of authority and norms concerning spiritual practices."[5] But this cannot be right. If so, Martin Luther and every Protestant after him would be an unbeliever, whereas, they would ardently disavow that label; likewise, all of the Christian heretics before and since—Arians, Nestorians, Gnostics, and Donatists to Albigensians and Mormons *ad infinitum*—not to mention Shi'ite Muslims and Mahayana Buddhists—would be classified as unbelievers, despite the fact that they most assuredly have beliefs and usually quite strong ones. In a word, unorthodox belief is not unbelief, except from the perspective of the orthodox believer, but I am reasonably confident that the unbelief camp does not mean to take that perspective.

This moves us to a further contradiction, which is that unbelief in their sense is not necessarily *less* belief but often precisely *more* belief. When a heterodox or heretical belief branches off from an orthodox one, we now have *two* beliefs. We might better call the outcome not unbelief but *alterbelief*, another belief, an "other" belief; at the most, from the orthodox standpoint, it is *dys*belief, wrong-belief, but not no-belief. In other words, contrary to Conrad's pronouncement of the decline of religion, at least in a quantitative sense, what we witness is a multiplication of religions, demonstrated by the fact that there are more sects, denominations, cults, and new religious movements in the world today than ever before. If we are to take seriously Conrad's admonition not "to impose a type of belief [or unbelief] (and an ambiguous one) that they never confessed,"[6] then we cannot honestly call heterodox beliefs "unbelief," since the believers would never confess that of themselves.

The second issue that I, as a confessed atheist, have is the (mis)characterization of atheism, which allegedly drives the urgent need for a new and better term. Conrad writes, for instance, that atheism "implies a

---

[5] Conrad, "An Argument for Unbelief," 2.
[6] Conrad, "An Argument for Unbelief," 7.

social rupture and clean break with religion—a kind of identity politics—and not a partial or ambiguous rupture."[7] This is not entirely so and represents the first, but hardly the last, instance of the conflation of levels of analysis that we will see in the pro-unbelief camp. Strictly speaking, atheism (*a-theos*-ism) only entails the absence of god-beliefs (not even necessarily the informed and militant rejection of such beliefs). As there are many religions and other kinds of "spirituality" that do not include god(s), atheism is not by definition a "clean break with religion"; in practice, of course, most modern Western atheists are a-religious or anti-religious, but there is nothing logically or terminologically inconsistent with an atheist still entertaining beliefs about ancestor spirits or nature spirits or ghosts or nirvana, etc. (Ideally, if atheists' godlessness is based on evidence and logic, they would also dismiss spirits, ghosts, and such.) Furthermore, we know full well that many avowed atheists do not break cleanly with religion, sometimes attending religious services, celebrating religious holidays, enjoying religious music, or nursing lingering religious sentiments.

Some of the other concerns of the unbelief advocates vis-à-vis atheism are also unfounded. For example, Conrad warns us that "there are many 'atheisms'"[8] as if this is a surprise and a mortal blow to the term. Actually, the literature has productively illustrated that there are indeed multiple local atheisms across cultures and through history, including ones that were ascribed derogatorily to believers who happened to believe the wrong things, as with Roman accusations of atheism against early Christians. In the contemporary world, we are acquainted with numerous local variations and interpretations of atheism or godlessness, from French *laïcité* and Turkish *laiklik* to Scandinavian indifference to religion. India has been explored particularly thoroughly, by Johannes Quack and Renny Thomas among others. Quack reports on the Atheist Centre and the Maharashtra Andhashraddha Nirmulan Samiti or ANiS ('Organisation for the Eradication of Superstition'), finding that organized Indian atheism does not dwell on the existence of god(s) or the separation of church and state. Even Indian atheist organizations spend less time arguing about god(s) and more time on social issues such as "sex education, environmental concerns, gender equality, and [the] problem of alcohol addiction and ...'consumerism.'"[9] And when they attack religion their attacks are trained on domestic foes like Brahmanism or the Satya Sai Baba movement and such self-appointed "god-men." Similarly, Thomas discovers

---

[7] Conrad, "An Argument for Unbelief," 3.
[8] Conrad, "An Argument for Unbelief," 3.
[9] Quack, "Organised Atheism in India," 77.

that Indian scientists, some of whom are quite vocal in their atheism, see no incongruity in participating in religious activities; such scientific atheists "are comfortable practicing the lifestyle of a religion while identifying themselves as atheists."[10] No clean break from religion for them, apparently. As Grace Davie summarizes the situation from Europe, the specific forms of atheism will depend on the native cultural heritage, the prior model of church/state relations, new emergent models of religion, the diversity of the population, and the presence and actions of secular constituencies (organizations, scientists, and so on).[11]

Without belaboring the point, there have been plentiful previous attempts to specify typologies of atheism, and their precise merits are less relevant than the fact that alert researchers are fully aware that atheism is not a single monolithic entity. This realization overrules the pro-unbelief objection that atheism is inflexible and absolute, let alone that it is "biased towards Anglophone history."[12]

But we said that unbelief as promulgated by its sponsors is also too narrow, and this problem arises because belief/unbelief is virtually always presented in terms of religious belief. But of course, it goes without saying that religious beliefs are one subset—albeit a large and problematic subset—of beliefs in general, so we cannot use unbelief as an antonym for religion. This is acknowledged in Conrad's mention of "aliens" in his list of unbeliefs, which presumably opens the door to UFOs, Big Foot, and all manner of wacky ideas and conspiracy theories. Nevertheless, if we peruse the topics in Flynn's voluminous encyclopedia, they are more or less exclusively related to religion, and to the Christian religion to boot, an unsupportable narrowing of the scope of their concept.

The most serious fault with the current incongruous construction of unbelief is its ambivalent relationship with atheism. Backers of unbelief might respond that they understand that unbelief is not identical to atheism, that atheism is only one form or variety of unbelief—which is true enough—yet, if Conrad's paper is any indication, atheism seems to be the primary antagonist of the unbelief campaign: the word "atheism" and its permutations (atheist, etc.) occur 124 times in a 6,000-word essay and the whole thrust of the exercise is to make "a proposal to call the subject of this research *unbelief* versus *atheism*, the *secular*, or *irreligion*."[13] But unbelief cannot be employed

---

[10] Thomas, "Atheism and Unbelief among Indian Scientists," 63.
[11] Davie, "Belief and Unbelief: Two Sides of a Coin."
[12] Conrad, "An Argument for Unbelief," 3.
[13] Conrad, "An Argument for Unbelief," 1.

as a substitute for atheism or any of its cognates, because the two terms operate at very different conceptual levels. (Moreover, atheism is not a synonym for secularism or irreligion.) We would contend instead, as the title of this article suggests, that atheism is a species of the broader genus unbelief. But unbelief and atheism are actually still further apart taxonomically. If we imagine a Linnaean classification scheme, with 'species' at the lowest level, rising to 'genus,' then 'family,' 'order,' 'class,' 'phylum,' and at the highest and most inclusive level 'kingdom,' atheism is about midway in the classificatory chain and unbelief two levels above (see Figure 1).

Figure 1: A Taxonomy of Belief

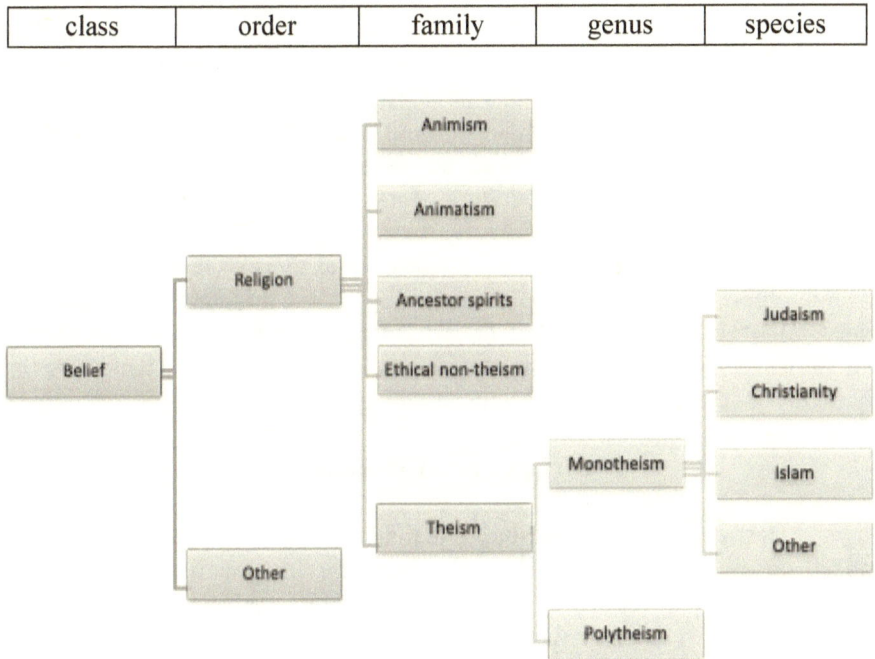

Atheism would apply as the antithesis or contrary of the family "theism," a category that co-exists with other families that would be exempt from the critique of atheism (animism, animatism, and ancestor-spirit religions posit other supernatural beings and forces besides gods, and ethical non-theism, like Theravada Buddhism, lacks gods by definition). Belief, as a Linnaean class, subsumes the order "religion" and other-than-religious belief, and unbelief would apply at this level and apply to all belief, not only religious. Parenthetically, we might envision that "belief" falls within the wider phylum "statements" or "propositions" where belong also the classes of knowledge, predictions, guesses, lies, and so forth (see below). Statements would join non-propositional utterances like questions, imperatives, and expletives in the kingdom "language" or "culture."

In conclusion, atheism is a perfectly fine and appropriate term and subject for scholarly research if we understand where and to what it refers. It is not the negation or refutation of all religion (religion residing one level above theism) nor of monotheism or Christianity specifically (lying one or two levels below, respectively). To deny atheism its rightful place as a subject of study would be like arguing that scientists should not study hominids (family) but only mammals (class)—or worse yet, that "mammal" is a satisfactory substitute for "hominid." Atheism is a fit object of analysis for those who are interested in that level of human thought and language; unbelief, at a different and higher position, is also fit for analysis if we understand and maintain unbelief at its appropriate classificatory level. However, unbelief in the current work of its exponents appears to vacillate up and down the taxonomic tree: properly a class opposed to the class of belief, it sometimes aims at religion (order), sometimes at theism (family), sometimes at monotheism (genus), and often enough at Christianity in particular (species). If unbelief-ers intend their term to refer to religion specifically, which it usually does implicitly, they should define it as such (which distorts the term) or select another level-appropriate term.

The Case for Unbelief

Despite this stern critique, I actually think that there is a valuable, indeed an essential, seat at the analytical table for unbelief. But that seat cannot be occupied until the term is considerably clarified and disciplined. Only then can we adopt unbelief as a master category that includes atheism most narrowly and irreligion less narrowly—as well as doubt and denial of other beliefs that have nothing to do with religion whatsoever. But expressly because unbelief is or should be an omnibus concept, it cannot be equated to its constituents; Figure 2 portrays unbelief as a domain encompassing irreligion, which in turn encompasses atheism. The figure also leaves plenty of room for other-than-religious unbelief.

Figure 2: Unbelief and its Subdomains Irreligion and Atheism

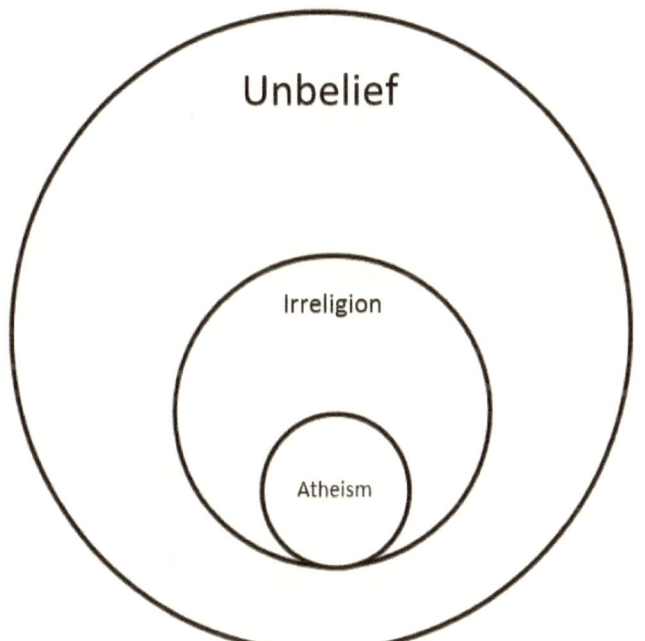

Secularism does not fall neatly and completely within the realm of unbelief or its subrealm of irreligion, because secularism is not universally anti-religious. As many observers have noted, especially in our post-secular age, secularism could mean (or could have meant) the utter annihilation of religion á la Marx, but it also can mean and has meant the reduction in the importance of religion for individuals or for society as a whole, the evacuation of religion from politics and the public square, the confinement of religion to a specific institutional setting, and/or the invasion of religious territory by "worldly" cultural elements and interests. For instance, Christian rap music marries the religious and the secular, and Raelianism constitutes a secularized version of some basic religious notions (e.g., that the "gods" are really advanced extraterrestrial beings called Elohim). Heterodoxy, on the other hand, usually represents a novel form of religion but not a form of unbelief, except from the viewpoint of the defenders of orthodoxy, and should be detached from unbelief conceptually (see Figure 3).

Figure 3: The Relationship between Unbelief, Heterodoxy, and Secularism

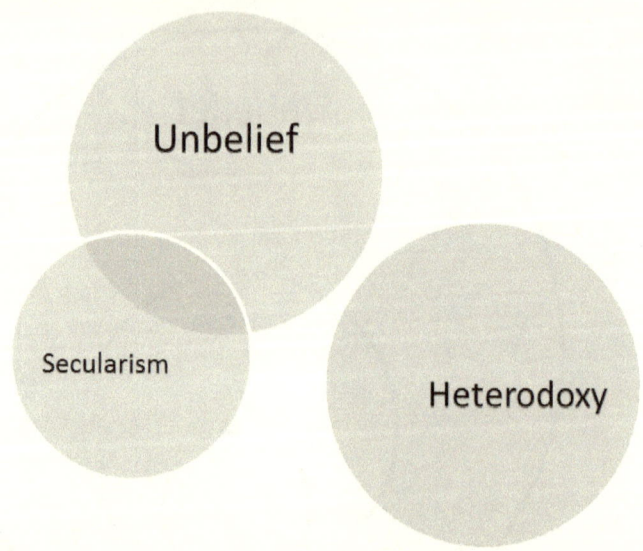

Having prepared the ground somewhat, a model for a future Unbelief Studies might be the Credition Research Project based at the University of Graz, Austria. Described most succinctly by its spokesman, Hans-Ferdinand Angel, in his contribution to the *Encyclopedia of Sciences and Religions*, its researchers replace the weary term "belief" with the more technical and unburdened term "credition" (from the Latin *credere*, believe, which also yields such words as "creed" and "credible"), intending to put belief on par with other psychological phenomena like cognition, emotion, perception, and so forth. Credition draws attention to belief as a process—"that is, on what happens 'while someone is believing,' rather than on the relationship between belief and knowledge" and links it with other mental processes including "empathy, perception, action control, memory, and the self-concept."[14] So far, credition researchers have identified four functions that drive belief/credition:

1. An enclosure function, which generates and modifies "those subsets of mind-sets, which are activated when a process of believing starts," i.e., "emotionally shaped propositions, such as vague ideas, confirmed

---

[14] Angel, "Credition, the Process of Belief," 536.

knowledge, values, moral claims, and intuitions," some of which are "mightier" than others.[15]
2. A converter function, which translates belief into action by, among other things, "reducing the number of choices and abbreviating the time of decision-making."[16]
3. A stabilizer function, which tends to "maintain" and "reduces the volatility" of creditions by putting them in contact and consonance with other "attitudes and mind-sets."[17]
4. A modulator function, which "highlights in a specific way the differences of individuals and the differences of situations," understanding that beliefs are not static entities but rather that credition is affected by body states, circumstances, and (although he does not discuss it) cultural context.

In the flagship publication of the project, *Processes of Believing: The Acquisition, Maintenance, and Change in Creditions*, Angel et al. assemble essays across a range of disciplines from philosophy and theology to economics and anthropology, but predominantly neuroscience, exposing the highly neurological and cognitivist thrust of the enterprise. Whether the project will bear fruit is yet to be determined, but for now it reveals the complex, dynamic nature of belief and, therefore, (although it is not their subject) unbelief, which is simultaneously epistemic and emotional and not by any means limited to religion.

Despite the intrinsic relation between belief and unbelief, *The New Encyclopedia of Unbelief* offers only one entry on belief, a limited treatment of the psychology of belief. And there is much more to consider than has been plumbed by credition researchers so far. In natural language usage, belief is a promiscuous term, and sorting out the language sharpens the analysis of belief. For example, English speakers use the word when what they mean is a propositional truth-claim ("I believe in God/that God exists," "I believe in vampires/that vampires exist," or "I believe in the Loch Ness monster/that the Loch Ness monster exists"), but also when they make other non-propositional statements like prediction ("I believe that it will rain tomorrow"), opinion ("I believe that Donald Trump is a great president"), taste or preference ("I believe that vanilla is the best flavor of ice cream"), extrapolation based on previous experience ("I believe that the sun will rise tomorrow"), valuation ("I

---

[15] Angel, "Credition, the Process of Belief," 537.
[16] Angel, "Credition, the Process of Belief," 538.
[17] Angel, "Credition, the Process of Belief," 538.

believe in straight marriage/that gay marriage is wrong"), more or less informed comparison, often without specification of criteria ("I believe that Tom Brady is the greatest quarterback in NFL history"; "No, I believe that Peyton Manning is the greatest quarterback in NFL history"). Most analyses and critiques of belief entertain only the first of these, the propositional/factual usage of belief, and most unbelief targets it exclusively as well.

However, the sprawling semantic range of belief cannot be pruned to propositional truth-claims alone—and in some languages, truth-claims are not the first or only function of belief. In an enlightening essay titled "Christians as Believers," Malcolm Ruel insisted that the ancient Greek and Hebrew equivalents of "to believe"—*pisteuo* and *'mn*, respectively—"express centrally the notion of trust or confidence….In classical Greek literature *pistis* [belief] means the trust that a man may place in other men, or gods; credibility, credit in business, guarantee, proof of something to be trusted."[18] The Hebrew term in particular "denotes even more directly a quality of relationship: it was used of the reliability or trustworthiness of a servant, a witness, a messenger, or a prophet, but it also served to characterize the relationship between God and his people, reciprocally trusted and trusting."[19] More interestingly, he traced the evolution of "belief" in Christian discourse from simple confidence to official creed ("I believe that...") to Reformation/Lutheran personal/internal commitment and finally to the present-day "adventure of faith rather than belief as a body of doctrine"[20]—in which, paradoxically, belief becomes the unbelief of Stein, Flynn, and Conrad, a liberated heterodox space of inventive ideas and practices. Worst of all for fans of belief, Ruel, like other informed researchers, declared that there is "little evidence that there is anything equivalent to Christian Belief in other world religions," let alone ancient and tribal religions.[21]

Some ancients employed belief in yet other senses. The great sceptic Sextus Empiricus taught that the verb form *piethesthai* could mean "to assent to something by choice," sometimes "with a kind of affinity that comes from desiring it strongly," whereas, it could also imply "not resisting by simply following, without strong inclination or attachment, as a boy is said to 'mind' his tutor."[22] As we see, the Greek word meant belief in the form of being persuaded but also the much weaker state of obeying, minding, or going

---

[18] Ruel, "Christians as Believers," 38.
[19] Ruel, "Christians as Believers," 38.
[20] Ruel, "Christians as Believers," 50.
[21] Ruel, "Christians as Believers," 51.
[22] Hallie, *Sextus Empiricus*, 95.

along. Fascinatingly and significantly, the antonym *apeitho* has just one meaning—*to disobey*—suggesting that from among its synonyms, obedience or conformity may be more central to belief than propositional agreement.

We encounter a similar situation in modern French, according to Jean Pouillon. Depending on the preposition, the verb *croire* (to believe) conveys divergent meanings and moods. "To believe [*croire*] is to state a conviction; it is also to add a nuance to that conviction: 'I believe' [*je crois*] often signifies 'I'm not sure.' This ambiguity involves the subjective side of belief [*croyance*]."[23] He explained that *"Croire á* is to state that something exists; *croire en* ... is to have confidence; *croire que* is for something to be represented in a certain way."[24] Belief in French, as in English, is hopelessly polysemous, the meanings of which are by no means mutually exclusive. But he went beyond this key point to make a more controversial one:

> [If] a believer believes in [*croire en*, "trusts in"] God, he feels no need to say that he believes in [*croire á*] God's reality; he believes in [*croire á*] it, one would say, implicitly. But is this certain? In fact, the believer not only need not say that he believes in [*croire á*] the existence of God, but he need not even believe in [*croire á*] it; precisely because in his eyes there can be no doubt about it: the existence of God is not believed in [*crue*], but perceived. On the contrary, to make God's existence an object of belief, to state this belief, is to open up the possibility of doubt—which begins to clarify the ambiguity with which we started. So one could say that it is the unbeliever who believes that the believer believes in [croire á] the existence of God.[25]

A mature field of Unbelief Studies must confront this semantic diversity of belief. The work of Ruel, Pouillon, and others suggests that even in the West the semantic range of "belief" covers three distinct but often overlapping denotations. One, to be sure, is a truth-claim—that X exists or possesses Y qualities. Let us call this the "correctness" denotation. The second is an expression of trust, "I believe that my wife will pick me up at the airport" is a trust statement, more or less well-founded depending on how reliable my wife has been in the past. Let us call this the "confidence" denotation. The third (e.g., "I believe in love" or "I believe in America") is a profession of attachment or partisanship; it establishes what side you are on. Let us call this

---

[23] Pouillon, "Remarks on the Verb 'To Believe,'" 1.
[24] Pouillon, "Remarks on the Verb 'To Believe,'" 2.
[25] Pouillon, "Remarks on the Verb 'To Believe,'" 2.

the "commitment" denotation. For a familiar illustration of the distinctions, garden-variety Christians may acknowledge the reality of Satan (correctness) but not trust (confidence) him or devote themselves (commitment) to him; a Satanist, on the other hand, holds that Satan is real, places trust in him, and pledges allegiance to him. Unbelief Studies cannot ignore the non-propositional aspects of belief, just as the credition project has tried to integrate emotional and even corporal variables. Belief must be regarded as a multi-dimensional phenomenon with three axes, each with a sliding scale—uncertain to certain correctness, hesitant to enthusiastic confidence, and tepid to rabid commitment—each varying independently and all subject to change over time, yielding quite an array of belief positions and intensities.

The complications are considerably amplified when we add linguistic and cultural diversity, which neither the creditionists nor most religionists and irreligionists have contemplated. We should not be surprised to hear, as anthropologist Rodney Needham taught almost fifty years ago, that concepts of belief vary across cultures and that, at the extreme, "there are apparently languages in which ... there is no verbal concept at all which can convey exactly what may be understood by the English word 'believe.'"[26] A few ethnographic examples will suffice. The eminent ethnographer E. E. Evans-Pritchard, in his classic study of Nuer (east Africa) religion, concluded that there is "no word in the Nuer language which can stand for 'I believe.'"[27] Instead, the Nuer said that they *ngath* their god/spirit (*kwoth*), which he contended we should translate as "trust," not "believe in." I can confirm from my own fieldwork in Australia that Aboriginal peoples like the Warlpiri lack an indigenous term for belief and would not indulge in or recognize talk like "I believe in the *jukurrpa* (Dreaming or Dreamtime)" or "I believe in the ancestor spirits."

In places where an indigenous concept of belief does appear, it often functions quite unlike the Western variety. The Akha of highland Burma have a word for belief (*tjhya*) and a word we might translate as religion (*zán*). However, according to Deborah Tooker, *zán* is not a matter of belief, "For the Akha, you cannot *believe* or *not believe* in *zán*."[28] Rather, *zán* is something to do, not religion in the Western sense but "something like a 'way of life,' 'way of doing things,' 'customs,' or 'traditions,'" including some elements we would call religion but others we would not, such as the proper way to plant rice, build a house, or boil an egg. The Akha say that they "carry" *zán* rather

---

[26] Needham, *Belief, Language, and Experience*, 37.
[27] Evans-Pritchard, *Nuer Religion*, 9.
[28] Tooker, "Identity Systems of Highland Burma," 804.

than "believe in" it. Behaviors may be "correct" (*zán-tsha-e*) or "incorrect" (*zán ma tsha-e*) by the standards of *zán*, but "truth and falseness are not an issue."[29] The Akha worldview even features spirits, but Akha "do not say anything like *neq djan-e* ('to believe in spirits')."[30] If one is Akha, one carries *zán*; if one is not Akha, one does not carry *zán*; and if one stops carrying *zán*, one ceases to be Akha. As one final example, practitioners of Orisa (Yoruba-based) religions in Trinidad are reportedly "uncomfortable with the term 'belief' and make fine distinctions between 'following the Orisa,' 'acknowledging the Orisa,' 'recognizing the Orisas,' and/or 'believing in the Orisa.'"[31] While among devotees the Orisa spirits "are accepted as givens—a taken-for-granted category of experience" and not subject to propositional assent or dissent, Stephen Glazier adds that even non-members including Christians may attest that the Orisa are real, although those people are not personally dedicated to them; these folks "'recognize' and 'acknowledge' the Orisa yet do not 'believe' that Orisa should be worshipped"[32]—that is, in our terminology, they accept the correctness of Orisa claims but they do not avow confidence in (or commitment to) those beings.

The potentially painful fact is that "belief" is a linguistic and cultural concept, not an absolute and certainly not a universal one, limiting the utility of an approach like the Credition Project: indisputably there are mental and brain states involved in belief, but it is not quite true that "creditions are purely mental processes."[33] It is also patently clear that belief or unbelief is not always an emic concept, throwing an obstacle at one of the main alleged advantages of Unbelief Studies—to ascribe a term like unbelief "only when the subject of the study declared and identified themselves as such."[34] "Unbelief" is no more emic than "atheism" and other problematic terms.

To return to the question of processes and models for Unbelief Studies, Ara Norenzayan and Will Gervais contribute to our understanding of unbelief with their four "pathways" to religious disbelief (which, in the perennial category error, they conflate with atheism). On the surely valid premise that "the same pathways that encourage religious beliefs, if altered or disrupted, yield disbelief instead,"[35] they postulate four different ways to

---

[29] Tooker, "Identity Systems of Highland Burma," 804.
[30] Tooker, "Identity Systems of Highland Burma," 802.
[31] Glazier, "Demanding Deities and Reluctant Devotees," 19.
[32] Glazier, "Demanding Deities and Reluctant Devotees," 26.
[33] Angel, "Credition, the Process of Belief," 538.
[34] Conrad, "An Argument for Unbelief," 7.
[35] Norenzayan and Gervais, "The Origins of Religious Disbelief," 20.

arrive at unbelief. The first depends on the much-touted theory of mind and its "hyperactive agency detection device."[36] People who are less prone to perceiving minds in the non-human world—who have weaker or more restrained "mentalizing abilities"—tend toward what Norenzayan and Gervais call "mind-blind atheism,"[37] although I object rather strenuously to the designation, as it implies that atheists are blind to some actually-existing non-human minds. The second type of disbelief flows from lack of motivation to believe ("apatheism"), not in the sense of individual interest but in the sense of social conditions that foster belief, in the case of gods specifically "existential insecurities" that promote hope in super-human intervention. They note that religiosity declines in a society as life becomes more secure and comfortable. Third, and perhaps most profitably, they stress the role of cultural support or lack thereof for beliefs, in the form of "credibility enhancing displays" or CREDS, like "frequent religious attendance, costly ritual participation, religious prosociality, and religious sacrifice" or merely endlessly hearing and seeing religion in the environment.[38] People who are "simply not receiving cultural inputs that encourage the belief" are literally "incredulous,"[39] reminding us that belief is learned and sustained socially, whatever our evolved intuitions might be. Finally, of course, there are those who think and reason their way out of belief, the "analytic" disbelievers, who overcome the intuitions that lead others to belief. Analytic thinkers, they find, are less likely to believe in god(s) at all and, if they do, are more likely to "favor less anthropomorphic and more intellectualized religious concepts, such as a distant, non-intervening God (Deism), and belief that the universe and God are identical (Pantheism)."[40] The key conclusions from their research are that "religious disbelief is not a unitary phenomenon that results from a single process," that "disbelief does not always require hard work or explicit cognitive effort, and that rational deliberation is only one of several routes to disbelief."[41] These lessons are more or less applicable to other-than-religious beliefs.

    A third model to learn from or emulate is the emerging field of unknowledge or agnotology. Contrasting with the overcrowded field of epistemology and recognizing that not-knowing is not a mere void but a

---

[36] Barrett, *Why Would Anyone Believe in God?*
[37] Norenzayan and Gervais, "The Origins of Religious Disbelief," 21.
[38] Norenzayan and Gervais, "The Origins of Religious Disbelief," 23.
[39] Norenzayan and Gervais, "The Origins of Religious Disbelief," 23.
[40] Norenzayan and Gervais, "The Origins of Religious Disbelief," 23.
[41] Norenzayan and Gervais, "The Origins of Religious Disbelief," 20.

condition that may be constructed and perpetuated, often intentionally and cynically, scholars began to perceive a need to examine non-knowledge. As early as the mid-1800s James Frederick Ferrier coined the term "agnoiology" for such a science (*a-gnosis-ology*, no/without-knowledge-study), but Robert Proctor and Londa Schiebinger's 2008 *Agnotology: The Making and Unmaking of Ignorance* gave us the term that has stuck. In addition to, or instead of, ignorance being the default state (prior to knowledge), Proctor explained and warned that ignorance can be achieved and sustained, sometimes as "a deliberately engineered and *strategic ploy*."[42] Further, not-knowing overlaps and "is generated by" such factors and tactics as "*secrecy, stupidity, apathy, censorship, disinformation, faith*, and forgetfulness."[43]

Prior to Proctor and Schliebinger, and without benefit of the word "agnotology," Michael Smithson performed a detailed inspection of ignorance, which he defined as follows, "A is *ignorant* from B's viewpoint if A fails to agree with or show awareness of ideas which B defines as actually or potentially valid."[44] He also built a taxonomy of ignorance (9), divided into two main branches, "irrelevance" and "error,"[45]

1) Irrelevance
    a) Untopicality
    b) Taboo
    c) Undecidability
2) Error
    a) Distortion
        i) Confusion
        ii) Inaccuracy
    b) Incompleteness
        i) Absence
        ii) Uncertainty
            (1) Ambiguity
            (2) Probability
            (3) Vagueness
                (a) Fuzziness
                (b) Nonspecificity

---

[42] Proctor, *Agnotology*, 3.
[43] Proctor, *Agnotology*, 2.
[44] Smithson, *Ignorance and Uncertainty*, 6.
[45] Smithson, *Ignorance and Uncertainty*, 9.

Others have added categories such as denial, obfuscation, and outright lying. In fact, it is not without import that the predominant studies of agnotology (whether or not they invoke the term), have explored how powerful entities, from corporations to governments, foment ignorance to advance their interests.[46] This rich literature is deeply relevant to, yet incomprehensibly neglected by, scholars of belief and unbelief, its relevance stemming from the insights that believing X often demands disbelieving Y; that, as we discovered in our semantic treatment of belief above, believing/disbelieving X or Y is often a matter of trusting/mistrusting those who espouse X or Y; and, finally, that many, if not most, situations of believing or disbelieving are social constructions and social achievements, often serving someone's interests.

We see these forces at play when we consider campaigns to induce people to distrust scientists (e.g., on the health effects of smoking, on global warming, etc.) or the mainstream media (e.g., "fake news"). The consequence is that people will not give credence to, will not accept as true, will not be persuaded by the claims that those sources make, but in this case untrusting precedes and facilitates unbelieving. For example, individuals who have no confidence in mainstream media will reject its statements as false and transfer their trust to other sources (like Fox News or Breitbart), receiving and believing different news—even different "facts"—in a circular loop of (mis)trust and (mis)belief.

While agnotology is immanently germane to Unbelief Studies, it is surprising that the unknowledge literature makes almost no reference to religion (e.g., churches and preachers are seldom named as purveyors of ignorance), whereas the unbelief literature is obsessed with it. Both initiatives would profit from touring the other's territory—more religion for agnotology, more non-religion for Unbelief Studies. Unbelief Studies can also incorporate agnotology's taxonomy or craft a classificatory scheme of its own; either way, unbelief scholars will appreciate that, like unknowledge, unbelief is not a void, an empty space where belief will be or formerly was, but a complex, dynamic social construction in its own right. Indeed, I am particularly eager to see how Unbelief Studies handles the fact that in some domains of knowledge unbelief is the default position and belief is the exception needing explanation. When it comes to topics like Bigfoot, the Loch Ness monster, flat earth, and all manner of conspiracy theories, why is it, despite usually overwhelming

---

[46] See for instance Michaels *Doubt is the Their Product*; Oreskes and Conway *Merchants of Doubt*; Mirowski *Never Let a Serious Crisis Go to Waste*; and Markowitz and Rosner *Deceit and Denial*.

evidence to the contrary, that some people essentially abdicate unbelief and accept blatantly unlikely if not thoroughly discredited and nutty claims? In this regard, I ponder geologist and Harvard Ph.D. Kurt Wise, a devout Christian who proudly and defiantly declared, "if all the evidence in the universe turned against creationism, I would be the first to admit it, but I would still be a creationist because that is what the Word of God seems to indicate."[47]

Unbelief: Analysis, Critique, Activism

I hope I have made myself clear that I am no foe of unbelief. Properly formulated, it can be a crucial and vital field of inquiry. In its current state, though, unbelief is a terribly confused concept, undone by its ambiguity and grandiose ambitions. It wants to be an exhaustive category, but its nearly sole obsession is religion; it throws its net spuriously around things that are, in every sense of the term, beliefs (i.e., heterodox beliefs are still beliefs), while it exalts itself against a constellation of similarly vague and abused terms like atheism, secularism, and irreligion as if they and it are synonyms. If it means to introduce precision into the analysis of unbelief, it is unsuited for the task in its unreformed state. The second part of this essay launched the reformation movement, and I would be the first to concede that atheism, secularism, and the lot also need reforming and discipline, some of which I have tried to interject here and elsewhere.

Yet, I not only welcome (rehabilitated) unbelief into the terminological fold, but I give it another charge, especially in view of the revelations about agnotology and the deliberate conjuring of ignorance which I have called agnomancy. I take a cue, ironically enough, from the Christian theologian Richard Swinburne, who advised that the philosophy of religion should undertake "an examination of the meaning and justification" of religious beliefs.[48] A robust field of Unbelief Studies, likewise, could and should not only investigate, but evaluate, beliefs of all types and belief as such, determining when beliefs are unjustified. And for those who want to pursue the project, I contend that belief itself will emerge as undesirable and indeed pernicious in virtually every instance.

First, if we isolate the natural language form of belief as a propositional truth claim (which is perhaps the most common everyday usage

---

[47] Ashton, *In Six Days*, 355.
[48] Swinburne, "Religion, Problems of the Philosophy of," 763.

and the only one that really catches the fancy philosophers and theologians), we emphasize that belief implies doubt, (because of) lack of information, and potentially if not probably falsehood. (Predictions, tastes, preferences, values, etc. are not truth claims, do not occupy the same semantic domain as truth claims, and are neither true nor false, except as personal testimony; for instance, a prediction cannot be true or false, yet, as its referent has not happened at the time of utterance.) When speakers say, "I believe in dragons," "I believe in vampires," or "I believe in god(s)," they are asserting that (a) they hold the claim of dragons/vampires/god(s) to be true but that (b) they have inadequate facts and/or logic to support the claim and may even be unsure of it themselves. I regard this situation as diagnostic of belief as opposed to knowledge and therefore define a belief as a truth-claim held without sufficient evidence or logic, or in the face of disconfirming evidence and logic. To believe is to hold a truth-claim without sufficient evidence or logic, or in the face of disconfirming evidence and logic. Accordingly, Scott Atran defined religion as belief in and commitment to 'counterfactual' claims[49]—counterfactual serving as a polite term for false.

I concur with W. K. Clifford when he judged in his classic essay "The Ethics of Belief" that "it is wrong in all cases to believe on insufficient evidence; and where it is presumption to doubt and to investigate, there it is worse than presumption to believe."[50] But if belief by definition is holding claims with insufficient evidence, then it is inadvisable—in Clifford's judgment, unethical—by definition to believe. Thus, in circumstances where knowledge is unclear or unavailable, unbelief is always preferable to belief. (This also puts the lie to the philosophical platitude that "knowledge is justified true belief"; first, knowledge does not inhabit the semantic range of belief as we have discovered it, and even if knowledge were a species of genus belief, that would leave the other species of belief as unjustified, untrue, or both, which I am sure no believer would like to admit.) Insofar as it is a counterfactual truth-claim, I would argue that all belief is what Nikolaj Nottelman called "blameworthy belief," a state of mind "that is undesirable from an epistemic perspective and for whose epistemic undesirability the believer has no adequate excuse."[51] In other words, given the freedom to believe or not and the ample resources to measure any particular belief, the honest and rational person who indulges in belief commits a grievous error.

---

[49] Atran, *in Gods We Trust*, 4.
[50] Clifford, "The Ethics of Belief," 309.
[51] Nottelman, *Blameworthy Belief*, 2.

This is the first reason to be suspicious of, and as often as possible to avoid, propositional belief. As a simple act of caution and mental hygiene (i.e., critical thinking), no one should embrace a claim that lacks empirical foundation or that is challenged at its core by empirical facts; that is, after all, Thomas Huxley's original maxim for agnosticism, not to profess knowledge when the grounds for our putative knowledge "are not demonstrated or demonstrable."[52] (Agnosticism, it is plain to see here, is not some kind of indecisiveness or epistemological skepticism, that knowledge or choice is impossible, but an honest acknowledgement of when one can make a justified knowledge claim and when one cannot.) But there is a second and more worrisome reason to shun belief, for which I turn once again to Clifford: "Every time we let ourselves believe for unworthy reasons, we weaken our powers of self-control, of doubting, of judicially and fairly weighing evidence."[53] Belief is, bluntly put, a bad habit, one that softens our mental faculties and leaves us vulnerable to further counterfactual/false claims and to surrendering our trust and our commitment to the wrong people and institutions. Research on the aforementioned "fake news" highlights the problem. If we understand "fake news" as (dis- or dys-) information "that is presented as real but is patently false, fabricated, or exaggerated to the point where it no longer corresponds with reality" and "operates in the express interests of deceiving or misleading a targeted or imagined audience,"[54] we can begin to grasp the toxic effect of such poison in the blood stream of the body social. False reports circulating in the public sphere erode confidence in institutions and in facticity itself, with at least three noxious results—(a) the "production of misinformed citizens" who (b) "are likely to stay wrongly informed in echo chambers" of counter factuality and belief and (c) who are easily "emotionally antagonized or outraged given the affective and provocative nature" of fake news and other such specious belief.[55] In the memorable but chilling words of Claire Wardle, the epistemological "ecosystem is now so polluted" with lies, distortions, and beliefs that too many people cannot tell what is true and are gullible for more counterfactual claims and alternative facts.[56]

So as caring scholars, we should not only study but promote unbelief, the unequivocal rejection of belief. I have said as much elsewhere, proposing a

---

[52] Huxley, "Agnoticism," 13.
[53] Clifford, "The Ethics of Belief," 294.
[54] Reilly, "F for Fake," 141.
[55] Bakir and McStay, "Fake News and the Economy of Emotions," 159.
[56] Wardle, "Fake News—It's Complicated."

neologism without the tortured history of atheism, secularism, or indeed unbelief, which is hardly as pristine as Conrad and Flynn suppose.[57] The term was *discredism*, from the same root *credere* as in Angel's credition; the prefix *dis-*, as opposed to *un-*, has the advantage of connoting action—to part with, to separate from, to exclude or expel. Discredism suggests not just the passive or indifferent absence of belief but an active, purposeful, and principled *dis*missal and *dis*carding of belief, a *dis*approval of the entire business of believing and a decisive *dis*mantling of the power of belief.

Discredism might serve better as the umbrella term that Conrad, Flynn, and Stein seek, since it is mercifully free of historical baggage and emphasizes the *cred-* root that features in many belief-related words. Sadly, it still suffers as a derivative term, like *un*belief, *a*theism, and *ir*religion, but so far no one has imagined a non-derivative option. Either way, a fully-realized project of unbelief/discredism puts atheism, secularism, irreligion, and other such terms in their proper place without invalidating any of them; recognizes its own place in the grand scheme of ideas (not limited to religious unbelief or certainly to Christian unbelief but not including heterodox religious belief which remains belief); and, insofar as individual practitioners choose, contributes to clarity of human thought by stressing the perils of belief in any guise.

BIBLIOGRAPHY

Angel, Hans-Ferdinand. 2013. "Credition, the Process of Belief." In *Encyclopedia of Sciences and Religions*, edited by Anne L. C. Runehov and Lluis Oviedo, 536–39. Dordrecht, Netherlands: Springer Science + Business Media, 2013.
Angel, Hans-Ferdinand, Lluis Oviedo, Raymond F. Paloutzian, Anne. L. C. Runehov, and Rüdiger J. Seitz, eds. *Processes of Believing: The Acquisition, Maintenance, and Change in Creditions*. Cham, Switzerland: Springer International Publishing, 2017.
Ashton, John F. *In Six Days: Why 50 Scientists Choose to Believe in Creation. Creation Ministries International*. Green Forest, AR: Master Books, 2000.
Atran, Scott. *In Gods We Trust: The Evolutionary Landscape of Religion*. Oxford: Oxford University Press, 2002.
Bakir, Vian and Andrew McStay. "Fake News and the Economy of Emotions." *Digital Journalism* 6, no. 2 (2018): 154–75.
Barrett, Justin. *Why Would Anyone Believe in God?* Lanham, MD: AltaMira Press, 2004.

---

[57] Eller, *Atheism Advanced*.

Clifford, W. K. "The Ethics of Belief." *The Contemporary Review* 29, no. 2 (1876): 289–309.

Conrad, Nickolas G. "An Argument for Unbelief: A Discussion about Terminology." *Secularism and Nonreligion*, 7, no. 11 (2018): 1–8.

Davie, Grace. "Belief and Unbelief: Two Sides of a Coin." *Ecclesiastical Law Journal* 15, no. 3 (2013): 259–66.

Eller, David. *Atheism Advanced: Further Thoughts of a Freethinker*. Parsippany, NJ: American Atheist Press, 2007.

Evans-Pritchard, E. E. *Nuer Religion*. New York and Oxford: Oxford University Press, 1956.

Flynn, Tom, ed. *The New Encyclopedia of Unbelief*. Amherst, NY: Prometheus Books, 2007.

Glazier, Stephen. D. "Demanding Deities and Reluctant Devotees: Belief and Unbelief in the Trinidadian Orisa Movement." *Social Analysis* 52, no. 1 (2008): 19–38.

Hallie, Philip P., ed. *Sextus Empiricus: Selections from the Major Writings on Scepticism, Man, & God*, trans. S. G. Etheridge. Indianapolis, IN: Hackett Publishing Company, 1985.

Huxley, Thomas. "Agnosticism." 1889. fountainheadpress.com/expandingthearc/assets/huxleyagnosticism.pdf, accessed June 14, 2019.

Markowitz, Gerald and David Rosner. *Deceit and Denial: The Deadly Politics of Industrial Pollution*. Berkeley: University of California Press, 2013.

Michaels, David. *Doubt is the Their Product: How Industry's Assault on Science Threatens Your Health*. Oxford and New York: Oxford University Press, 2008.

Mirowski, Philip. *Never Let a Serious Crisis Go to Waste: How Neoliberalism Survived the Financial Meltdown*. London and New York: Verso, 2003.

Needham, Rodney. *Belief, Language, and Experience*. Chicago: The University of Chicago Press, 1972.

Norenzayan, Ara and Will M. Gervais. "The Origins of Religious Disbelief." *Trends in Cognitive Science* 17, no. 1 (2013): 20–6.

Nottelman, Nikolaj. *Blameworthy Belief: A Study in Epistemic Deontologism*. Dordecht, Netherlands: Springer, 2007.

Oreskes, Naomi. & Erik Conway. *Merchants of Doubt: How a Handful of Scientists Obscured the Truth about Issues from Tobacco to Global Warming*. New York: Bloomsbury, 2010.

Pouillon, Jean. "Remarks on the Verb 'To Believe.'" in *Between Belief and Transgression: Structuralist Essays in Religion, History, and Myth*, edited by Michael Izard and Pierre Smith, 1-8. Chicago: The University of Chicago Press, 1982.

Proctor, Robert. N. and Londa Schiebinger, eds. *Agnotology: The Making & Unmaking of Ignorance*. Stanford, CA: Stanford University Press, 2008.

Quack, Johannes. "Organised Atheism in India: An Overview." *Journal of Contemporary Religion* 27, no. 1 (2012): 67–85.

Reilly, Ian. "F for Fake: Propaganda! Hoaxing! Hacking! Partisanship! and Activism! in the Fake News Ecology." *The Journal of American Culture* 41, no. 2 (2018): 139–52.

Ruel, Malcolm. "Christians as Believers." In *Belief, Ritual, and the Securing of Life: Reflexive Essays on a Bantu Religion.* Leiden: E. J. Brill, 1997.

Smithson, Michael. *Ignorance and Uncertainty: Emerging Paradigms.* New York: Spring-Verlag, 1989.

Stein, Gordon, ed. *The Encyclopedia of Unbelief.* Buffalo, NY: Prometheus Books, 1985.

Swinburne, Richard. "Religion, Problems of the Philosophy of." in *The Oxford Companion to Philosophy*, edited by Ted Honderich, 763-6. Oxford: Oxford University Press, 1995.

Thomas, Renny. "Atheism and Unbelief among Indian Scientists: Towards an Anthropology of Atheism(s)." *Society and Culture in South Asia* 3, no 1 (2017): 45–67.

Tooker, Deborah. "Identity Systems of Highland Burma: 'Belief,' Akha Zan, and a Critique of Interiorized Notions of Ethno-Religious Identity." *Man* (n.s) 27, no. 4 (1992): 799–819.

Wardle, Claire. 2017. "Fake News—It's Complicated. *First Draft.*" 2017. https://medium.com/1st-draft/fake-news-its-complicated-d0f773766c79, accessed August 3, 2019.

ABOUT THE AUTHOR

Jack David Eller holds a PhD in anthropology and has conducted fieldwork on religion and religious change among Australian Aboriginals. His other areas of interest include ethnic/religious violence, and atheism/secularism, and he is the author of a number of books on cultural anthropology, anthropology of religion, psychological anthropology, and atheism/secularism.

MORE FROM THE AUTHOR

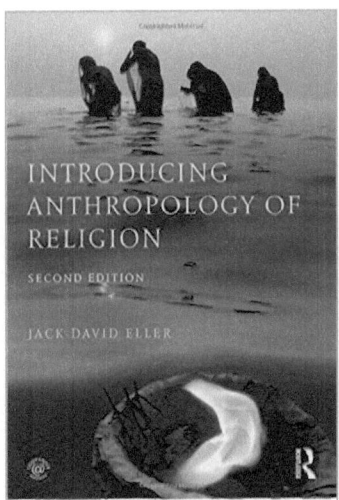

Introducing Anthropology of Religion, 2nd edition
Routledge, 2015

Atheism Advanced: Further Thoughts of a Freethinker
American Atheist Press, 2007

Trump and Political Theology
GCRR Press, 2020

A New Publication by Raul Casso
From Palmetto Publishing

A professional lawyer seeks to demonstrate just how the Bible could not possibly have a divine origin. And it seeks to prove this by using the Bible's own words against itself.

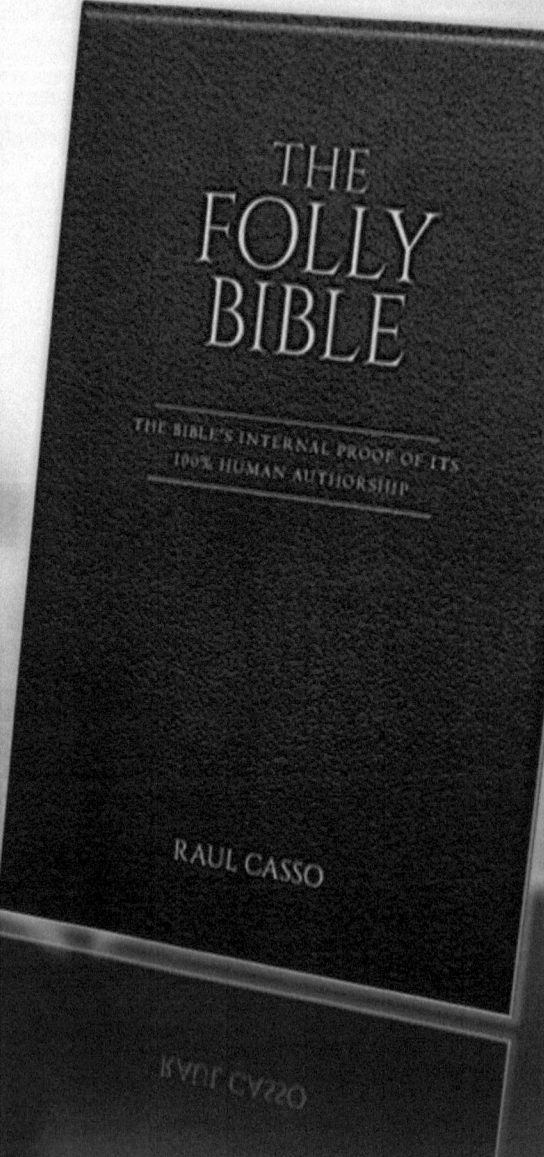

Buy Now at amazon.com

Inference to the Best Explanation and Rejecting the Resurrection

David Kyle Johnson,
King's College (PA)

Abstract: *Christian apologists, like Willian Lane Craig and Stephen T. Davis, argue that belief in Jesus' resurrection is reasonable because it provides the best explanation of the available evidence. In this article, I refute that thesis. To do so, I lay out how the logic of inference to the best explanation (IBE) operates, including what good explanations must be and do by definition, and then apply IBE to the issue at hand. Multiple explanations—including (what I will call) The Resurrection Hypothesis, The Lie Hypothesis, The Coma Hypothesis, The Imposter Hypothesis, and The Legend Hypothesis—will be considered. While I will not attempt to rank them all from worst to best, what I will reveal is how and why The Legend Hypothesis is unquestionably the best explanation, and The Resurrection Hypothesis is undeniably the worst. Consequently, not only is Craig and Davis' conclusion mistaken, but belief in the literal resurrection of Jesus is irrational. In presenting this argument, I do not take myself to be breaking new ground; Robert Cavin and Carlos Colombetti have already presented a Bayesian refutation of Craig and Davis' arguments. But I do take myself to be presenting an argument that the average person (and philosopher) can follow. It is my goal for the average person (and philosopher) to be able to clearly understand how and why the hypothesis "God supernaturally raised Jesus from the dead" fails utterly as an explanation of the evidence that Christian apologist cite for Jesus' resurrection.*

Keywords: Inference to the Best Explanation, Jesus' Resurrection, The SEARCH Method, The Legend Hypothesis, Willian Lane Craig, Stephen T. Davis, Robert Cavin and Carlos Colombetti, Abduction

---

William Lane Craig has argued that it is rational to believe that God raised Jesus from the dead because the hypothesis that such an event happened provides the best explanation of the available evidence (e.g., the biblical witness and the martyrdom of the apostles).[1] According to Craig, if you consider what an explanation must do—the criteria it should meet—the resurrection hypothesis meets them better than its naturalistic

---

[1] See Craig, *Assessing the New Testament Evidence* and also Craig, *Reasonable Faith*.

competitors. Robert Cavin and Carlos Colombetti, however, very skillfully refuted his argument by revealing, not only the problems with Craig's criteria and his criteria-based approach, but also how the resurrection hypothesis actually fails to meet the criteria Craig proposed.[2]

Later, in the pages of this very journal, Stephen T. Davis tried to defend Craig's argument,[3] but Cavin and Colombetti (again, in this journal) not only refuted his argument as well, but fully explained why the resurrection hypothesis cannot be the best explanation.[4] The standard model of physics "entails that God never supernaturally intervenes in the affairs of the universe that lie within its scope,"[5] and thus the resurrection hypothesis is necessarily implausible and has low explanatory power. They even go on to give a rigorous Bayesian analysis of why the Legend hypothesis—the idea that "the New Testament Easter traditions that relate group appearances of the Risen Jesus did not originate on the basis of eyewitness testimony but arose, rather, as legend"[6]—is a much better explanation of the available evidence than the resurrection hypothesis.

Their argument is devastating for those who claim to believe in the resurrection because it is the best explanation of the evidence. From start to finish, however, the debate between Craig, Davis, and Cavin and Colombetti is difficult to follow—most definitely for the lay person, and even for some professional philosophers. Not everyone is familiar with the relevant nuances of inference to the best explanation and philosophy of science, and Bayesian analysis can go over the head of even analytically trained philosophers. It is the goal of this essay, therefore, to explain in more easily understandable terms why the resurrection hypothesis cannot be the best explanation for the evidence that those like Craig and Davis offer in its favor. To do so, I am going to use a method of reasoning, a version of inference to the best explanation, I teach to college students every semester—one popularized by Ted Schick and Lewis Vaughn in their textbook, *How to Think About Weird Things*. They call it the SEARCH method. I will explain the criteria it utilizes and how the method

---

[2] Cavin and Colombetti, "Assessing the Resurrection Hypothesis," 205–28.

[3] Davis, "Craig on the Resurrection," 28–35.

[4] Cavin and Colombetti, "The Implausibility and Low Explanatory Power of the Resurrection Hypothesis," 37–94.

[5] Cavin and Colombetti, "The Implausibility and Low Explanatory Power of the Resurrection Hypothesis," 67.

[6] Cavin and Colombetti, "The Implausibility and Low Explanatory Power of the Resurrection Hypothesis," 85–86.

works before going on to apply it to the resurrection hypothesis and its competitors.

In doing so, I do not take myself to be breaking new ground, or even presenting an argument that is immune to objection. Indeed, while Cavin and Colombetti would undoubtedly agree with the conclusion of my argument, they would also point to shortcomings of the SEARCH method and argue for the superiority of the Bayesian approach. I would not presume to argue that they are wrong (although, as I will explain, I do not think the shortcomings prevent my argument from establishing its conclusion). But I believe that the following is an argument that the average person, and average philosopher, can more easily wrap their head around—and having such an argument, clearly articulated, is not only useful, but can do nothing but provide further reason to think that Cavin and Colombetti are right. The resurrection hypothesis not only fails to be the best explanation, but it is not even a good one.

Abduction and Inference to the Best Explanation

The procedure for identifying and embracing the best explanation for something is very appropriately named: "Inference to the Best Explanation" (IBE). When employing IBE, one compares multiple possible explanations for something, and then infers (i.e., accepts) what is determined to be the best one. In the literature, IBE is often equated with "abduction," but as William H. B. Mcauliffe explained in "How did Abduction Get Confused with Inference to the Best Explanation?", the person who coined the term abduction, C.S. Peirce, did not originally conceive of abduction as IBE.[7]

As Mcauliffe demonstrates, according to Peirce, *abduction* is the process by which one *generates* hypotheses or explanations to be tested, considered, or compared. Now, as Harry Frankfurt points out, the process Peirce describes does not actually generate any new ideas; and what Peirce is most concerned with are the criteria by which one can determine which hypotheses we should bother to consider or test (once they have been generated).[8] Peirce did argue that "the only way to discover the principles upon which anything ought to be discovered is to consider what is to be done with the constructed thing after it is constructed,"[9] so perhaps "the problem of constructing a good hypothesis is ... analogous to the problem of choosing a good hypothesis."[10]

---

[7] Mcauliffe, "How did Abduction Get Confused with Inference," 300–19.
[8] Frankfurt, "Peirce's Notion of Abduction," 593–96.
[9] Peirce, *The Essential Peirce*, 107.
[10] Fann, *Peirce's Theory of Abduction*, 42.

But, strictly speaking, the actual formulation or creation of hypotheses to explain certain phenomena does not really follow a pattern; it must truly be creative, like art.[11] Nevertheless, since some of the criteria Peirce described are also useful for determining which explanation is the best one, later philosophers like Harman,[12] Lipton,[13] and Thagard,[14] folded those criteria into their articulations of IBE, and also used the term "abduction" to refer to IBE.[15]

One shortcoming of IBE is the so-called "best of a bad lot" problem; if the list of hypotheses you are considering does not include the true one, determining which among them is the best cannot reveal the truth.[16] This is where recognizing and developing what Peirce called abduction could be very useful; a process aimed at generating hypotheses that are likely to be true would make "bad lots" less of a threat. Fortunately, however, for our purposes, we do not have to worry about this. Not only are the hypotheses we will consider already generated—they are already discussed in the literature and even anticipated by some of the gospel authors—but to prove that the belief in the resurrection hypothesis is irrational, all we have to do is find one that is better. It need not even be true. If even one possible explanation that we consider is better than the resurrection hypothesis, we will have shown belief in the resurrection to be irrational.

In my opinion, the clearest, easiest to understand, and most useful articulation of IBE belongs to Theodore Schick and Lewis Vaughn. In their book *How to Think about Weird Things*, they divide IBE into steps that they call The SEARCH method. **S**tate the claim. **E**xamine the evidence for the claim. Consider **A**lternative hypotheses. **R**ate, according to the **C**riteria of adequacy, each **H**ypothesis.[17] Because I take this to be relatively easy to understand, this is what we shall use. Before we begin, however, it will be useful to clarify each step.

---

[11] Schick and Vaughn, *How to Think about Weird Things*, 170.

[12] Harman, "The Inference to the Best Explanation," 88–95.

[13] Lipton, *Inference to the Best Explanation*.

[14] Thagard, "Best Explanation: Criteria for Theory Choice," 76–92.

[15] One important reason for making this distinction is that philosophers, including those that argue for the resurrection, will sometimes claim they are performing an inference to the best explanation, when in fact (at best) they are only doing what Peirce called abduction or (worse yet) merely declaring what seems to them, based on their own assumption, to be the best explanation. This would include Bayesian arguments in support of the resurrection.

[16] Notice that this entails that, even if the resurrection hypothesis could be shown to be the better of those we are about to consider, that would not entail that it is true. There are other explanations that have not yet been considered that could turn out to be better.

[17] Schick and Vaughn, *How to Think about Weird Things*, 233.

When **stating a claim**, one needs to be as specific and precise as possible. This will make clearer what evidence should be considered. When **evaluating the evidence for the claim**, one must determine whether the cited evidence is relevant and then bring to bear all the critical thinking lessons that philosophers should know (and that Schick and Vaughn teach in their book). What is the nature and limit of the evidence? Could the shortcomings of our perception and memory be at work? Are there logical fallacies involved? Are there probabilistic or statistical errors? One must be very careful to not be fooled by bad evidence. **Considering alternative hypotheses** really involves two steps: stating alternative hypotheses and evaluating the evidence for them as well. A person can state one, or many, but of course, it is most efficient to restrict oneself to the hypotheses that are most likely. And when **rating the hypotheses**, to figure out which one is the best, one must use the criteria of adequacy.

The criteria of adequacy are what a good explanation should be (or do), by definition. A good explanation should:

1. be testable: make novel predictions by which the explanation can be falsified.
2. be fruitful: get the novel predictions it makes right.
3. be wide-scoping: explain a variety of phenomena without raising unanswerable questions or replacing one unexplained thing with another.
4. be simple/parsimonious: not make more (especially existential) assumptions than are necessary.
5. be conservative: cohere with that which we already have good reason to believe (e.g., established scientific knowledge).

Now a good, or even the best explanation, need not always be or do all these things. Indeed, scientific revolutions happen when non-conservative explanations become accepted because they proved themselves to be more testable, fruitful, wide-scoping, and simpler than their "established" competitor. Einstein's theory of relativity, for example, was not conservative when it was first proposed because it contradicted Newton's, which was the established theory at the time. But relativity proved itself by being testable, more fruitful,[18]

---

[18] Relativity was more fruitful than Newton's theory when it successfully predicted the position of a star during a solar eclipse. For a readable rundown of this historical event, see Siegel, "This is How."

wide-scoping,[19] and simple[20] than Newton's theory. Or take the germ theory of disease. It introduced new entities, and thus was not simple, but it proved itself by successfully predicting things like the efficacy of handwashing,[21] vaccines,[22] and explaining how diseases spread.

That is also not to say that there cannot be ties. In my opinion, this is why it is currently impossible to delineate between the major interpretations of quantum mechanics. For example, neither David Bohm's pilot wave theory nor Hugh Everett's multiverse theory make any new novel predictions; and both seem to have the same explanatory power. But whereas Everett's multiverse interpretation is not simple (because it requires the existence of multiple universes), Bohm's interpretation is not conservative (because it violates relativity by requiring faster than light signaling). Which is better? It is a matter of preference. Which do you think is more valuable: simplicity or conservatism?

But the fact that there can be ties does not mean that, when there is not, one explanation is not the best. If you compare competing hypotheses according to the criteria, and one clearly turns out to adhere to them the most, then that is the best explanation and it is irrational to embrace the others. You might refrain from endorsing it, in hopes of an even better one coming along, but that possibility cannot make embracing the worse hypotheses rational. Or, alternately, if one hypothesis does not emerge as the best, but others are clearly demonstrated to be inferior, embracing the inferior one(s) cannot be rational. And as we shall now see, among the proposed explanations for the cited evidence of Jesus' resurrection, the resurrection hypothesis is the worst. Thus, it cannot be rationally accepted.

State the Claim and Evaluate the Evidence

In the case of Jesus' resurrection, stating the hypothesis that we need to evaluate first, clearly and precisely, seems easy enough to do: "God

---

[19] Relativity proved itself to be a very wide-scoping explanation by "accidentally" explaining the apparent "wobble" in Mercury's orbit. For a readable explanation, see *Lumen Learning*, "Tests of General Relativity."

[20] Relativity is simpler than Newton's theory because it does not require the existence of gravity; it reveals that gravity is only an apparent force. For a readable explanation, see Davis, Rickles, and Scott, "Understanding Gravity."

[21] For a great example of how handwashing saved lives and in doing so served as evidence for the germ theory of disease, see Explorable.com, "Semmelweis' Germ Theory."

[22] For a readable rundown of how the success of vaccines was evidence for the germ theory of disease, see *Science History Institute*, "Louis Pasteur."

supernaturally raised Jesus from the dead."[23] But Craig also believes that Jesus' post-resurrection body was a "soma pneumatikon" (spirit body image) that was immortal, imperishable, and able to de- and re-materialize. So, to align with Schick's suggestion that one should state the hypothesis as precisely as possible, it should be stated like this:

> *The Resurrection Hypothesis: A first century Palestinian apocalyptic preacher named Jesus was crucified and then raised from the dead; this was accomplished by the supernatural powers of a supernatural being we now call "God," who gave him a spiritual body that was immortal, imperishable, and able to de- and re-materialize.*

In other words, *Jesus' resurrection happened pretty much as the Bible described*. Evaluating the evidence for this claim, however, is a bit more complicated than stating it.

The first piece of evidence is the biblical account itself, and its report that Jesus was crucified, died, was placed in a tomb which was later found empty, and then appeared to the apostles (by, for example, just appearing out of thin air in a room they were in). But this piece of evidence must be rated as low, given that the Bible is in no way a reliable historical document. For example, scholars generally agree that the Old Testament is mostly ahistorical;[24] neither Abraham, nor Moses, or even King David, for example, likely ever existed.[25] The New Testament does not fare much better. Even if one sets aside the (often convincing but unpopular) view that Jesus never existed either, the New Testament is not considered by most biblical scholars to be historically reliable.[26] Indeed, it is especially unreliable when it comes to the details of Jesus' life. It is full of historical contradictions. The two nativity stories in *Luke* and *Matthew*, for example, are impossible to reconcile historically.[27] And the same is true for the different gospels' accounts of Jesus' crucifixion and resurrection.

The latter is worth elaboration. The gospels say two things about when Jesus was crucified. *Mark* (14:12; 15:25) says he was crucified on the day of

---

[23] Craig has two different articulations which he says are equivalent but are not. Cavin and Colombetti generously correct this error by clearly stating the hypothesis this way. See Cavin and Colombetti, "Assessing the Resurrection Hypothesis," 205

[24] For a readable rundown as to why, see Eisendrath, "The Old Testament Wars."

[25] Rainey, "Early History of the Israelite People," 156–60.

[26] Humphreys, *Jesus Never Existed*.

[27] Johnson, *The Myths that Stole Christmas*, 16–21.

Passover at the third hour, but *John* (19:14–16) says it was the day *before* Passover at the sixth hour.[28] In the synoptic gospels (Mark 15:23; Matt. 27:48; Luke 23:36), Jesus refuses to drink while on the cross, but in *John* (19:29–30) he does not refuse. Historically, the Romans usually did not crucify thieves—crucifixion was reserved for enemies of the state—but the synoptics say the men crucified with Jesus were thieves. Additionally, those the Romans did crucify were not taken down and put into a grave but were instead left up to rot and later thrown into a pit.[29] Indeed, the list of discrepancies in the story is vast and numerous.[30] More importantly, for our purposes, discrepancies also exist in the biblical account of the resurrection.[31] How many people saw the resurrected Jesus, for example? Paul says it was over 500 (1 Cor. 15:6), but the gospels never mention this crucial event. Were the women joyful or sad? Could the apostles touch Jesus, or not? Was he recognizable? Did he appear in Galilee or Jerusalem? Different gospels say different things. If two people told you so such wildly conflicting stories about anything, you would know that one is lying, and would not be able to believe either without corroborating evidence.

Such discrepancies are not surprising given that we now know the gospels were not written by followers of Jesus named Matthew, Mark, Luke, and John right after the events happened—but instead by non-eyewitnesses decades after Jesus would have lived.[32] (The first clue was that the gospels are written in Greek and the apostles and other followers of Jesus would have spoken Aramaic.) *Mark* was written first, and whoever wrote *Matthew* and *Luke* used it as source material, but *John* was written independently—that is why it is so different and contradictory. Therefore, the resurrection accounts in the gospels cannot be considered a reliable account of what happened after Jesus' death because the people who wrote them were not around when Jesus' resurrection supposedly happened. The gospel accounts, therefore, do not provide good evidence that a resurrection occurred.[33]

Of course, some have claimed that the gospels are simply written accounts of oral traditions that were started by the apostles and perfectly

---

[28] Barrett, "The Gospel According to St. John," 58.

[29] Ehrman, "Why Romans Crucified People."

[30] For a readable rundown, see Cline, "Gospel Discrepancies of Jesus' Crucifixion" and *RationalWiki*, "Contradictions in Jesus' Crucifixion."

[31] For a readable rundown, see Seidensticker, "Contradictions in the Resurrection Account."

[32] Ehrman, *Forged: Writing in the Name of God.*

[33] It is worth noting that, even if they were eyewitness accounts, the Gospels still would not be that reliable. For a quick readable explanation of why, see Azar, "The Limits of Eyewitness Testimony," 26.

preserved by the Christian community. But as Bart Ehrman proves in his book *Jesus Before the Gospels*,[34] there is no way that actually happened.[35] Oral traditions are no different than rumors; all research suggests that they change and are added to drastically as they are passed on. Add to that how unreliable our senses and memories are to begin with, and we have every reason to not take this notion seriously.[36] To put it simply, I would not believe my neighbor if he said he saw someone raise from the dead with his own eyes yesterday—and justifiably so. How much less should I believe non-eyewitness accounts passed through multiple languages for 2000 years?

Outside the biblical witness, proponents of the resurrection will often cite other factors—like the tradition that the apostles died as martyrs for their faith. "Why would they be willing to do that," the argument goes, "if they were not convinced the resurrection happened?" But there are two things to say in response.

First, the evidence that the apostles actually died for their faith is poor. In his book, *The Fate of the Apostles*, Sean McDowell lays out the evidence and argues that (at best) Peter, Paul, James (son of Zebedee) and Jesus' brother (James) were martyred.[37] But even the evidence he mentions for their martyrdom was written down decades after it would have happened—which means the stories would have been preserved by oral tradition and thus are not reliable. It is just as likely that all such stories are church traditions that were invented to try to convince skeptics. Indeed, as we shall soon see, Christians confabulating stories to convince skeptics was quite common.

Second, and more importantly, the apostles being convinced that the resurrection occurred would not be good evidence that it happened—even if they were so convinced that they were willing to die for it.[38] Some people are convinced Elvis still lives, and people in cults die for (demonstrably and obviously) false things they are convinced are true all the time.[39] Again, as we shall soon see, there are many (more likely) reasons the apostles could have been that convinced that Jesus rose, even though he did not.

---

[34] Ehrman, *Jesus Before the Gospels*.
[35] Johnson, "Book Review: Bart Ehrman's *Jesus Before the Gospels*."
[36] Schick and Vaughn, *How to Think About Weird* Things, 106–126.
[37] McDowell, *The Fate of the Apostles*; see also McDowell, "Did the Apostles Really Die as Martyrs for Their Faith?"
[38] McDowell, "Did the Apostles Really Die as Martyrs for their Faith?"
[39] For a readable rundown of Elvis sightings, see *Wikipedia*, "Sightings of Elvis Presley." For a nice example of people dying for obviously false beliefs, see Conroy, "An Apocalyptic Cult, 900 Dead."

Something similar could be said about the "success" of Christianity. The fact that Christianity spread and is still thriving today is not a testament to the fact that Jesus indeed rose—any more than the fact that Islam is thriving today is testament to the fact that Muhamad was Allah's prophet and rode a flying horse named Burāq up to heaven. Religions succeed or fail primarily because of historical accident (e.g., the conversion of Constantine), not because they are (or are not) rooted in historical events. Besides, to think that something is true because it has been believed by a lot of people for a long time is a doubly fallacious argument: one that combines "appeal to tradition" with "appeal to the masses."

So the evidence for the resurrection hypothesis is not convincing.

Consider Alternative Hypotheses

To consider an alternative hypothesis is to state it and to evaluate the evidence for and against it. Of course, given how far back in the past the resurrection would have occurred, no evidence we will consider here will deductively settle the matter. But the discussion will be very useful when comparing the hypothesis to the criteria of adequacy in the next step.

The obvious alternative hypothesis is that Jesus did not actually raise from the dead but people ended up believing that he did anyway. But that is far from specific, as there are a number of ways that could have happened. So, let us consider the four specific hypotheses that seem to be the most likely.

> *The Lie Hypothesis: The apostles lied and said that Jesus rose; they knew he did not but made it seem like he did. The disciples stole his body out of his tomb and buried it somewhere else, so that the women who went to the tomb on Sunday morning would find it empty and conclude that Jesus rose from the dead. People believed them, and the story grew.*

The best reason to doubt this hypothesis is the suggestion that the disciples were martyred; although it is not impossible, it seems unlikely that they would be willing to die for a lie that they knowingly told. But, as was mentioned above, the evidence for the suggestion that the disciples died as martyrs is unreliable, so this cannot be a reason to dismiss this hypothesis.

The best evidence for this hypothesis is the fact that the author of Mathew felt it necessary to try to knock it down.

> While the women were on their way, some of the guards went into the city and reported to the chief priests everything that had happened. When the chief priests had met with the elders and devised a plan, they gave the soldiers a large sum of money, telling them, "You are to say, 'His disciples came during the night and stole him away while we were asleep.' If this report gets to the governor, we will satisfy him and keep you out of trouble." So the soldiers took the money and did as they were instructed. And this story has been widely circulated among the Jews to this very day. (Matt. 28:11–15, NIV)

Given the low historical value of the gospels, and since there is no way the author of Matthew could have been privy to this secret meeting,[40] these verses cannot be good evidence against this theory. Indeed, clearly the idea that this meeting took place was invented by the author to "shoot down" this alternative explanation. As the author makes clear, "the disciples stole the body" was a retort that early Christians often heard when they tried to convince people that Jesus rose from the dead. So this passage actually provides at least *some reason* to think this hypothesis is true.

At the same time, however, the mere fact people were saying the disciples stole the body is not *good evidence* that they did. It probably just occurred to people as a better explanation for the stories about an empty tomb. And we will have to wait until later in this process to determine whether it actually is.

One thing this does demonstrate, however, is that elements that seem to have been added to the story—like secret meetings and the guards and stone in front of the tomb—which were clearly designed to "head off" objections or alternate explanations, do not actually provide good evidence against the alternative explanations in question (and thus for the resurrection hypothesis). Yes, it is possible that there was a giant boulder in front of Jesus' tomb, but it is at least equally possible (indeed it is more likely) that such notions were fabricated by someone in response to people saying that the apostles lied. As Christian origins scholar James Tabor put it, "What is clearly the case is that neither Matthew nor Luke are relating history, but writing defenses against charges that are being raised by opponents who are denying the notion that Jesus literally rose from the dead."[41]

The second alternative explanation would be along these lines.

---

[40] No scholars think a tomb guard or a chief priest is the author of Matthew.
[41] Tabor, "What Really Happened Easter Morning?"

> *The Coma Hypothesis: Jesus did not die on the cross but was sent into a temporary coma due to his wounds. This was mistaken for death, and he later awoke and left his tomb, leaving it empty.*

This hypothesis is sometimes chidingly called the swoon theory, but the condition described would be much more serious than Jesus simply passing out.

The evidence usually cited against it is actually, once again, some evidence for it: the part of the crucifixion story where the soldiers at the cross do not break Jesus' legs to hasten his death, but instead stick a spear in his side to confirm he already died. This bit appears nowhere else but in the Gospel of John, the last and least historically reliable gospel to be written. It is, therefore, more likely that it was added to the story as a way to head off reasons people were giving at the time to doubt the resurrection hypothesis. After all, even given the story they were told, people at the time had good reason to suspect that Jesus did not actually die on the cross. It usually took most who were crucified days to die, and even those who were nailed to a cross would likely live up to 24 hours; and even according to those telling the story, Jesus was only on a cross for a few hours.[42] Moreover, it is not like Roman guards usually stuck around and made sure people who were crucified actually died; again, the crucified were usually just left to die (and then tossed into a mass grave if wild animals did not get to them first).

One might argue that comas are never as short as 36 hours (roughly the time that passes between Friday evening and Sunday morning). But (a) I was unable to find any evidence that comas cannot last this long, and (b) this hypothesis does not require that the time between the crucifixion and finding the empty tomb was 36 hours. It could have actually taken much longer, and the "3 days" part of the story was added later.

Evidence that such things happened in first century Palestine is bolstered by the fact that they still happen today. Consider the many stories from the modern world where even medical professionals thought someone was dead when they were not[43]—like 29-year-old Gonzalo Montoya Jiménez who was declared dead by 3 separate doctors before later awakening and completely recovering (even after being in cold storage).[44] How much more common must

---

[42] Jha, "How Did Crucifixion Kill?"

[43] For some modern-day examples, see Valentine, "Why Waking Up in a Morgue isn't Quite as Unusual as You'd Think."

[44] For the news report of this happening, see Dockrill, "Man Declared Dead by 3 Doctors Wakes Up."

mistaking a coma (or illness) for death have been in the ancient world? How much more unqualified (than modern medical doctors) to tell whether someone was really dead must the illiterate apostles have been? The fact that Jesus' inerudite apostles thought Jesus had died and then been raised would not be a valid reason to think that he had. (Notice that Christians would be very quick to embrace this hypothesis to explain non-Christian resurrection stories, like that of Mr. V. Radhakrishna.)[45]

The Coma Hypothesis does raise questions, however. For example, if Jesus did not die, and walked away from the tomb, what happened to him afterwards? Well, it is possible such an event would have convinced Jesus himself that he had risen from the dead. If so, things could have unfolded basically as the gospels suggest: The women found the empty tomb, Jesus appeared to them and the apostles, he and they believed he had risen, and he sent them to convert the nations. But it is just as likely that Jesus simply went on to die of his wounds somewhere else, and his body was never found or identified. (It would likely have been eaten by animals and left unrecognizable.) And then the merely empty tomb convinced the apostles that he had risen.

But if Jesus did die (whether on the cross or after) but did not rise, this makes one wonder about all those post death appearances. How do we account for those? This brings us to our last two alternate hypotheses: *The Imposter Hypothesis,* and *The Legend Hypothesis.* Let us deal with the former first.

The Imposter Hypothesis: Jesus died but the apostles came to believe that he rose because they came to believe that a different (live) person was Jesus.

There are a number of ways this could be true, so this hypothesis is not as specific as it should be; but the different possibilities are all about equally likely, so that should not matter for our purposes here.

On this hypothesis, the disciples may not have even known where Jesus was buried. Again, victims of crucifixion were usually just thrown in mass graves. If so, perhaps other people later claimed to be the resurrected Jesus, and without a way to prove them wrong with a body, people (including the Apostles) believed it. After all, apocalyptic preachers were common at the time; and claiming to be Jesus could have been an easy way to gain a following—like gurus in India today often claim to be reincarnations of Vishnu, or others (like

---

[45] For the account of his supposed resurrection, see Saibaba.ws, "The Resurrection of Mr. V. Radhakrishna."

Texas' David Koresh and Siberia's Sergey Torop) claim to be Jesus.[46] Such persons could have easily excused away why they looked different. "The resurrection changed me." But perhaps they did not need to because Jesus had a doppelganger (or even twin brother) that people mistook for Jesus, after his death. We know that twins exist, and even unrelated doppelgangers are not that uncommon.[47] Any of these possibilities could very easily make sense of the strange biblical story (from Luke 24) where two apostles, on the road to Emmaus, did not quite recognize the person they were talking to "as Jesus" until after he was gone.

On this view, all the subsequent details—like the empty tomb, and doubting Thomas story where Thomas sticks his fingers in Jesus' side, which were obviously later added to the story to squelch doubts—were fabricated after the fact. But this is not unreasonable at all. As we have already seen (and biblical scholars agree), those who passed them on, whether in written or oral form, embellished the gospel stories readily, and for this very purpose. And the doubting Thomas story only appears in the latest and least historical of the gospels: *John*. But that brings to mind the possibility that the entire story was fabricated, and leads us to our final hypothesis:

> *The Legend Hypothesis: The idea that a man named Jesus rose from the dead is a complete fabrication, a legend that arose in 1st century Palestine—one that people, like the apostle Paul, came to believe, and that later inspired the writings of the gospels, and the religion of Christianity.*

One way that this hypothesis would be true is if Jesus never existed at all, and his entire story is legend—especially the part about his crucifixion and resurrection, which bears certain resemblance to the stories of other resurrected deities. On this view, Christianity was essentially invented by Paul, which accounts for why he (and not any eyewitness) was the first to write about it. Although it is not mainstream, a number of scholars have argued for this idea; as such, all the evidence they present would be evidence for this theory.[48]

---

[46] For a readable rundown of such examples, see *Wikipedia*, "Sathya Sai Baba," and "List of people claimed to be Jesus."

[47] For some (silly but relevant) modern day examples, see *Brightside*, "25 People Who Didn't Expect to Meet Their Doppelgangers."

[48] See for example Doherty, *Jesus: Neither God nor Man* and Carrier, *Proving History*. Counter evidence that Jesus existed, however, would not be evidence against *The Legend Hypothesis* since it still can be true, even if Jesus existed.

The (arguably) more conservative interpretation of *The Legend Hypothesis*, however, is that an apocalyptic preacher named Jesus did exist, and was crucified and died—but that his followers were so distraught as a result that they simply began to believe that he had resurrected out of despair. Because of this belief, "sightings" occurred and oral legends emerged—and they, in turn, were believed by Paul,[49] later embellished by the gospel writers (who, again, were not apostles), and believed by the early church.

That such a thing can and does happen, especially in cults of personality, is not uncommon. Indeed, there are modern-day examples. It could have been that the disciples, much like fans of Elvis, despite the obvious evidence, simply could not accept his death and began to believe they saw him alive as a result. Such rumors spreading (especially among illiterate first century Palestinians) would have made "sightings" more frequent, and easily laid the groundwork for a widespread belief that Jesus was still alive. From this, the stories about an empty tomb, his subsequent appearances, and even his early miracles, could have easily emerged.

Direct evidence that any of these things happened is, of course, as impossible to obtain as direct evidence that a resurrection occurred. However, there is one bit of indirect evidence that favors the legend hypothesis over all the others: the amount of time it took for the belief in Jesus' resurrection to take hold, to be professed in writing (by Paul), and to later be written in the gospels. On the *Lie*, *Coma*, and *Imposter* hypotheses, belief in Jesus' resurrection would have risen immediately because the evidence (faulty as it was) would have been obvious and available. The empty tomb, the post-coma Jesus, or the imposter, would have been right there! You would have therefore expected a written account of it within a year, and for the church to have preserved such an important document.[50] As it stands, we do not get even a bare-bones statement of the resurrection until the writings of Paul, which were written at best 20 years later (ca. 50 C.E.), and the subsequent accounts proceed just as legends do: they become more grandiose over time.[51]

---

[49] Paul came to believe the stories perhaps because of a temporal lobe seizure. See Johnson, "Why Religious Experience Can't Justify Religious Belief," 26–46.

[50] Granted, most of the earlier followers were illiterate but probably not all. Indeed, it is widely held that a document, called Q, containing the sayings of Jesus was written down during his lifetime. If his followers were writing down what he said right after he said it, why did they not write about his resurrection right after he rose? See Millard, "Literacy in the Time of Jesus."

[51] It is worth noting that this, and all subsequent statements about how long after Jesus' death certain things were written, relies on the very generous assumption that Jesus was born (as church tradition holds) in year 0 and was crucified around year 30. There is scant evidence for

This last point is worth some elaboration. From Paul we just get a creed. "That Christ died for our sins according to the Scriptures, and that He was buried, and that He was raised on the third day according to the Scriptures." (I Cor 15:3–4, NASB).[52] He mentions earlier in the letter that Jesus died by crucifixion (I Cor 2:1–2), but that is it.[53] It is not until twenty years later (ca. 70 C.E., at least 40 years after Jesus would have died) that the author of Mark adds details to the crucifixion (Ch. 15) and resurrection story (Ch. 16). But even then, we do not get much; after the crucifixion, Jesus never physically appears again. The women just meet a young man who tells them Jesus was raised.[54] Not until still another 20 years later (ca. 90 C.E.), after all the eyewitnesses would have been dead, do we get Matthew's and Luke's accounts about the crucifixion and personal appearances made by Jesus to eyewitnesses, which add even more (divergent) details to the resurrection story. And then, as much as 20 years after that (ca. 110), we get John's gospel, which not only neglects many details in Luke's and Matthew's gospels but adds many more of its own. This is exactly how legends develop; it decidedly is not how history is accurately preserved.

Indeed, James Tabor has argued that how the stories developed indicates that the earliest Christians did not believe that Jesus was physically raised and physically appeared to the disciples, but instead that Jesus was "'lifted up' or 'raised up' to the right hand of God," and that his followers merely experienced "epiphanies of Jesus once they returned to Galilee after the eight-day Passover festival and had returned to their fishing in despair."[55] Only decades later, after all the original followers had died, did the belief that Jesus physically resurrected become common.[56] This comports precisely with *The Legend Hypothesis*.

---

this as well, and Jesus was just as likely born much earlier. If so, the case against the resurrection hypothesis is even more damning. See Abruzzi, "When Was Jesus Born?"

[52] The creed itself may have been recited orally earlier, but still, likely was not commonly embraced until about a decade after Jesus would have died. For a readable argument as to why, see Turner, "An Analysis of the Pre-Pauline Creed."

[53] To be fair, Paul also mentions that Jesus appeared to Cephas, the twelve, and to "five-hundred brethren at one time," to James, and then "all the apostles"—but he equates such appearances to his own, which was not a physical appearance but a vision. So Paul's statement actually comports with the legend hypothesis.

[54] Forged verses were added to the end of Mark (16:9–20) centuries later, where Jesus appears and chastises people for not believing those who said they physically saw him alive, but scholars do not consider these verses to be legitimate. Indeed, it's another obvious case of an author adding details to the story to stave off objections. See Tabor, "The 'Strange' Ending of the Gospel of Mark."

[55] Tabor, "The 'Strange' Ending of the Gospel of Mark."

[56] Tabor, *The Jesus Discovery*.

According to the Criteria of Adequacy, Rate Each Hypothesis

We have five hypotheses: *Resurrection*, *Lie*, *Coma*, *Imposter*, and *Legend*. The fact that there is no way to directly test any of these hypotheses, since they deal with far, distant beliefs and actions of first century Palestinians, might lead one to think that we are forced to just shrug our shoulders and say we cannot know what happened. "You cannot *prove* one hypothesis over the other, so it is just a matter of faith." But there are two important responses here. First, knowledge does not require *proof.* If one hypothesis can be shown to be much more likely than the others, belief in it will at least be justified, if not be knowledge. Second, *knowing what happened* is not the issue here. The question is whether *The Resurrection Hypothesis* is, as Davis and Craig suggest, the best explanation; and we can determine that even if we are not able to directly test any of the hypotheses, or even know exactly what happened.

We can do so because testability and fruitfulness—the only criteria that deal with whether a hypothesis makes correct, novel, observable predictions—are only two of the five criteria of adequacy. We can still use the other three: scope, simplicity, and conservatism. If I go downstairs to find my TV missing but have no video surveillance or way to lift fingerprints, I can do no testing…but I can still know that "I was robbed" is a better explanation than "a ghost took my TV." Why? Because the former is simpler, more conservative, and has wider scope. The former does not require ghosts to exist, does not contradict the laws of physics and facts of neuroscience, and does not raise unanswerable questions about how non-material objects can move TVs. We can do something very similar with the above five hypotheses.

That said, testability and fruitfulness are still somewhat relevant. Although you cannot test any of the hypotheses in a lab—as I mentioned in the previous section—on *The Legend Hypothesis*, one would expect the development of Jesus' crucifixion and resurrection story to develop a certain way: to become more elaborate over decades. That type of development is not what to expect on the *Resurrection, Lie, Coma,* or *Imposter* hypotheses. Since that is what happened, the legend hypothesis is more fruitful. Indeed, since such hypotheses have been around for centuries, but only until relatively recently (historically speaking) did we date and order the letters of Paul and the gospels, and discover that the gospels were written decades later by non-eyewitnesses, we could even say that the legend hypothesis made a novel prediction that turned out to be right.

The simplicity of the hypotheses is much easier to compare. *The Resurrection Hypothesis* requires the existence of a supernatural entity operating with supernatural powers. That is two enormous, grandiose assumptions that none of the other hypotheses have to make. Thus, it is the least simple. (And the fact that it says Jesus was given a unique spiritual body makes it even less simple.) Yes, the *Lie, Coma, Imposter*, and *Legend* hypotheses also make certain kinds of assumptions—but they do not assume the existence of an entirely new kind of force, entity, or body. We know that lies, comas, imposters, and legends exist. Indeed, scholars already know that additions were made to Jesus' story, how legends develop, and that misdiagnoses of death readily occurred before the advent of modern medicine.

Granted, *The Imposter Hypothesis* requires the existence of an imposter/doppelganger, and *The Lie Hypothesis* requires a bit of a conspiracy;[57] and that does make them less simple than the *Coma* or *Legend Hypothesis*. But even the *Imposter* and *Lie* hypotheses are simpler than *The Resurrection Hypothesis*. At least we know that doppelgangers, twins, and conspiracies can and do exist. If Princess Diana appeared on TV tomorrow claiming to be back from the dead, saying that she had faked her death or had a long-lost twin would both be simpler explanations than, say, "aliens resurrected her corpse with advanced technology." None of this entails that the other hypotheses we have considered are contrary to belief in God. Indeed, even if we granted that God exists, since such explanations do not *require* God or his supernatural powers to exist, by definition, they are simpler than the resurrection hypothesis.

The scope of the hypotheses is also easy to compare. *The Resurrection Hypothesis* has little scope because it invokes the inexplicable: an infinite, incomprehensible being who uses unknown, un-understandable powers, to create a body made of an inexplicable substance that has mysterious magic powers. As Schick might point out, this is a bit like trying to explain why a bridge collapsed by saying "a mysterious gremlin zapped it with a magical ray gun." Such explanations actually explain nothing. (Notice that the alien explanation would not help you build a more stable bridge next time). To paraphrase Plato, to say "the gods did it" is not to offer an explanation, but to just offer an excuse for not having one.

The Legend Hypothesis, however, has very wide scope because it can explain not only the evidence cited for the resurrection but a vast number of other phenomena, like other legends, and things like Elvis and Hitler

---

[57] It should be noted, however, that only two or three apostles needed to be involved - not necessarily all twelve.

sightings.[58] It explains the contradictions in the biblical accounts of the resurrection, and why those accounts were written so much later than the events they purport to relay by non-eyewitnesses. It could even explain a host of other religious beliefs about the resurrection of other supposedly dead persons (although the *Lie, Coma,* and *Imposter* hypotheses could also explain those as well).[59]

The Legend Hypothesis is also monumentally conservative because it conflicts with nothing that we know is true. We know that (and how and why) false beliefs, even in the face of contrary evidence, can arise—even the belief that someone who has died is still living (again, like Elvis and Hitler).[60] It coheres with what we know about how and who the Romans crucified, how long it took those they crucified to die, and how the Romans disposed of their bodies. It even aligns with what Bart Ehrman revealed about how unreliable group memories and "oral traditions" are. (Even the *Lie, Coma,* and *Imposter* theories require the unlikely assumption that the stories about Jesus' "resurrection" were reliably preserved orally for decades.)

Most notably, however, all but *The Resurrection Hypothesis* aligns with perhaps one of the most established facts there is: the dead stay dead. And this brings us back around to Cavin and Colombetti. They argue that, regardless of whether God exists, *The Resurrection Hypothesis* is contrary to the Standard Model of physics. Defenders of the resurrection, like Davis and Craig, argue that the Standard Model comes with a proviso: the laws operate as usual *unless there is divine intervention*. They thus argue that the resurrection is not scientifically impossible. But, as Cavin and Colombetti very skillfully explain, such a proviso is either superfluous or "renders [the] laws untestable metaphysical pseudo-science."[61] Consequently, the standard model "entails that God never supernaturally intervenes in the affairs of the universe that lie within its scope."[62] And that would include raising Jesus from the dead.[63]

---

[58] For a readable rundown of conspiracy theories about Hitler's death, see *Wikipedia*, "Conspiracy Theories about Adolf Hitler's Death."

[59] For an example of a non-Christian resurrection story, see Saibaba.ws, "The resurrection of Mr. V. Radhakrishna."

[60] For a readable rundown of Elvis sightings, see Raffa, "The King of Rock and Roll Lives."

[61] Cavin and Colombetti, "The Implausibility and Low Explanatory Power of the Resurrection Hypothesis," 84.

[62] Cavin and Colombetti, "The Implausibility and Low Explanatory Power of the Resurrection Hypothesis," 67.

[63] It is worth noting that Cavin and Colombetti point out that a dead person spontaneously coming back to life is not outside the realm of physical possibility; it would not

In other words, the Standard Model of physics—along with all of the research that has established it over the years—is in direct conflict with *The Resurrection Hypothesis*. The Standard Model thus entails that the resurrection did not happen. This means that *The Resurrection Hypothesis* is practically as non-conservative as a hypothesis can be—not only less conservative than the *Lie, Coma, Imposter,* and *Legend* hypotheses but even less conservative than creationism, geocentrism, and the flat Earth theory. It is contrary to all of science.

The Verdict

This, by all accounts, is one reason Cavin and Colombetti's paper is so devastating to *The Resurrection Hypothesis;* it is its death nail. The unconservative nature of *The Resurrection Hypothesis* that Cavin and Colombetti reveal puts an evidential burden on it that it cannot overcome. If *The Resurrection Hypothesis* could prove itself—by being vastly more fruitful, simpler, and wider scoping than its competitors—it might have a fighting chance. As we have seen, that is how unconservative scientific theories win scientific revolutions. But (also as we have seen), *The Resurrection Hypothesis* is none of those things; indeed, by its very nature, it cannot be. It invokes inexplicable entities, acting in the unobservable and inexplicable ways; it is

---

necessarily break physical laws. To put it simply, because completely random events happen at the quantum level, it is statistically possible for all the subatomic particles in a dead body to, randomly and simultaneously, all leap to a state they would have to be in to make the body alive again. But this does not affect the argument I have made here. First, this is possible in the same way that it is possible for the molecules in the air next to you to spontaneously recognize themselves into your clone. Yes, such things (in the loosest sense of the word) *could* happen—but we know they have not, and we know they will not. The universe is not large enough, nor will it exist long enough, to make the occurrence of such things anywhere, at any time, even remotely likely. (No, we cannot be *certain* they do not happen, but certainty is not required for knowledge. Such events are so statistically improbable that we can be justified in believing they do not occur.) Second, the point of Cavin and Colombetti's argument is that, while a dead person *spontaneously* coming back to life is not (technically speaking) contrary to the Standard Model, *God bringing a dead person back to life* is contrary to the Standard Model. So, since God raising Jesus is what *The Resurrection Hypothesis* says happened, *The Resurrection Hypothesis* is monumentally unconservative. And third, even if we took "God did it" out of *The Resurrection Hypothesis,* and instead suggested that Jesus rose because of a random convolution of quantum events, it would still be unconservative. Yes, the hypothesis would no longer be "contrary" to the Standard Model; but given how unlikely the Standard Model entails that such an event would be, the Standard Model would still give us very good reason to think that such an event did not happen. If we saw Princess Diana on the news tonight, "she faked her death" would still be a more conservative (and better) explanation than *quantum resurrection.*

untestable, cannot be fruitful, has virtually no explanatory power (i.e., scope), and is, by definition, not simple. Even the ridiculous idea that Jesus had a long-lost twin brother who just happened to show up three days after Jesus was crucified, would be a better explanation.

But, of course, as we saw above, the most likely explanation is *The Legend Hypothesis*. It is not only simpler than the resurrection hypothesis, but is also simpler than the *Lie*, *Coma*, and *Imposter* hypotheses. It was more successful in predicting what we discovered about how Jesus' story evolved over time, is more consistent with what we know about the reliability of oral traditions, and what the early Christians seemed to have believed. It is therefore, by definition, the best explanation of the evidence that Davis, Craig, and others cite for *The Resurrection Hypothesis*. That does not necessarily mean that *The Legend Hypothesis* is true; perhaps there is an even better explanation out there that we have not considered. But it certainly is better than *The Resurrection Hypothesis*, and thus belief in the resurrection hypothesis is irrational.

As I mentioned in the introduction, Cavin and Colombetti would undoubtedly point out the shortcomings of the SEARCH method and argue for the superiority of their Bayesian approach. For example, the SEARCH method does not show how the criteria of adequacy "fit" together or when and how one criterion should take precedence over another. What do you do in in case of ties, where one hypothesis is simpler, but another has wider scope? By factoring in conservatism and simplicity into prior probability, and scope and fruitfulness being a factor of Bayesian likelihood, the Bayesian approach can potentially answer these kinds of questions.[64] But this shortcoming of the SEARCH method in no way affects the strength of the argument I have presented here because there is not a tie. *The Legend Hypothesis* is the best explanation in every respect; and *The Resurrection Hypothesis* is the worst in every respect. There is no tie for the Bayesian approach to break.

But none of this should be surprising. Supernatural explanations *never* fare well against their competitors because, by their very nature, they do not meet the criteria of adequacy—they do the exact opposite of what good explanations must, by definition, do.[65] They invoke inexplicable, extra,

---

[64] For more on this, see Cavin and Colombetti "Assessing the Resurrection Hypothesis,"

[65] I point out that these are the things they must do, *by definition*, to circumvent the inevitable objection that using the criteria of adequacy "rigs the game" against the resurrection hypothesis. There is no rigging; the criteria express what good explanations must do or be to be *good explanations*—like have *explanatory* power, or not invoke extra entities (a criteria first

supernatural assumptions that are contrary to the laws of science and are thus, by definition, non-simple, unconservative, and cannot have scope. Indeed, Theodore Schick has argued that "God did it" can never be an adequate explanation of anything,[66] and I have argued that the same is true for "a miracle occurred."[67] Since the resurrection would have been a miracle caused by God, it is no wonder that it fails so monumentally at being a good explanation.

BIBLIOGRAPHY

Abruzzi, William S. "When Was Jesus Born? A Critical Examination of Jesus' Birth Year as Presented in the Infancy Narratives." Preprint submitted January 2016. https://www.researchgate.net/publication/334577128_When_Was_Jesus_Born_A_Critical_Examination_of_Jesus'_Birth_Year_as_Presented_in_the_Infancy_Narratives.

Azar, Beth. "The Limits of Eyewitness Testimony." Monitor on Psychology 42, no. 11 (2011): 26. https://www.apa.org/monitor/2011/12/eyewitness.

Barrett, C. K. *The Gospel According to St. John: An Introduction with Commentary and Notes on the Greek Text*. 2nd ed. Philadelphia, PA: Westminster John Knox Press, 1978.

BrightSide. "25 People Who Didn't Expect to Meet Their Doppelgangers." Accessed May 28, 2021. https://brightside.me/wonder-people/25-people-who-didnt-expect-to-meet-their-doppelgangers-431260/.

Carrier, Richard. *Proving History: Bayes's Theorem and the Quest for the Historical Jesus*. Amherst, NY: Prometheus Books, 2012.

Cavin, Robert Greg and Carlos A. Colombetti. "Assessing the Resurrection Hypothesis: Problems with Craig's Inference to the Best Explanation," *European Journal for Philosophy of Religion* 11, no. 2 (2019): 205–28, https://doi.org/10.24204/ejpr.v11i2.2836.

———. "The Implausibility and Low Explanatory Power of the Resurrection Hypothesis – With a Rejoinder to Stephen T. Davis." *Socio-Historical Examination of Religion and Ministry* 2, no. 1 (2020): 37–94, https://doi.org/10.33929/sherm.2020.vol2.no1.04.

Cline, Austin. "Gospel Discrepancies of Jesus' Crucifixion." *Learn Religions*, June 25, 2019. https://www.learnreligions.com/contradictions-in-gospel-accounts-of-jesus-crucifixion-250140.

---

identified by a Christian philosopher, William of Ockham). These criteria work across the board and are consistently utilized in IBE.

[66] Schick, "Can God Explain Anything?" 55–63.

[67] Johnson, "Justified Belief in Miracles is Impossible," 61–74.

Conroy, J Oliver. "An Apocalyptic Cult, 900 Dead: Remembering the Jonestown Massacre, 40 Years On." *The Guardian*, November 17, 2018. https://www.theguardian.com/world/2018/nov/17/an-apocalyptic-cult-900-dead-remembering-the-jonestown-massacre-40-years-on.

Craig, William Lane. *Assessing the New Testament Evidence for the Historicity of the Resurrection of Jesus*. New York: NY: The Edwin Mellen Press, 1989.

———. *Reasonable Faith: Christian Truth and Apologetics*. Wheaton, IL: Crossway Books, 2008.

Davis, Stephen T. "Craig on the Resurrection: A Defense." *Socio-Historical Examination of Religion and Ministry* 2, no. 1 (2020): 28–35, https://doi.org/10.33929/sherm.2020.vol2.no1.03.

Davis, Tamara, Dean Rickles, and Susan Scott. "Understanding Gravity – Warps and Ripples in Space Time." Australian Academy of Science. February 03, 2016. https://www.science.org.au/curious/space-time/gravity.

Dockrill, Peter. "Man Declared Dead by 3 Doctors Wakes up in Morgue Just Hours Before Autopsy." Science Alert. January 10, 2018. https://www.sciencealert.com/man-declared-dead-3-doctors-wakes-up-morgue-hours-before-autopsy-prisoner-catalepsy.

Doherty, Earl. *Jesus: Neither God nor Man: The Case for a Mythical Jesus*. Ottawa, ON: Age of Reason Publications, 2009.

Ehrman, Bart. *Jesus Before the Gospels: How the Earliest Christians Remembered, Changed, and Invented Their Stories of the Savior*. New York, NY: Harper One, 2016.

———. *Forged: Writing in the Name of God – Why the Bible's Authors are Not Who We Think They Are*. New York, NY: 2012.

———. "Why Romans Crucified People (The Story Beyond the Cross & Nails." The Bart Ehrman Blog: The History & Literature of Early Christianity, July 7, 2014. https://ehrmanblog.org/why-romans-crucified-people/.

Eisendrath, Craig. "The Old Testament Wars: Is the Bible History or Fiction?" *The Baltimore Sun*, August 31, 2003, https://www.baltimoresun.com/news/bs-xpm-2003-08-31-0309020483-story.html.

Explorable.com. "Semmelweis' Germ Theory." August 21, 2010. https://explorable.com/semmelweis-germ-theory.

Fann, K.T. *Peirce's Theory of Abduction*. The Hauge: Holland: Springer, 1970.

Frankfurt, Harry. "Peirce's Notion of Abduction." *Journal of Philosophy* 55, no. 14 (1958): 593–96, https://doi.org/10.2307/2021966.

Harman, Gilbert. "The Inference to the Best Explanation." *Philosophical Review* 74, no. 1 (1965): 88–95, https://doi.org/10.2307/2183532

Humphreys, Kenneth. *Jesus Never Existed: An Introduction to the Ultimate Heresy*. Charleston, WV: Nine-Banded Books, 2014.

Jha, Alok. "How Did Crucifixion Kill?" *The Guardian*, April 8, 2004. theguardian.com/science/2004/apr/08/thisweekssciencequestions.

Johnson, David Kyle. "Book Review: Bart Ehrman's Jesus Before the Gospels." A Logical Take (blog). Psychology Today, April 10, 2016. https://www.psychologytoday.com/us/blog/logical-take/201604/book-review-bart-ehrman-s-jesus-the-gospels.

———. "Justified Belief in Miracles is Impossible." *Science, Religion and Culture* 2, no. 2 (2015): 61–74, http://dx.doi.org/10.17582/journal.src/2015/22.61.74.

———. *The Myths that Stole Christmas: Seven Misconceptions That Hijacked the Holiday (and How We Can Take It Back)*. Washington, DC: Humanist Press, 2015.

———. "Why Religious Experience Can't Justify Religious Belief." *Socio-Historical Examination of Religion and Ministry* 2, no. 2 (2020): 26–46.

Keys, David. "Leading Archaeologist Says Old Testament Stories are Fiction." *Independent*, March 28, 1993. https://www.independent.co.uk/news/leading-archaeologist-says-old-testament-storeis-are-fiction-1500431.html.

Lipton, Peter. *Inference to the Best Explanation*. 2nd ed. New York: NY: Routledge, 2004.

Lumen Learning, "Tests of General Relativity." https://courses.lumenlearning.com/astronomy/chapter/tests-of-general-relativity/.

Mcauliffe, William H. B. "How did Abduction Get Confused with Inference to the Best Explanation?" *Transactions of the Charles S. Peirce Society* 51, no. 3 (2015): 300–19, https://doi.org/10.2979/trancharpeirsoc.51.3.300.

McDowell, Sean. "Did the Apostles Really Die as Martyrs for Their Faith?." Biola Magazine (blog), November 4, 2013. https://www.biola.edu/blogs/biola-magazine/2013/did-the-apostles-really-die-as-martyrs-for-their-f.

———. *The Fate of the Apostles: Examining the Martyrdom Accounts of the Closest Followers of Jesus*. New York: NY: Routledge, 2016.

Millard, Alan R. "Literacy in the Time of Jesus. Could His Words Have Been Recorded in His Lifetime?" *Biblical Archaeology Review* 29, no. 4 (2003). baslibrary.org/biblical-archaeology-review/29/4/4.

Peirce, Charles S. *The Essential Peirce*, Vol.1, ed. N. Houser and C. Kloesel, Vol.2, ed. The Peirce Edition Project, Indiana University Press, 1982–1992.

Raffa, Julia. "The King of Rock and Roll Lives." *The Psychology of Extraordinary Beliefs: Ordinary students exploring extraordinary beliefs* (blog), April 18, 2018. https://u.osu.edu/vanzandt/2018/04/18/the-king-of-rock-and-roll-lives/.

Rainey, Anson F. *Early History of the Israelite People from the Written & Archaeological Sources. Studies in the History of the Ancient Near East*. Leiden: E. J. Brill, 1992. https://doi.org/10.1017/S036400940000636X.

RationalWiki. "Contradictions in Jesus' Crucifixion." Last modified July 5, 2019. rationalwiki.org/wiki/Contradictions_in_Jesus%27_crucifixion.

Saibaba.ws. "The Resurrection of Mr. V. Radhakrishna." http://saibaba.ws/miracles/resurrectionradhakrishna.htm.

Schick, Theodore. "Can God Explain Anything?" *Think* 2, no. 4 (2003): 55–63, https://doi.org/10.1017/S1477175600000634.

Schick, Theodore and Lewis Vaughn. *How to Think about Weird Things: Critical Thinking for a New Age*. New York, NY: McGraw-Hill Education, 2019.

Science History Institute. "Louis Pasteur." Last modified December 14, 2017. https://www.sciencehistory.org/historical-profile/louis-pasteur.

Seidensticker, Bob. "Contradictions in the Resurrection Account." Cross Examined: Clear Thinking About Christianity (blog). Patheos.com. March 22, 2013. https://www.patheos.com/blogs/crossexamined/2013/03/contradictions-in-the-resurrection-account-3/.

Siegel, Ethan. "This is How, 100 Years Ago, A Solar Eclipse Proved Einstein Right and Newton Wrong," *Forbes* May 29, 2019, https://www.forbes.com/sites/startswithabang/2019/05/29/this-is-how-100-years-ago-a-solar-eclipse-proved-einstein-right-and-newton-wrong/#634f1b9b1610.

Tabor, James. *The Jesus Discovery: The New Archaeological Find that Reveals the Birth of Christianity*. New York: NY: Simon & Schuster, 2013.

———. "The 'Strange' Ending of the Gospel of Mark and Why It Makes All the Difference." *Biblical Archaeology Society*, April 1, 2018. https://www.biblicalarchaeology.org/daily/biblical-topics/new-testament/the-strange-ending-of-the-gospel-of-mark-and-why-it-makes-all-the-difference/.

———. "What Really Happened Easter Morning – the Mystery Solved?" *Taborblog (blog)*, December 31, 2015. https://jamestabor.com/what-really-happened-easter-morning-the-mystery-solved/.

Thagard, Paul. "Best Explanation: Criteria for Theory Choice." *Journal of Philosophy* 75, no. 2 (1978): 76–92. https://doi.org/10.2307/2025686

Turner, Ryan. "An Analysis of the Pre-Pauline Creed in 1 Corinthians 15:1–11." *Christian Apologetics & Research Ministry*. October 1, 2009. https://carm.org/analysis-pre-pauline-creed-1-corinthians-151-11.

Valentine, Carla. "Why Waking Up in a Morgue isn't Quite as Unusual as You'd Think." *The Guardian*, November 14, 2014. https://www.theguardian.com/commentisfree/2014/nov/14/waking-morgue-death-janina-kolkiewicz.

Wikipedia. "Sightings of Elvis Presley." Last modified May 25, 2021. https://en.wikipedia.org/wiki/Elvis_sightings.

———. "Sathya Sai Baba," Last modified May 17, 2021. https://en.wikipedia.org/wiki/Sathya_Sai_Baba.

———. "List of people claimed to be Jesus," Last modified May 27, 2021. https://en.wikipedia.org/wiki/List_of_people_claimed_to_be_Jesus

———. "Conspiracy Theories about Adolf Hitler's Death," Last Modified May 27, 2021. https://en.wikipedia.org/wiki/Conspiracy_theories_about_Adolf_Hitler's_death.

ABOUT THE AUTHOR

David Kyle Johnson is professor of philosophy at King's College (Wilkes-Barre, Pennsylvania) who also produces lecture series for The Teaching Company's *The Great Courses*. His specializations include metaphysics, logic, philosophy of science, and philosophy of religion; his "Great Courses" include *Sci-Phi: Science Fiction as Philosophy*, *The Big Questions of Philosophy*, and *Exploring Metaphysics*. Kyle has published in journals such as *Sophia, Religious Studies, Think, Philo,* and *Science, Religion and Culture* and is the editor-in-chief of *The Palgrave Handbook of Popular Culture as Philosophy*. He is the editor of popular books such as *Black Mirror and Philosophy: Dark Reflections* (Wiley-Blackwell, 2019) and *Exploring the Orville* (McFarland, 2021), and has also written numerous book chapters on popular culture and logic, including eleven entries in *Bad Arguments: 100 of The Most Important Logical Fallacies in Western Philosophy* (Wiley-Blackwell, 2018). He maintains two blogs for *Psychology Today* (*Plato on Pop* and *A Logical Take*), and most of his academic work is available for free download on academia.edu.

ACKNOWLEDGEMENT

Kyle would like to thank his student aide, Sabrina Traver, for her herculean formatting, typesetting, and proofreading efforts. The debt she is owed cannot be calculated. He would also like to thank Darren Slade, and the anonymous reviewers of earlier versions of this paper.

MORE FROM THE AUTHOR

Sci-Phi:
Science Fiction as Philosophy
The Great Courses, 2018

The Big Questions of Philosophy
The Great Courses, 2016

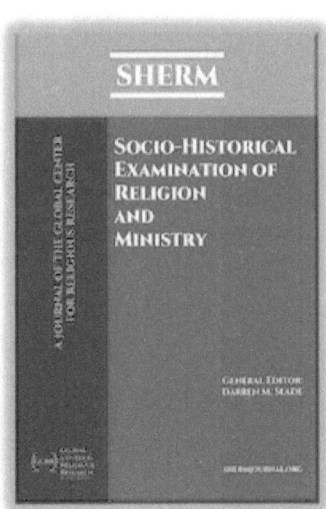

A Fruitful or Wild French Vineyard? Distinguishing the Religious Roots of Albigenses and Waldensians in the Twelfth Century

Ottavio Palombaro,
Free University of Amsterdam

Abstract: *Much like how fruitful and wild branches are mixed in the same vineyard, there is a great deal of confusion when someone tries to discern the religious roots of heretical movements grown out of the Middle Ages. Two peculiar cases are often associated by confessional literature: Waldensians and Albigenses, demonized by Roman Catholic literature or romanticized by Protestant and modern Medieval fictional literature. In the quest for historical accuracy this paper intends to argue for the supremacy of certain contextual theological beliefs rather than socio-economic features alone in discerning the true nature of these movements despite their similarities and common persecution by the dominant Catholic religion. While the Albigenses reintroduced the ancient heresy of Gnosticism, the Waldensians were driven by a return to apostolic Christianity. The study also points out the need to analyze those movements beyond a one-dimensional approach in order to see the heterogeneity inside each movement, especially in their progressive evolution through time. Results point toward the need to reject an ancient origin thesis for the case of the Waldensians, whereas still allowing, in their case, a possible proto-Protestant connection.*

Keywords: Albigenses, Cathars, Middle Ages, Religious Movements, Waldensians

Introduction

Fruitful or wild vineyards may look alike on the outside but only one produces genuine fruits. In the same way, two religious movements of the Middle Ages have often suffered an unfair association among scholars, and it is time to bring such associations to a close.[1] Confessional history on the Protestant side boasted of the Albigenses as ancestors of the Reformation,[2] whereas on the Catholic side many described Protestantism as a

---

[1] Walther, "Were the Albigenses and Waldenses," 178. See also, Cross, *The Oxford Dictionary of the Christian Church*, 1726-27.

[2] Beavis, "The Cathar Mary Magdalene," 419.

new form of the old Albigenses heresy.[3] A host of contemporary fictional stories about Catharism reduced their history to a tourist ploy or as a source of revenue for many bestsellers. Scientific history and secularists, on the other hand, classified these movements as "medieval anticlerical movements" and interpreted them both as the fruit of political struggle driven mostly by economic considerations.[4] This could not be farther from the truth.

Southern France, being the center of commercial routes, allowed new ideas to circulate, yet the nature of these movements was primarily religious. Christendom as a whole, whether among Catholic or heretical factions, during this period witnessed the spread of movements aiming at returning to apostolic simplicity. This was the case not just of the Waldensians and Albigenses but also of other movements such as: Vita Apostolica, Humiliati, Cistercians, Joachimites, Dominicans, Franciscans, Hospitallers, Fraticelli, Petrobrusians, Publicans, Beghards, Henricians, Tisserantes, Free Spirits, Hussites, Lollards, Dolcinians, Arnaldists, Patarines, Passagini, and Josephini. Given this variety of movements, there is a risk of grouping them all together despite their differences. These movements were united only in their desire to counteract the pomp and spiritual "sickness" of the corrupted religious structure of the official church during the Middle Ages. They were movements signaling a crisis in the medieval church and not necessarily a revival.[5] But how exactly did these two movements of Waldensians and Albigenses differ from each other?

This paper shows that in discerning respectively the gnostic roots of the Albigenses and the biblical roots of the Waldensians it is of primary importance to consider the role of biblical teachings in each of them regardless of similarities or changes over time. In the pages that follow, these two religious movements will be analyzed and compared first by tracing their roots, and then by presenting a brief overview of their spread and the major events connected with them. Furthermore, the main beliefs of each group will be examined, focusing on the role of the biblical message for their faith and practice; and where opportune, a discussion on the doctrine of salvation of the specific movement will be included. Lastly, mention will be made of their respective community organization, persecution, and subsequent extinction or survival, giving some concluding thoughts on the implications of the findings.

Before analyzing the doctrinal features of each of these religious groups, it is important to make a methodological note. There are contrasting

---

[3] Gui, "The Waldensians Heretics," 207. See also, Vicaire, *Les Albigeois Ancetres des Protestants*, 23.

[4] Kaelber, "Weavers into Heretics?," 112–13.

[5] Zeman, "Restitution and Dissent," 7.

types of literature on the subject ranging from idealistic and at times fictional representations of the matter[6] to condemning and denigrating depictions.[7] Torn between these extremes, it is not always easy to distinguish their historical accuracy. This is also aggravated by the fact that dealing with clandestine groups during the Middle Ages, very little direct documentary evidence was written or survived persecution. Therefore, the majority of historical recollections end up relying on indirect and at times questionable documents from the hands of the persecutors of these groups.[8] Reconstructions based on speculations and chronological imprecisions prevent drawing a line between history and historical fiction. For this reason, considering the specific beliefs of these groups will be of primary importance. This paper will trace the general doctrinal features of these groups and then draw some significant conclusions on the role of beliefs for the comparative study of religious movements.

The Gnostic Sect of the Albigenses

The Albigenses obtained this title due to their strong presence in the town of Albi in southern France, where they were also called Cathars (καθαρός: pure), and known as Bulgari, Bugari, or Burges in Eastern Europe. They represented the most widely distributed and most enduring heresy among the sects of the Middle Ages, as well as Europe's first and greatest counter-religion to the Roman Catholic church.[9] The religious movement of the Albigenses had no founder. However, it is possible to trace back their origin to the Paulicians of Armenia. These were gnostic groups active in Asia Minor during the fifth century that were pushed toward Constantinople and toward the Balkans (known there as Bogomil). Much later on, in 1167, the Bogomil bishop, Nicetas, arrived in Languedoc and founded a Cathar congregation.[10] From there, the heresy spread in parts of Italy, the Rhine, northern Spain, and England.

Customary relations with the East due to the First Crusade increased the number of Cathars in the West.[11] Midway through the twelfth century, the Albigenses were present in more than 1,000 villages and had four million Occitan adherents in southern France alone.[12] In Italy, they relied on

---

[6] McCaffrey, "Imaging the Cathars," 411.
[7] Vasilev, "Heresy and the English Reformation," 785.
[8] Lansing, "Power and Purity," 102.
[9] Schaff, *History of the Christian Church*, 470.
[10] Barber, *The Cathars*, 181.
[11] Previté-Orton, *The Shorter Cambridge Medieval History*, 661.
[12] Lambert, "The Cathars," 339.

independent civic authorities and informal ties; and by the end of the twelfth century, they outnumbered the Catholics in big cities, such as Milan or Florence. They were able to expand their own local communities in other areas, such as those documented in Orvieto, even sending some of their members to study at important universities.[13] The movement was found to be attractive because of its communal living, imitating an apostolic poor and simple lifestyle. Their ideological alternative to the official social organization saw purity as the real source of power. Also, the Albigenses were characterized by a disciplined conduct that sharply contrasted with the opulence and corruption of the official church.[14]

The episcopal weakness of southern France, as well as the vacuum of central authorities, made the ethical appeal of the Albigenses suitable for the Languedocian noble patronage of people, such as Roger Trencaval, viscount of Béziers, and his local networks, in growing opposition to the ecclesiastical conspicuous owning of proprieties.[15] In light of this corrupt and negligent clergy, the Albigenses rejected the established church as the "great Babylon" of Revelation with all its corruptions, rituals, and structure of powers, presenting themselves as a true spiritual alternative.

However, like the Bogomils and Paulicians, the Albigenses doctrinally professed a strict dualism, with two equal deities (a good god and an evil god) guided by principles of eternal good and evil. They considered all matter as evil, created by the evil god, Lucifer, who was given a material body after being cast out of heaven. They rejected the Hebrew Bible, baptism, the Mass, the use of any religious items, the priesthood, marriage as well as reproduction,[16] and in particular the material presence of Christ in the Eucharist.[17] Their denial of the real presence in the host was the core of their fiercest opposition to the religious system of the day, and it was seen by the official church as a direct, dangerous attack at the foundation of their ecclesiastical and sacramental order. The Cathars believed themselves to be the only true "church of the righteous" bearer of salvation, but at the same time, they were highly divided among themselves on doctrine with more than seventy sects.

Not all Cathars, therefore, believed the same thing, but there existed instead a wide spectrum of belief and stress on concerns that varied in time and

---

[13] Miller, "Power and Purity," 163.
[14] Costen, "The Cathars and the Albigensian Crusade," 81.
[15] Cannon, *History of Christianity in the Middle Ages,* 222.
[16] Their numerical growth is surprising even because, given their prohibition of reproduction, it happened only through personal conversion.
[17] Costen, "The Cathars and the Albigensian Crusade," 950.

place. At times, in fact, heterodox views coexisted alongside the conventional practices of the Catholic majority. The Albigenses translated the New Testament in Occitan with the addition of other writings of a gnostic nature, such as the "Gospel of the Secret Supper" and the "Book of the Two Principles." When approaching the Bible, they believed it to be erroneous. They allegorized many biblical passages, describing the Hebrew Bible as a "demonic book of an evil god" and John the Baptist as a "major demon." The Cathars believed that their god, married with two wives, could not be found anywhere in the material world, which was instead made by the devil, the lesser creator who stole particles of light from heaven when creating the universe.[18]

Being a non-Christian movement that acquired Christian coloration, Catharism as a form of medieval neo-Manichaeism[19] also denied the incarnation of Christ, his death on the cross (suffered instead by the devil), as well as Christ's eternal pre-existence and the hypostatic union, which for them was less than God. The sect was divided between *credentes* (common sympathizers) and *perfecti*, (proper members) often living in a community of goods. Even the *perfecti*,[20] however, were involved in manual labor in order to support themselves and the community. This venerated status of the *perfecti* was accessible through the *consolamentum*, a baptism of the Holy Spirit through the laying of hands on the head of the novices as a sign of their entrance into the community. The *consolamentum* was the only sacrament and means of salvation among the Albigenses. It gave assurance of the forgiveness of sins and restoration to the spiritual kingdom of God, but it needed to be taken under strict dietary and celibacy laws. Other rituals were added to this, such as the *benedictio panis*, the collective penance (*servici*), and the ritual of *endura*, a voluntary starvation that caused several cases of death.[21]

The use of anything material in their worship, oaths, eating of milk, meat, cheese, and eggs was condemned, as well as participation in war. This did

---

[18] Davenport, "The Catholics, the Cathars, and the Concept of Infinity," 267.

[19] Manicheism was a syncretic dualistic philosophy taught by Mani (third century CE) that, combining elements of Christianity and Gnosticism, believed in a primordial battle between good and evil, light and dark, where all matter is evil.

[20] The *Perfecti* were commonly called: "bons hommes et bonnes femmes." Inside this category there were bishops (highest degree with power of ordination), deacons (responsible of administration and discipline of the religious houses) and major and minor sons ("fils," co-helper of bishops, the major was the successor at the bishop's death). Apart from the *consolamentum* the *perfecti* ministered several rituals, one of them, the "adoration," was a term used by the Inquisition to define the ritual of blessing (*melioramentum*) that the *perfecti* were ministering to the believers.

[21] Tsiamis, et al., "The 'Endura' of The Cathars Heresy," 174.

not mean complete and actual pacifism since they were sometimes willing to murder their enemies in order to preserve their secret establishment. According to the Albigenses, marriage was not only to be avoided, as well as any sexual contact, but they also believed that no one living in sexual relations could be saved.[22]

Since the Albigenses believed in the reincarnation of spirits in animals, they forbade the killing of any animal, even insects.[23] After death, there was no resurrection since the doctrine of creation was denied. The body was believed to be made by the devil. At death the human spirit, in tune with medieval Neo-Platonism, went back to heaven since it originated from God.[24] The end of the world was conceived as the final and complete removal of beings from actual nothingness and culminated in the universal salvation of all fallen souls. From this evidence, it is possible to conclude that Catharism was outside the Christian circle and should be referred to as another religion. As their members used the Bible and assembled in fellowship, their movement was neo-pagan and theologically opposite to the fundamental beliefs of orthodox Christianity.[25] Cathars, for instance, placed a strong emphasis on the Gospel of John, but their religious practice clearly went against John's central teachings.

A Variety of Waldensianisms

The Waldensians, Waldenses, or Vaudois, were a different biblical sect of the Middle Ages, founded by Peter Waldo or Valdes (1140–1205), a rich unlearned merchant of Lyon in south-eastern France who, after witnessing the death of a friend, was touched by listening to a ballad on St. Alexis and its call to poverty. After he was counseled by a priest, he felt a compelling call to give his fortunes away to the poor people of Lyon. In 1173, Waldo immediately started a movement of "the poor of Lyon" (*pauperes spiritu or pauperes Christi*), characterized by itinerant preaching, translating several portions of the Bible into the vernacular, and living out the ideals of apostolic simplicity. Since Waldo was unable to read Latin, parts of the Christian Bible were commissioned and translated by one of his followers in Provençal, becoming

---

[22] Hamilton, "The Yellow Cross," 154.
[23] The Cathars taught that in order to regain the spiritual and angelic pure status, a believer had to renounce the material completely. Until this was achieved the soul was believed to be stuck in a cycle of reincarnation, condemned to live on the corrupt earth. See also, Schaff, *History of the Christian Church*, 493.
[24] Langermann, "Of Cathars and Creationism," 161.
[25] Shriver, "A Summary of 'Images of Catharism and the Historian's Task'," 52.

accessible to the common people. Waldo believed that in order to be "perfect" all material benefits were to be refused *a priori*.[26]

The intention of this movement, like many religious movements of the Middle Ages, was to restore the austere ideals of the early apostolic communities.[27] Some scholars have even suggested a more obscure origin[28] long before Waldo, hypothesizing the presence of primitive forms of *Vaudois* Christianity in the area joined later on by the followers of Waldo of Lyon in the same area.[29] Those ancient examples of local dissidents in the Italian valleys are said to trace back their line to the "night of time" of primitive Christianity even up to 120 CE. Their presence is said by those scholars of Protestant leaning who follow this view to have become evident only as the church of Rome was moving farther and farther away from its apostolic origins.[30] This "ancient origins thesis," often instrumentally idealized by Protestants, Mormons, Jehovah's Witnesses, and Adventists to prove their own standing, is today largely discounted.[31]

Rather than being related with the heresy of the Albigenses, the Waldensians were in origin much closer, and in fact gave direct influence, thirty years later to the rising Franciscan movement.[32] The case of the Waldensians and Albigenses in this regard shows the impact that heretical movements had in shaping the religious practices of the medieval Catholic Church. By 1179, Waldo and his followers, at first recognizing the authority of Pope Alexander III, journeyed to Rome and appeared at the third Lateran council asking for the recognition of their "Rule." At first, they were only considered schismatic and disobedient to authority, but not heretical. Later, under influence of the Archbishop of Lyon Jean aux Belles-Mains, the Waldensians in 1184 were expelled from Lyon and excommunicated by Pope Lucius III at the Synod of Verona with the charge of preaching as laymen without the bishop's consent.[33]

To this charge, Waldo and his followers in 1182 answered that it was "better to obey God than men" in the face of those who "want to bind the Word of God according to their personal wish." The situation was aggravated by divisions internal to the movement. The "poor men of Lyon" rejected manual

---

[26] Tourn, *The Waldensians*, 25. On the same author: Snyder, "The Waldensians," 396.
[27] Kaelber, "Other- and Inner-Worldly Asceticism," 92.
[28] Cameron, *The European Reformation*, 70.
[29] Comba, *History of the Waldenses of Italy*, 81.
[30] Barnett, "Where Was Your Church before Luther?," 21.
[31] Stephens, "Never Failing Light. The Waldensian Story," 235.
[32] Marthaler, "Forerunners of the Franciscans: the Waldenses," 133–42.
[33] See for example, Grant, "The Elevation of the Host," 232.

labor but the "poor of Lombardy" instead of making vows of absolute poverty wanted to remain involved in trade.[34] The controversy resulted in an internal division where the Waldensians of northern Italy remained involved with manual work, without being dependent on alms.[35] The Spanish Waldensian Durand of Huesca (1160-1224), on the contrary, believed that preachers should leave all manual work to dedicate themselves to the meditation of Scriptures. As the movement shifted from being just a schismatic group to a heretical movement, Huesca decided to return to the Catholic church. A problem to factor in was that, in contrast to the Albigenses and other religious dissident groups like the Hussites or Lollards, the Waldensians lacked any support from lords, viscounts, or local governments.

Despite the efforts of unification with a conference in Bergamo (1218), where several issues of faith were examined by the Waldensian leadership, part of the group eventually rejoined the Catholic church. Although being historical contemporaries of the Albigenses, the Waldensians were not doctrinal sympathizers with them. On the contrary, Waldensians were untainted by Manicheanism and went a great way to dissociate from the heretical, dualist teachings of the Albigenses, according to which good and evil are juxtaposed as opposite equal forces. As a former Waldensian, Durand of Huesca wrote a treatise against the Cathars without, however, condemning the Waldensians. Waldensians were often labeled by other Inquisitors as "Donatists" because of their rejection of the validity of Catholic sacraments.

As the Waldensians were expelled from Lyon and the bloody massacres against the Albigenses approached southern France, many Waldensians fled from Provence and Languedoc to other parts of Europe, mostly to the more secure alpine regions between the Dauphiné and Piedmont. From an urban movement focused on poverty, they became a rural clandestine community increasingly opposed to the official clergy. They professed biblical literalism, believing in the supreme authority of Scripture in matters of faith and practice long before the Protestant Reformation. They believed in the right of lay people to preach the gospel (*libere praedicare verbum Dei*) in their common tongue. They defended liberty of conscience, considering several traditions of the church at the time inconsistent with orthodox teachings.[36]

In accordance with certain New Testament teachings, they denied several Catholic traditions: seven sacraments, priestly vestments, sacred images, taking of oaths, veneration of Mary or the saints, purgatory, mass for

---

[34] Brown, *Heresies*, 263.
[35] Brown, *Heresies*, 264.
[36] Walther, "A Survey of Recent Research," 148.

the dead, indulgences, etc.[37] The Waldensians saw themselves as part of the universal church who had experienced divine love and grace.[38] They distinguished themselves from the "church of the wicked" (*ecclesia malignantium*). They were organized with the apostolic pattern of bishops-presbyters and deacons with the addition of a "majoral" super-intender, as well as other sympathizers (amici, "friends" or secret associates). Due to persecution, leaders were constantly moving among the religious communities, which were centered on meetinghouses (*hospitia*).[39] Later, leaders developed the role of barbes, a specific body of lay itinerant preachers trained to preach two-by-two across Europe.[40] Many of them could circulate through disguise as physicians or merchants.[41]

Some scholars suggested that the Waldensians, until the advent of Martin Luther, should not be too easily labeled as "forerunners of the Reformation," "evangelical" or "proto-Protestant." Contrary to the portrait of some confessional histories, Schaff notes, it is not possible to find mention of justification by faith alone (*sola Fide*) among early Waldensians, a doctrine crucial to the identity of the Protestant faith.[42] Instead, Waldo emphasized from the beginning of his movement that faith without works is dead. Humanity, therefore, is neither justified by faith alone, nor by deeds on their own, but by faith and good works.[43] It is nevertheless significant that in an historical recount by Samuel Morland, mention is made of an ancient confession of faith dating to 1120. Supposedly, this creed even precedes Waldo and his profession of faith dating between 1179-1180. The intention of the creed is to go back to a primitive church pattern of poverty and defense of the faith. Articles 5 through 7 confess:

> That Christ was born in the time appointed by God the Father. That is to say, in the time when all iniquity abounded, and not for the cause of good works, for all were Sinners; but that he might shew us grace and mercy, as being faithful. That Christ is our life, truth, peace, and righteousness, as also

---

[37] Cameron, "The Reformation of the Heretics," 99.
[38] Cantor, *Medieval History*, 416.
[39] Biller, "Goodbye to Waldensianism?," 16.
[40] Audisio and Davison "Preachers by Night," 853. See also, "How to Detect a Clandestine Minority," 208.
[41] Wakefield, "Heretics as Physicians in the Thirteenth Century," 328.
[42] Schaff, *History of the Christian Church*, 493.
[43] Gonnet, "The Influence of the Sermon on the Mount," 34.

our Pastour, Advocate, Sacrifice, and Priest, who died for the salvation of all those that believe and is risen for our justification.[44]

In these words, as well as from the context of the whole confession of faith, it is possible to derive a view of justification closer to the one in Protestantism than the one of Medieval Catholicism. The application of this instance on Waldensianism remains questionable also in light of Morland's use of sources written after Waldo and given other dissonant testimonies with confused dates and false quotations. In order to be saved, the Waldensian believer needed, in fact, to make a profession but also to "observe the true law of Christ."[45]

It is only by the time of Oecolampadius and Bucer that by 1532, the Waldensians officially incorporated the Reformed doctrine of justification by faith alone. Furthermore, it is important to consider the existence of doctrinal differences among streams of Waldensianism, such as leadership structure, women teaching,[46] or other issues. In addition to this, during times of harsh persecution, cases of backslidings into the Catholic church were common among Waldensians. In order to elude the Inquisition, oftentimes many made compromises, displaying a double religious commitment, being formally Catholic but secretly remaining in contact with the Waldensian clandestine community.[47]

A Common Bloody Destiny

Despite their different doctrines, because of their common condemnation and refusal to submit to the established Roman Catholic Church, Albigenses and Waldensians both experienced brutal and systematic persecution. First, the Catholic Church made attempts to quell the heresy of the Albigenses through itinerant preachers sent to southern France, like Dominic of Guzman sent to combat the heresy in Languedoc around 1206.[48] Because of the little success of this strategy, Pope Innocent III launched a Crusade led by Simon de Montfort against the Albigenses (1208-1209) in order to extirpate the

---

[44] Morland, *The History of the Evangelical Churches*, 32-33.
[45] Cegna, "La Tradition Pénitentielle des Vaudois et des Hussites," 141.
[46] Kienzle, "Women in a Medieval Heretical Sect," 261.
[47] For example, the visit in Piedmont of the founder of Seventh-day Adventism, Ellen G. White, in 1885. See also, Conder, *The Waldensians and the Seventh-day Sabbath*, 1-4.
[48] Vicaire, *Persequutor Hereticorum*, 75.

growing threat of Catharism in southern France.⁴⁹ By 1218, the Albigenses were exterminated in southern France. The Catholic crusaders destroyed entire cities, systematically burning at the stake hundreds of Albigenses men, women, and children. Most important for the Catholics was the defeat of castle owners who had been the securest patrons, sympathizers, and defenders of the heresy.

Yet the Cathars faced death and persecution with dedication. The Synod of Toulouse of 1229 forbade the use of vernacular translations of the Bible.⁵⁰ The crusade moved from a spiritual battle into a political struggle between southern and northern France. The counteroffensive of Franciscan and Dominican friars, although successful in devastating the region of Languedoc, were not enough to break the local networks of the heresy in the region. Alarmed by the persisting force of the heresy, Gregory IX established the Inquisition by 1233, a secret ecclesiastical court that used torture, capital punishment, and criminal investigation in order to break the strong ties of the local networks of different heresies. Although experiencing some decades of revival in the fourteenth century, by 1244, during the siege of the castle of Montsegur, the movement of the Albigenses came to an end.⁵¹

Unlike Catharism, the Waldensians survived despite recurrent harsh persecution.⁵² Across the centuries, they endured trials before the Inquisition where they were burned at the stake or suffocated inside caves set on fire by their enemies.⁵³ Peter Liegé gives an account of the massacre of 1,700 Waldensians perpetrated by the troops of the Duke of Savoy, which took place during Easter week, commonly known as "Pasque Piemontesi":

> Little children were torn from the arms of their mothers, clasped by their tiny feet, and their heads dashed against the rocks; or were held between two soldiers and their quivering limbs torn up by main force. Their mangled bodies were then thrown on the highways or fields, to be devoured by beasts. The sick and the aged were burned alive in their dwellings. Some had their hands and arms and legs lopped off, and fire applied to the severed parts to staunch the bleeding and prolong their suffering. Some were flayed alive, some were roasted alive, some disemboweled; or tied to trees in their own orchards, and their hearts cut out. Some were horribly mutilated, and of others the brains were boiled and eaten by these cannibals. Some were

---

[49] Hamilton, "The Cathars and the Albigensian Crusade," 610.
[50] Cairns, *Christianity through the Centuries*, 223–24.
[51] The last four *perfecti* were burned at Carcassonne on September 8, 1319.
[52] Ward, "The Waldensian Story," 123.
[53] Deane, "Archiepiscopal Inquisitions in the Middle Rhine," 197.

fastened down into the furrows of their own fields, and ploughed into the soil as men plough manure into it. Others were buried alive. Fathers were marched to death with the heads of their sons suspended round their necks. Parents were compelled to look on while their children were first outraged [raped], then massacred, before being themselves permitted to die.[54]

    The slaughter became infamous through the British poet, John Milton, who, with the sympathy of Oliver Cromwell, penned his famous sonnet "On the Late Massacre in Piedmont."[55] Under this context of geographical and cultural isolation, risking genocide, the Waldensians saw the advent of Protestantism as a necessary lifeboat. Already, by the Synod of Chanforan (1532), the *barbes* conferred in the Angrogna Valley with the Swiss Reformers led by William Farel and issued a new Confession of Faith, openly embracing the Reformed Protestant faith.[56] Waldensians gradually changed from being a rural movement of dissidents into becoming a Genevan-style reformed church.[57]

    Such change seems unexpected since the earlier Waldensian movement was closer to Anabaptism.[58] Waldensian theology, like the Czech Brethren, Taborites or Bohemian Brethren, was much more focused on the New Testament teachings of the Sermon on the Mount.[59] This theological shift was also surprising in light of the existing connection between Waldensians and Hussites already established by the fifteenth century.[60]

    The acceptance of the Protestant Reformation involved the implementation of a number of significant changes in their beliefs, practices, and organization. For example, the Waldensians abandoned their original pacifist tendencies and decided to view war as a legitimate form of defense under the Cattaneo's crusade of 1488 under the leadership of Henri Arnaud (1641-1721). Among other significant and lasting changes, the Waldensians also changed their attitude toward public and ecclesiastical authorities. The itinerant preachers (*Barba*) were sent directly to study theology in Geneva, resulting in the adoption of Calvinist theology.[61]

---

[54] Wylie, *History of the Waldenses*, 132.
[55] Accardy, "Calvin's ministry to the Waldensians," 45.
[56] Ferrario, "The Peaks and Valleys of the Waldensian Church," 53.
[57] Muston, *The Israel of the Alps*, 93.
[58] DeWind, "'Anabaptism' and Italy," 20.
[59] Lochman, "Not Just One Reformation," 218.
[60] MacCulloch, *The Reformation*, 38.
[61] Treesh "The Waldensian Recourse to Violence," 294.

Embracing the Reformation meant the increase of persecutions from the Catholic church, culminating in the joint effort between the King of France Louis XIV and Duke Amedeo II of Savoy to wipe them out in 1686, after the revocation of the Edict of Nantes. During this period even some French Protestant Huguenots sought refuge in the Waldensian Valleys. Even the Waldensians themselves were later on forced to migrate to Switzerland. After such exile, in 1689, Arnaud led a "glorious return" to their homeland, making their survival possible. In that occasion the Waldensians held off a French regiment in what today is known as the battle of Salbertrand.[62]

The Waldensians Today

Only after the late nineteenth century, Waldensians living in the valleys of Piedmont started to enjoy relative religious and political freedom, first under Napoleon then with the Risorgimento, joining the unification process and supporting Count Cavour's unsuccessful effort to promote a "free church in a free state" for the Italian peninsula.[63] Although full separation between church and state in Italy still remains fictitious today, their emancipation became apparent with the "Patenti Letters" enacted by King Alberto of Savoy on April 17, 1848. After centuries of isolation, not being allowed to leave their area, Waldensians were allowed to cross their borders and started to become active in Italian society.[64]

However, their struggle for freedom continued during the time of Italian fascism.[65] As the Catholic Church signed the Concordat with the fascist regime (1929), Waldensians instead took weapons during the resistance movement in 1943-1945.[66] The Waldensians are a rare case of survival representing 10% of the Protestant Italian community today,[67] and in other parts of the world.[68] Their church polity today is a mixture between Presbyterian and Congregationalist with an elected executive committee ("Tavola Valdese").[69]

In recent times, under a climate of granted religious freedom, the Waldensian movement has embraced more pluralistic ecumenical ideas. In

---

[62] Cunsolo, "You are My Witnesses," 116.
[63] Homer, "Seeking Primitive Christianity," 12.
[64] Brauer, ed., *The Westminster Dictionary of Church History*, 854-55.
[65] Rochat, "Le Valli valdesi nel regime fascista: appunti sul controllo poliziesco," 3.
[66] Bowden, ed., *Encyclopedia of Christianity*, 1222-23.
[67] Root, "The Waldensians," 1105.
[68] Vinay, "Storia dei Valdesi III," 670.
[69] Fahlbusch et al., *The Encyclopedia of Christianity*, 702-5.

terms of practical theology, they became closer to the "Social Gospel" and to various aspects of public opinion (euthanasia, remarriage, etc.) that in some Protestant circles are considered forms of liberal theology.[70] The Waldensians also established a theological school now located in Rome, as well as a publishing house where they are involved in an inter-religious dialogue with Methodist and Baptist churches.

Conclusions

Having examined these two dissident movements evolving out of the Middle Ages, it is possible to reach some conclusions. First of all, the field of studies of religious movements requires the recourse to an objective methodological approach that has not always been pursued in the past. Analyzing the specific beliefs of these religious groups requires necessary distinctions to be made and to avoid the generalizations found in existing literature. Despite their apparent commonalities, the "branches" of the Albigenses and Waldensians originated from very different and incompatible roots: Gnosticism versus a focus on poverty. Both groups claimed very ancient origins in their roots that date back to the first centuries of Christianity, yet, it is an error to contemplate an "ancient origin thesis" for the Waldensians, a theory abandoned today by much of the literature.

This becomes particularly relevant when considering the documentary evidence for the doctrine of justification among the Waldensians. It should not come as a surprise that not every aspect of the doctrine was present in the Waldensian pre-Reformation period as even the official church for centuries did not have a clear and uniform position on justification. But this, however, should not lead any competent scholar to simply reject the essence of a possible form of partial proto-Protestantism in Waldensianism. A similar case should be made for those pre-Reformation analogies to Waldensianism that are traceable among the Lollards of John Wycliffe or the Hussites of John Hus. This research indeed warns about the twofold risk of considering the Albigenses as a Christian movement and on the other hand inappropriately rejecting the Waldensians as a heretical movement alien to ancient Christianity.

For both the Waldensians and Albigenses, their roots are not always traceable and easy to distinguish. Nevertheless, the desire to imitate primitive Christianity is still traceable in both, at least outwardly. This study shows that religious beliefs operate as a test for whether a specific religious movement

---

[70] Cottin, "The Evolution of Practical Theology," 131.

should be considered a part of Christianity proper. This paper pointed out how Waldensianism, in its first formulations, can only in part be considered a form of proto-Protestantism, whereas it should be rightly recognized as proto-Franciscan for its vows of poverty.[71] This correlates with the necessity to consider the impact that institutional factors had both for heterodox and orthodox religious movements in shaping and transforming their nature over time. It is therefore useful to speak of a plurality of Waldensianisms, from its Catholic beginning, through an almost Anabaptist season, then to a Calvinist Reformed church polity, and finally the ecumenical tendencies of today. Future research should try to examine more in detail the doctrine of salvation among Waldensians prior to the Reformation as well as trying to analyze the collateral effects of heresy in shaping the practices of the orthodox church. This has implications even in how one should properly make sense of one's own ministry setting in the fragmented church settings of today. Religious movements must be seen more as evolving through time and less for what they might have in common on the surface. Specific core beliefs have far deeper ramifications pastorally than the mere social settings. Such a study becomes crucial also when applied to the history of other religious movements, as well as in today's returning clash of worldviews between the Eastern and Western world.

Finally, this research also pointed out how both dissident groups underwent the major "pruning" of violent persecution. From a contemporary perspective, regardless of their differences, they were almost exterminated during the Middle Ages. Yet, it is important to take into account the time and culture of religious conformity, which was the foundation for the entire society of the Middle Ages. Despite the total absence of any diplomatic support, the Waldensians, however much they differed from the Albigenses, miraculously survived centuries of "pruning" persecution until they finally gained their freedom of religion just over a century ago.

BIBLIOGRAPHY

Accardy, Chris. "Calvin's Ministry to the Waldensians." *Reformation and Revival* 10, no. 4 (2001): 45–58.

Audisio, Gabriel, and Claire Davison. "Preachers by Night: The Waldensian Barbes (15th–16th Centuries)." *The Sixteenth Century Journal* 40, no. 3 (2009): 853–54.

———. *The Waldensian Dissent: Persecution and Survival, c.1170–c.1570.* Cambridge, UK: Cambridge University Press, 1999.

---

[71] González, ed. *The Story of Christianity*, 358.

———. "How to Detect a Clandestine Minority: The Example of the Waldenses." *The Sixteenth Century Journal* 21, no. 2 (1990): 205–16.

———. "Les Vaudois du Luberon: Une minorité en Provence (1460-1560)." *The Journal of Modern History* 59, no. 4 (1987): 853–56.

Barber, Malcolm. *The Cathars: Dualist Heretics in Languedoc in the High Middle Ages*. New York, NY: Longman, 2000.

Barnett, S. J. "Where Was Your Church before Luther? Claims for the Antiquity of Protestantism Examined." *Church History* 68, no. 1 (1999): 14–41.

Beavis, Mary Ann. "The Cathar Mary Magdalene and the Sacred Feminine: Pop Culture Legend vs. Medieval Doctrine." *Journal of Religion and Popular Culture* 24, no. 3 (2012): 419–31.

Biller, Peter. "Goodbye to Waldensianism?" *Past and Present*, no. 192 (2006): 3–33.

Bowden, John, ed. *Encyclopedia of Christianity*. New York, NY: Oxford University Press, 2005.

Brauer, Jerald C., ed. *The Westminster Dictionary of Church History*. Philadelphia, PA: The Westminster Press, 1971.

Brown, Harold O. *Heresies: The Image of Christ in the Mirror of Heresy and Orthodoxy from the Apostles to the Present*. Grand Rapids, MI: Baker Book House, 1984.

Cairns, Earle E. *Christianity through the Centuries: A History of the Christian Church*. Grand Rapids MI: Zondervan, 1996.

Cameron, Euan, "The Waldenses: Rejections of Holy Church in Medieval Europe." *Utopian Studies* 13, no. 1 (2002): 182–84.

———. *The European Reformation*. Oxford, UK: Clarendon Press, 1991.

———. "The Reformation of the Heretics: The Waldenses of the Alps, 1480–1580." *The Journal of Religion* 67, no. 1 (1987): 99–100.

Cannon, William Ragsdale. *History of Christianity in the Middle Ages: From the Fall of Rome to the Fall of Constantinople*, New York, NY: Abingdon Press, 1960.

Cantor, Norman F. *Medieval History. The Life and Death of a Civilization*. London, UK: MacMillan Company, 1969.

Cegna, Romolo. "La Tradition Pénitentielle des Vaudois et des Hussites et Nicolas de Dresde." *Communio Viatorum*, no. 25 (1982).

Colish, Marcia L. "The Cathars: Dualist Heretics in Languedoc in the High Middle Ages." *Church History* 71, no. 1 (2002): 181–84.

Comba, Emilio. *History of the Waldenses of Italy, From Their Origin to the Reformation*. London, UK: Truslove & Shirley, 1978.

Conder Darrell W. *The Waldensians and the Seventh-day Sabbath*, Sydney, AU: Friends of the Sabbath, 1996.

Costen, Michael. "The Cathars and the Albigensian Crusade." *The International History Review* 20, no. 4 (1998): 950–51.

Cottin, Jérôme. "The Evolution of Practical Theology in French Speaking Europe: France, Switzerland, Belgium, and the Italian Waldensian Church." *De Gruyter* 17, no. 1 (2013): 131–47.

Cross, F. L. ed. *The Oxford Dictionary of the Christian Church*. New York, NY: Oxford University Press, 2005, 1726–27.

Cunsolo, Ronald S. "You are My Witnesses: The Waldensians Across 800 Years." *Fides et Historia* 23, no. 1, (1991): 115–17.

Davenport, Anne A. "The Catholics, the Cathars, and the Concept of Infinity in the Thirteenth Century." *Isis* 88, no. 2 (1997): 263–95.

Deane, Jennifer Kolpacoff. "Archiepiscopal Inquisitions in the Middle Rhine: Urban Anticlericalism and Waldensianism in Late Fourteenth-Century Mainz." *The Catholic Historical Review* 92, no. 3 (2006): 197–24.

DeWind, Henry A. ""Anabaptism" and Italy." *Church History* 21, no. 1 (1952): 20–38

Fahlbusch, Erwin, and Jan Milic Lochman, eds. *The Encyclopedia of Christianity*. Grand Rapids, MI: William B. Eerdmans, 2008.

Ferrario, Fulvio. "The Peaks and Valleys of the Waldensian Church." *Lutheran Forum* 50, no. 1 (2016): 53–56.

Gonnet, Giovanni. "The Influence of the Sermon on the Mount upon the Ethics of the Waldensians of the Middle Ages." *Brethren Life and Thought* 35, no. 1 (1990): 34–40.

González, Justo L. ed. *The Story of Christianity: The Early Church to the Dawn of the Reformation*. New York, NY: Harper One, 1984.

Grant S. J., Gerard G. "The Elevation of the Host: A Reaction to Twelfth Century Heresy." *Theological Studies* no. 3 (1940): 228–50.

Gui, Bernard. "The Waldensians Heretics." in *The Portable Medieval Reader*. 1949. edited by James Bruce Ross, and Mary Martin McLaughlin, New York, NY: the Viking Press.

Hamilton, J. S. "The Yellow Cross: The Story of the Last Cathars, 1290–1329" *Journal of Church and State* 44, no. 1, (Winter 2002): 153–154.

———. "The Cathars and the Albigensian Crusade." *Journal of Church and State*, 41 no. 3 (1999): 610–11.

Homer, Michael W. "Seeking Primitive Christianity in the Waldensian Valleys: Protestants, Mormons, Adventists and Jehovah's Witnesses in Italy." *Nova Religio* 9, no. 4 (2006): 5–33.

Jones, William. *The History of the Waldenses: Connected with a Sketch of the Christian Church from the Birth of Christ to the Eighteenth Century*. London, UK: Gale and Fenner, 1816.

Kaelber, Lutz. "Weavers into Heretics? The Social Organization of Early-Thirteenth-Century Catharism in Comparative Perspective." *Social Science History* 21, no. 1 (1997): 111–37.

———. "Other- and Inner-Worldly Asceticism in Medieval Waldensianism: A Weberian Analysis." *Sociology of Religion* 56, no. 2 (1995): 91–119.

Kienzle, Beverly Mayne. "Women in a Medieval Heretical Sect: Agnes and Huguette the Waldensians." *Speculum* 78, no. 1 (2003): 261–62.

Lambert, Malcolm. "The Cathars." *The Catholic Historical Review* 88, no. 2 (2002): 339–40.

Langermann, Y. Tzvi. "Of Cathars and Creationism: Shemarya Ikriti's Polemic against a Dualist Eternalism." *Jewish Studies Quarterly* 13, no. 2 (2006): 159–70.

Lansing, Carol. "Power & Purity: Cathar Heresy in Medieval Italy." *The Catholic Historical Review* 86, no. 1 (2000): 102–3.

Latourette, Kenneth Scott. *A History of Christianity*. New York, NY: Harper & Row Publishers, 1975.

Lochman, Jan Milič. "Not Just One Reformation: the Waldensian and Hussite Heritage." *Reformed World* 33, no. 5 (1975): 218–24.

MacCulloch, Diarmaid. *The Reformation*. New York, NY: Viking, 2004.

Mark, Vera. "In Search of the Occitan Village: Regionalist Ideologies and the Ethnography of Southern France." *Anthropological Quarterly* 60, no. 2 (1987): 64–70.

Marthaler, Berard "Forerunners of the Franciscans: The Waldenses." *Franciscan Studies* 18, no. 2 (1958):133–42.

McCaffrey, Emily. "Imaging the Cathars in Late-Twentieth-Century Languedoc." *Contemporary European History* 11, no. 3 (2002): 409–27.

Miller, Maureen C. "Power and Purity: Cathar Heresy in Medieval Italy." *Church History* 68, no. 1 (1999): 162–64.

Morland, Samuel. *The History of the Evangelical Churches of the Valleys of Piemont*. London, UK: Henry Hills, 1658.

Muston, Alexis. *The Israel of the Alps: A Complete history of the Waldenses and Their Colonies*. London, UK: Blackie, 1978.

Previté-Orton, C. W. *The Shorter Cambridge Medieval History: The Twelfth Century to the Renaissance*. London, UK: Cambridge University Press, 1978.

Rochat, Giorgio. "Le Valli valdesi nel regime fascista: appunti sul controllo poliziesco." *Bollettino della Società di Studi Valdesi*, no. 156 (1985): 3–30.

Root, Robert. "The Waldensians." *The Christian Century* 64, no. 38 (1947): 1105–6.

Rubin, Miri, and Simons Walter, ed. *The Cambridge History of Christianity: Chistianity in Western Europe c. 1100-c.1500*. Cambridge, UK.: Cambridge University Press, 2009.

Schaff, Philip S. *History of the Christian Church. Volume V the Middle Ages: From Gregory VII 1049, to Boniface VIII, 1294*. Grand Rapids, MI: WM. B. Eerdmans, 1981.

Shriver, George H. "A Summary of 'Images of Catharism and the Historian's Task'." *Church History* 40, no. 1 (1971): 48–54.

Snyder, Arnold. "The Waldensians: The First 800 Years." *The Mennonite Quarterly Review* 56, no. 4 (1982): 396.

Stephens, R. M. "Never Failing Light. The Waldensian Story." *Anglican Theological Review* 44, no. 2 (1962): 235–36.

Tourn, G. *The Waldensians: The First 800 Years*. Turin, IT: Claudiana, 1980.

Treesh Susanna K. "The Waldensian Recourse to Violence." *Church History* 55, no. 3 (1986): 294–306.

Tsiamis, Costas, and Eleni Tounta, "The 'Endura' of The Cathars' Heresy: Medieval Concept of Ritual Euthanasia or Suicide?" *Journal of Religion and Health* 55, no. 1 (2016): 174–180.

Vasilev, Georgi. "Heresy and the English Reformation: Bogomil–Cathar Influence on Wycliffe, Langland, Tyndale and Milton." *Speculum* 84, no. 3 (2009): 785–87.

Vicaire, M. H. *Les Albigeois ancetres des protestants: Assimilations Catholiques.* Toulouse, FR: Centre D'Etudes Historique de Fanjeaux, 1979.

———. *Persequutor Hereticorum ou les 'Persécutions' de Saint Dominique.* Toulouse, FR: Edouard Privat, 1971.

Vinay, Valdo. "Storia dei Valdesi. III: Dal movimento evangelico italiano al movimento ecumenico (1848-1978)." *The Catholic Historical Review* 68, no. 4 (1982): 670–72.

Wakefield, Walter L. "Heretics as Physicians in the Thirteenth Century." *Speculum* 57, no. 2 (1982): 328–31.

Walther, Daniel. "Were the Albigenses and Waldenses forerunners of the Reformation." *Andrews University Seminary Studies* 6, no. 2 (1968): 178–02.

———. "A Survey of Recent Research on the Albigensian Cathari." *Church History* 34, no. 2 (1965): 146–77.

Ward, W. R. "The Waldensian Story: A Study in Faith, Intolerance and Survival." *Epworth Review* 26, no. 1 (1999): 123.

Wylie, James Aitken. *History of the Waldenses.* New York, NY.: Cassell & Company, 1860.

Zeman, J. K. "Restitution and Dissent in the Late Medieval Renewal Movements: The Waldensians, the Hussites and the Bohemian Brethren." *Journal of the American Academy of Religion* 44, no. 1 (1976): 7–27.

ABOUT THE AUTHOR

Ottavio Palombaro has a Doctorate (PhD) in Economic Sociology from the University of Milan and a Master of Divinity (MDiv) from Puritan Reformed Theological Seminary. His interests are in the sociology of religion and church history, having done research on Calvinism, Italian Waldensians, and figures of the Reformation.

MORE FROM THE AUTHOR

"Reality and Representations of the Doctrine of Justification in Early Waldensian Preaching,"
Medieval Sermon Studies 64, no. 1 (2020): 5–15.

"The Italian Waldensians During the Puritan Era,"
Puritan Reformed Journal 11, no. 1 (2019): 70–84.

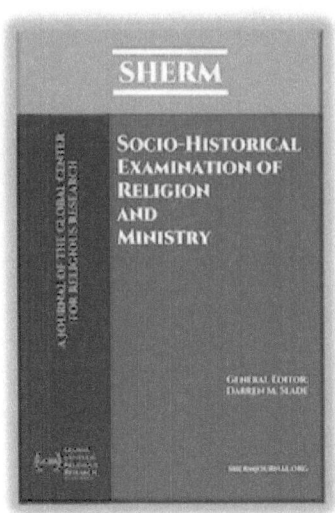

FaithX
Strategic Missional Consulting

- Data-grounded, missional assessment
- Vision-driven missional strategy
- For engaging missional opportunity

FAITHX.NET

Working to connect YOU with your mission.

Datastory
MAPDASH™ FOR FAITH COMMUNITIES

MAPDASH.DATASTORY.BIZ

- Reveal community insights
- Identify emerging missional opportunities
- Access congregational health and sustainability

Bayesian Reasoning's Power to Challenge Religion and Empirically Justify Atheism

Richard Carrier,
Independent Scholar

Abstract: *Bayes' Theorem is a simple mathematical equation that can model every empirical argument. Accordingly, once understood it can be used to analyze, criticize, or improve any argument in matters of fact. By extension, it can substantially improve an overall argument for atheism (here meaning the belief that supernatural gods probably do not exist) by revealing that god apologetics generally operates through the omission of evidence, and how every argument for there being a god becomes an argument against there being a god once you reintroduce all the pertinent evidence that the original argument left out. This revelation further reveals that god apologetics generally operates through the omission of evidence. This paper demonstrates these propositions by illustrating their application with examples.*

Keywords: Bayes' Theorem, Bayesian Reasoning, Atheism, Logic, Apologetics

Introduction

Bayes' Theorem (discovered by Thomas Bayes before his death in 1761 and developed by Pierre-Simon Laplace in 1774) is an equation that models all correct empirical reasoning. Take any argument for any conclusion about any question of fact, and Bayes' Theorem describes everything going on in it that decides how likely that conclusion really is. Once you understand this, it is like understanding how a car's engine works: you can pop the hood on any argument and see what is wrong with it or what it would take to fix it and make it work. This follows whether it is an argument you are making to others to persuade or convince them of some matter of fact, or an argument you are making to yourself in developing your own conclusions and beliefs, or an argument someone else is making or has made that you are being confronted or challenged with.[1]

---

[1] Carrier, *Proving History*, 106–14; Bovens and Hartmann, *Bayesian Epistemology*; Zenker, *Bayesian Argumentation*; Levitin, *Field Guide*; Tucker, *Knowledge*; Jaynes, *Probability Theory*; and Hunter, *Political-Military Applications*.

Most reasoners (especially atheists) will be more familiar with various forms of straightforward, deductive, syllogistic reasoning; for example, "if *p* is *q*, and *q* is *x*, then *p* is *x*," or "if *q* when *p*, and there is no *q*, then there is no *p*," etc. But that is of no direct use in answering questions of fact. Deductive logic can tell us what must be the case "if" something else is the case; but what you usually want to know is whether that "something else" is the case. And deductive logic cannot answer that question—or at least, once you deconstruct the convoluted syllogism you would need to do that, you will end up discovering exactly what Bayes and Laplace did hundreds of years ago. The principal problem is that, excepting basic Cartesian facts about present human experience, all matters of fact can only ever be known to a probability, and simple deductive syllogisms do not validly induce a probability. But a Bayesian syllogism does.

This article will explain Bayes' Theorem in the simplest terms possible and illustrate how it can be used to analyze arguments generally, and then it will show how this knowledge can be used to transform any argument for the existence of a supernatural god (meaning any sentient being powerful enough to create or alter our universe who is not just another evolved or constructed physical machine in the way humans are) into an argument against the existence of that god, by merely reintroducing evidence that the original argument left out, thus illustrating that all reasons given for believing that such a god exists depend on the omission of evidence.

Bayes' Theorem in a Nutshell

Bayes' Theorem can be formulated mathematically in many different ways, but they all reduce to each other and are therefore interchangeable with suitable translation. But the formula most readily understandable to most people relies on the human brain's more natural capacity to understand probability in terms of "odds" or "frequencies," whereby the chance something will turn out to be true might be, for example, "2 to 1" or "2 in 3" and the like.[2] The expression "2 to 1" means the same thing as "2 in 3" and translates to a probability of roughly 67%; likewise, "1 to 99" means "1 in 100" and translates to a probability of 1%, and "4 to 7,000" means "4 in 7,004" and translates to a probability of roughly 0.057%, or about a seventeenth of a percent.[3] Human

---

[2] On this disposition: Weber, Binder, and Kraus, "Why Can Only 24%?"

[3] Numbers in quotation marks are being given here as numerals to facilitate the reader's comprehension of the mathematical points to be made.

reasoners more readily grasp concepts like "twice as likely" or "twelve times less likely" than complex decimal percentages such as 66.67% or 8.33%.[4]

When represented in its odds form, Bayes' Theorem can be fully represented with the colloquial formula:

$$\text{Final Odds} = \text{Prior Odds} \times \text{Evidential Odds}$$

Where here "Final Odds" means simply the odds that your claim or conclusion is true; the "Prior Odds" means what those odds would usually be, based on past experience and before considering new or specific evidence in this particular case; and the "Evidential Odds" refers to the relative likelihood that this new or specific evidence would exist on either your claim being true, or your claim being false (in which case some other conclusion must be true).

For example, for the Prior Odds, one would state how often similar claims have turned out to be true in the past. What has *usually* turned out to be the case when such claims are made? And here, one might take into account the frequency of past claims being true given a particular source or circumstance (e.g., "more reliable" sources and circumstances will entail higher frequencies of certain kinds of claims that have turned out to be true). Given all that, how often have such claims turned out to be true? Is it "1 in 10" times? Or "1 out of 2" times? Or "99 out of 100" times? Stated in terms of the odds, "1 in 10" would be 1/9, since the 1 and the 9 must account for every possibility, and 1 + 9 = 10. Accordingly, "1 in 2" is 1/1, "99 out of 100" is 99/1, and so on.

Many arguments depend on explicit or implicit assumptions regarding this "Prior Odds" ratio. Indeed, this is always a stated or implied premise in every argument in matters of fact. It is, therefore, important to ascertain which assumption regarding the "Prior Odds" ratio the presenter of an argument is making (even if that presenter is you, and you are only reasoning with yourself), and then to examine whether that assumption is sound, given all that humankind knows to date. As with the premises in any other form of logic, an unsound assumption regarding the Prior Odds will have to be corrected in order to produce a sound conclusion.

---

[4] For readers who need more mathematical explanation, the odds that some claim or conclusion h is true are always the ratio of the probabilities that h is or is not true, e.g., if there is a 95% chance your conclusion is true then there is, by definition, a 5% chance it is not true, since its being true or not true sum all objective possibilities, and therefore must sum to 100%; and the ratio of 95/5 produces an "odds" on the claim being true that can be represented fractionally as 19/1 (as 95/5 = 19/1).

Then, for the Evidential Odds, one would state how much more (or less) likely is the entire collection of all the available evidence there is to present for or against the claim or conclusion being argued, which requires estimating two things: first, how likely all the available evidence is if the claim is true; and, second, how likely all that same evidence is if the claim is false. These two likelihoods then stand in ratio to each other to establish how strongly the total body of evidence argues for or against the claim. Is all that evidence ten times more likely if that claim is true than if it is false? Or two times less likely? Or only slightly less likely? Or equally likely? Etc. One would then write this out as a statement of relative odds—the odds of the evidence "based on the claim being true rather than false." So, evidence that is ten times more likely if the claim is true would give us an evidential odds of 10/1, because "10" is ten times "1"; if it were two times *less* likely, then it would be 1/2, because "2" is two times one, and in this case, the evidence is twice as likely if the claim is *false* than if it is true. Likewise, if one said the odds on the evidence were 99/100, true to false, then one would be saying the relative odds were 99/100, which is so close to 100/100 and thus 1/1, as to make little difference in practice. Whereas if all the evidence we have is equally expected whether the claim or conclusion is true or false, then the "evidential odds" are indeed 1/1.

Just Three Numbers

This is all the math you need to analyze an argument. And this means that all arguments about matters of fact are always arguments over just three numbers: the prior probability of a claim (how usually do claims like that turn out to be true; how typical is it), the probability of the evidence if that claim is true, and the probability of that same evidence if that claim is false. Most commonly, arguments surround the Evidential Odds: someone is asserting "the evidence" is so much more likely based on their claim being true than based on its being false that their claim "must" be true, i.e., the Final Odds have to be so good that their claim *must* have a high enough probability to believe it is true. And this is just another estimate of "usual frequency" (how often does "that kind of evidence" result from "that kind of cause," and how often without it). For example, starting out with equal Prior Odds—mathematically, 1/1, or one to one—someone might then claim that the evidence they are pointing to is twenty times more likely to be there (20/1) if their conclusion is correct than if it is not (and "something else" caused all that evidence to exist instead). Which amounts to asserting only "a twentieth of the time" would such evidence still come about in the absence of that claimed cause. And since it is incontrovertible that $1/1 \times 20/1 = 20/1$ in Final Odds, this argument would entail the conclusion is also twenty times more likely to be true than false. All one then need do is examine whether the premises are well-founded. *Is* that evidence "twenty" times more likely when that explanation is true than any other? *Are* the Prior Odds equal?

That assumption about prior probability is often a hidden premise. For example, if someone argues solely from the relative likelihood of the evidence, they are implicitly assuming the Prior Odds are even—that absent that evidence the claim is "50/50," or "just as likely" to be true as false. And if there are good reasons to doubt that such a claim has fully equal odds of being true before being presented the specific evidence referenced in the argument—if a vast database of *prior* evidence accumulated by humankind argues those odds do *not* "begin" equal in any argument today—then *that must be taken into account*, and the Prior Odds accordingly revised and included in the calculation of any Final Odds. Otherwise, the Final Odds will not be a soundly produced conclusion, but a conclusion depending on an untenable assumption, an assumption that essentially amounts to disregarding a great deal of pertinent evidence—leaving that evidence "out of account," as it were. But a sound conclusion cannot be reached with omitted-yet-available evidence. That evidence, therefore, must be reintroduced, and the effect of that reintroduction logically accounted for. In this case, "prior" evidence is usually referred to as "background knowledge" to distinguish it from the more limited selection of evidence being presented specifically to argue for or against the conclusion, which is thereby simply called "evidence" by abbreviation. But in a broader sense, it is all evidence, and it must all be accounted for to arrive at any sound conclusion.[5] A sound conclusion cannot be reached with omitted-yet-available evidence.

Imprecision and Uncertainty

To use Bayesian reasoning like this requires understanding other general principles of reasoning. One of which is the argument *a fortiori*, "from the stronger premise." Here this means using estimated probabilities that are so much higher or lower than needed that any correction toward a more accurate

---

[5] This is also mathematically *literally* the case: every Prior Odds is either actually or conceptually the Final Odds of a previous run (usually implicit) of the same Bayesian equation. "Background knowledge" is therefore really "prior evidence." Prior Odds therefore mathematically represent all human learning; and apart from thought experiments that counterfactually posit ignorance, arguments that ignore all human learning are unsound.

probability will only make the conclusion stronger. It is, thus, not necessary to know or to precisely prove *any* probability or odds in a Bayesian argument; all one needs to do is settle on any probability all sides agree is indisputable based on the available background understanding.

For example, I do not know the precise odds that a meteorite will destroy my house today. I could determine that from available background knowledge (such as data collected by NASA regarding the frequency-per-acre-day of destructive meteorite impacts on Earth). But I do not have to if I can proceed with any probability or odds *against* my expected conclusion that is, nevertheless, already obviously correct. If I am claiming that I need not worry about my home being destroyed by a meteorite today (and therefore I do not need to evacuate it), and that conclusion follows even with a much *higher* odds of an impact than I know to be actual, then my conclusion will follow *with even greater certainty* given any more accurate estimation of those odds. For example, it is indisputable that the real odds of a meteorite destroying my house today, whatever they are, are well above one in a thousand—because if they were not, I would have in my own personal background knowledge hundreds of friends and acquaintances who have lost their homes to meteorite impacts (since a daily rate of one in one thousand entails every home will be thus destroyed on average every three years or so). So, I can operate with the premise "the Prior Odds are higher than one in one thousand," and still know that the conclusion ("I need not evacuate my home today") is correct.

The utility of *a fortiori* reasoning eliminates any objection one might have to the impossibility or inaccessibility of mathematical precision in an argument; and this is the actual way everyone typically argues—most people are operating from implicit *a fortiori* assertions or assumptions regarding the Prior or Evidential Odds, almost all the time. That they never articulate these assumptions in precise numerical terms makes no difference. This is nevertheless what is going on in their heads. And we often don't even need to articulate numbers; usually it is enough to know that some probability is "more" than another, or "a lot more," and either way, *a fortiori*, it might not matter "by how much."

For example, that some collection of evidence is evidence "for" our claim being true requires only that the probability of that evidence be *higher* if our claim is true than on any other competing claim (or whatever competing claim we are comparing ours to); it does not matter "how much" higher. That would only matter insofar as we were asserting that that evidence is "very good" or "very strong" and the like (or the converse, that it is "very weak" or "not very compelling" and the like), but these assertions only entail declaring that whatever that difference in probabilities is, that it is nevertheless "large" (or, in the converse case, "small"). And as with the meteorite example, that claim can be known to be true without knowing any more precisely "how" large or small. If some collection of evidence is "very unlikely" on any other explanation than ours, and we can present "strong" evidence of that (as for example, the complete absence of frequently meteor-ravaged homes in our personal and investigative experience), we do not need to know anything more to support whatever conclusion follows. Mathematical logic is, therefore, in no way hindered by imprecision or uncertainty. One can simply include any needed imprecision or uncertainty in the math.

General Application:
Common Principles of Reasoning

To see how this works in a general respect, consider some common tropes of argument—for example, that "extraordinary claims require extraordinary evidence." Analyzed with the tool of Bayes' Theorem, one can entirely model what this is saying: an "extraordinary claim" means any claim with an "extraordinarily low" Prior Odds. Because this amounts to saying that a claim is "extremely unusual," and "extremely" is just a synonym of "extraordinarily," and "unusual" is just a synonym of "infrequent," and "infrequent" is just a synonym of "improbable." And "improbable" translates to "low odds." Bayes' Theorem then explains *why* such claims require extraordinary evidence to believe them.

If a claim starts out with extraordinarily low Prior Odds, and anyone's "belief" requires at least a minimally favorable "Final Odds" (any odds better than equal odds, or 1/1), then *only* an extraordinarily high Evidential Odds can warrant belief. This holds regardless of what precise definition is given to "extraordinary," so long as one maintains the same definition in both cases. For example, if one defined "extraordinarily low odds" as one in one million (mathematically, 1/1,000,000), then one must define "extraordinarily high odds" as at least a million to one (mathematically 1,000,000/1). If a claim starts out a million to one against, then one needs evidence that is over a million to one in favor to overcome that obstacle. The demonstration follows:

$$1/1 = 1/1,000,000 \times 1,000,000/1$$

It is thus indisputable that *any* Evidential Odds *below* extraordinary can never warrant belief; such would always produce a Final Odds that favored the claim *being false*. Belief is, therefore, only warranted to the degree the evidence is *even more extraordinary* than the claim itself is improbable.

Of course, "merely" extraordinary evidence (evidence that has Evidential Odds exactly the inverse of the Prior Odds) only warrants perfectly equivocal agnosticism (a belief that the claim is just as likely to be false as true); but the intent behind the aphorism is that one must have *at least* evidence that extraordinary to overcome the conclusion that such a claim is probably false. Most people set a much higher bar for belief than merely "more probable than not" (thus accounting for the epistemic position of "agnosticism" in the particular sense of "the state of being insufficiently certain"), so evidence must be not merely as extraordinary as a claim is improbable, but *also* sufficiently strong *over and above* that to warrant actual confidence in a claim's truth—just as with ordinary claims. For example, if a person's threshold for belief is that a claim must be at least 99% certain to be true in order for them to "believe" it (as in, to confidently operate as if it is true), and so far as they know the claim is as likely to be true as false (before receiving any specific evidence regarding it), then that person needs evidence that is at least a hundred times more likely if the claim is true than if any other competing explanation of the evidence were instead true. That evidence, therefore, must have less than a 1% chance of existing on any other explanation; otherwise, by their own standards, they might still accept that it is likely but still have to reserve some doubts. But when a claim is extraordinary, the evidence required must *also* meet that *extraordinary* bar, and Bayes' Theorem explains why—while proving that one cannot "get around" this.

The same follows for the aphorism "absence of evidence is not necessarily evidence of absence." If we expect the evidence in question to be missing *regardless* of whether a claim regarding it is true, then the Evidential Odds are equal, an even 1/1. In that case, the evidence is as likely to be missing if the claim is true as when the claim is false. Ergo, the absence of this evidence is not evidence of absence. But if we *do not* expect that evidence to be missing, then the more unlikely it is that we would not have found it, and, therefore, the more unlikely the claim is to be true. For instance, if it were five times more likely that a certain court record would be missing if a claim about it were false than if it were true (in other words, that document is so expected to be there that its absence *is unusual*), then the Evidential Odds would be 1/5. If we had started with equal Prior Odds, we would end up with a Final Odds of $1/1 \times 1/5 = 1/5$. The claim is then five times more likely *to be false* than to be true. The absence of *this* evidence *is* evidence of absence. Bayes' Theorem, therefore, explains why, as well as *when*, an absence of evidence is evidence of absence, *and* how strong that absence is as evidence: it is simply a function of how unexpected—how unusual—its being missing happens to be, all things considered.

Similarly, Ockham's Razor states that simpler explanations tend to be more likely, which follows from the fact that explanations with excess components are always more improbable than explanations (should any be available) that do not require those components, or any other components that are as unlikely as those. Again, Bayes' Theorem explains why. When two explanations perform equally well (e.g., they explain all the same observations), an explanation that has more components "added to it" will always be the less probable, owing to the Law of Total Probability: unless the additions are fully 100% certain (meaning, they are logically necessary; as in, they cannot logically be false and thus have *no* probability of being false), they will each always have some probability less than 100%, which necessarily reduces the total probability of their conjunction (any two probabilities multiplied always produces a probability smaller than both). So, a theory that is otherwise identical but does not have those added elements cannot fail to be more likely. However, most of the time, Ockham's Razor is applied not to *identical* theories (with only things added or taken away), but quite different ones, which are nevertheless being compared with respect to their relative complexity, and that is where Bayes' Theorem comes in.

For example, if the Evidential Odds are against a claim—say, that 1/5 just considered earlier, where the evidence is five times more likely to be as we find it if the claim *is false* than if it were true—one might try to change that by "adding" more assumptions to your claim ("invisible ninjas hid all the evidence"). Then, of course, the missing evidence is entirely expected ("the ninjas got to it"), so its being missing is now as expected if the claim is false as if it were true (and thus 1/1, instead of 1/5, a significant improvement in the theory's ability to predict the evidence). But usually to do that, one would have to add improbable assumptions to their claim, as in this toy example: someone invented a new kind of ninja, which they have no evidence for; and these ninjas just happen to have a motive to hide this particular evidence; *and* that person invented their remarkable success at doing so—since it does not automatically follow that if they tried, they'd succeed. Even if each of those assumptions were as likely true as false (and therefore "50/50"), that would still mean your claim requires *a set* of assumptions that is very unlikely (the "ninjas" explanation requires three assumptions, each no more likely to be true than false, and 50% × 50% × 50% = 12.5%). If your Prior Odds had been equal ("50/50," i.e. 1/1), now upon adding these assumptions you have to multiply your explanation's prior probability by the *new* improbability you just added on. Because that same Law of Total Probability still applies.

So when we take this 12.5% in our toy "ninja" example, we take a 50% prior probability (where we had started) and now must multiply it by a 12.5% chance that all those assumptions you added are even true. Which gets you to 6.25% (0.50 × 0.125 = 0.0625). When you include the effect of this on the total odds, your theory's Prior Odds are no longer "50/50" but 6.25/93.75, which reduces to 1/15.[6] So you went from 1/1 to 1/15. It is now fifteen times more likely something *else* is causing the evidence than what you are proposing. You just made your theory *less* likely, in your misguided attempt to make it fit the evidence better than it actually does. By adding your unproven assumptions, you took a claim that started out 50% likely, and ended up with a claim that's barely 6% likely; and you also obtained no increase to that at all from the probability of the evidence. "As likely as not" has thus become fifteen times more likely *to be false*. And since all you "got back" for that trick was to bump the Evidential Odds up from 1/5 to 1/1 (the evidence is now just as likely on your new assumption-reinforced claim being true as on its being false), you actually went from 1/1 × 1/5 = 1/5, for a Final Odds of 5 to 1 against your claim (where you started), to 1/15 x 1/1, for a Final Odds of 15 to 1 against your claim. So indeed all you did was make your claim less likely. You did not rescue it from the evidence at all. "Added assumptions" usually make theories less, not more probable.

The example above shows how Bayes' Theorem explains the validity of Ockham's Razor, even when comparing otherwise disparate theories: the more assumptions one would have to add to increase the predictive success of an explanation or claim necessarily reduces the overall probability that the claim is true. Usually, when this tactic is employed apologetically rather than rationally, this effect of "adding assumptions" on the overall probability *is ignored*. Bayes' Theorem thus explains why doing that is logically invalid. The only time adding assumptions does not have this effect is when there is abundant independent evidence the assumptions are true (so that their probability is high) or when their addition increases the Evidential Odds more than it reduces the Prior Odds. For example, in what it can predict and explain, the Periodic Table far outperforms Aristotle's much simpler Four Element model in Evidential Odds—far more than its complexity would diminish its Prior Odds. And that is

---

[6] For readers needing the mathematical reason: if a theory requires assumptions that reduce its prior probability to 6.25%, the prior probability that some other thing explains the evidence becomes 100% - 6.25% = 93.75%. The concurring odds ratio, therefore, becomes 6.25/93.75; and 6.25 goes into 93.75 fifteen times.

why we believe the former and not the latter, despite it being so much less simple.

Specific Application: Godless Naturalism

Of all the worldviews and belief-systems compatible with atheism as a general conclusion, ontological naturalism currently enjoys the highest Final Odds (on the basis of the findings of all the sciences to date). And if *any* version of atheism is more probable than theism, then *atheism* is more probable than theism. Therefore, this article will continue with the simplifying assumption that atheism means "ontological naturalism" (as no other variety of atheism needs to be considered here to warrant the conclusion that "atheism" is more likely).

Basic Argument for Naturalism

The basic argument for naturalism runs as follows: after centuries of inquiry now, countless times, millions even, claims of the "God did it" or "It requires God" variety have turned out to be false; whereas claims like "Nature did it" or "It only requires Nature" have turned out to be true instead. The evidence overall has accumulated in only one direction: that minds require physical machinery (brains) and cannot exist or function disembodied; supernatural powers do not exist; there is no magic or miracle that has ever been verified as anything but a product of fakery or mistake; and so on. In other words, the presumption of naturalism is not, in fact, a *presumption*: it is a conclusion built on extensive evidence and experience.[7] Had the world been the other way around—had supernatural powers existed, gods existed, disembodied minds existed—we should likely have found evidence of it by now. That we have not means there is not likely to be any, which is exactly what we expect if those things do not exist at all. And any excuses one might invent to "explain this away" only make their claim *less* likely, not more so, per Ockham's Razor as just explained. Conclusions to the contrary are now Extraordinary Claims, lacking even ordinary, much less extraordinary evidence. To the contrary, the profound absence of evidence now, after such meticulous and extensive investigation and observation over hundreds of years, is itself extraordinarily

---

[7] For surveys of this fact of modern naturalism, see Carroll, *The Big Picture*; Bashour and Muller, *Contemporary Philosophical Naturalism*; Clark, *Blackwell Companion*; and Carrier, *Sense and Goodness*.

improbable—exactly the opposite of what is needed to vindicate supernaturalism, much less specifically theism (as previously defined).

In Bayesian terms, the Prior Odds on theism are extraordinarily low. And this is not for arbitrary reasons of presumption. It is a consequence of a vast body of past evidence (the accumulated background knowledge of humankind). "God-causes" are not just extraordinarily rare in reliable observation; they are completely missing from reliable observation.[8] They are, therefore, not "usual" explanations in any subject of inquiry. They are, in fact, now the least likely explanation one could posit for anything.

Even the "rebuttal" that "god-causes" are evident in *non*-reliable observation (occasions in which real tests cannot be made of their authenticity) argues *against* the existence of god-causes rather than for them: all else being equal, it is improbable that this disparity would exist if gods exist (god-causes "appearing" precisely only ever in non-reliable observations, and conveniently never in reliable ones), whereas this disparity is exactly what we expect to observe if gods do not exist. Therefore, *this very observation* (the theist's own rebuttal) yields Evidential Odds favoring atheism against theism, not the other way around. Any effort to escape that logical consequence by "inventing excuses" for why gods deceptively ensure exactly this outcome (thereby intentionally making the world look exactly like a world with no gods in it) violates Ockham's Razor by requiring the addition of improbable assumptions (assumptions for whose truth no evidence exists, and thus no evidence exists to render them probable), which necessarily reduces the Prior Odds (as previously shown), while still not producing any Evidential Odds against atheism— because even such an excuse can only at best get this observed evidence to be *equally likely* on theism and atheism, not *more* likely on theism than atheism, which is what is needed to turn those odds around. So, this excuse *reduces* the overall probability of theism, thereby making *atheism* more probable—not less. As it happens, this same reasoning turns every argument for god against itself.

The Cosmological Argument

Consider the so-called Cosmological Argument. For example, "What begins to exist must always have a cause; the universe began to exist; therefore, the universe must have a cause; but without a universe only a god-cause can exist; therefore, a god caused the universe." This argument requires three

---

[8] For examples of how Bayesian argumentation can demonstrate this for ancient Christianity, see Carrier, "Why the Resurrection is Unbelievable" 291–315 and "Christianity's Success Was Not Incredible," 53–74.

premises no more likely to be true than false ("*everything* that begins requires a cause"; "there is a beginning to *everything* that exists"; and "only god-causes can exist apart from 'a universe'"). These assumptions are possibly even *less* likely to be true than false: many leading cosmological models involve no beginning to time, but since causes by definition precede effects in time, it does not seem plausible that time itself can be expected to have a cause; and based on all we know about what causes are necessary to produce thought and action, it is implausible that a disembodied mind with supernatural powers could exist and predate even time.[9] But even if we set those concerns aside and set these three assumptions at exactly 50% likely apiece (each "as likely true as not"), then the Prior Odds on "a god caused the universe" can then be no better than, again, 50% (initial odds) × 50% (first assumption) × 50% (second assumption) × 50% (third assumption) = 6.25%. Which leads us again to a mere 1/15 odds on the existence of a god. Thus, the Cosmological Argument, when subjected to the correct application of logic, is an argument for atheism: even if the remaining evidence is equally likely on atheism and theism (for an Evidential Odds of 1/1), we end up with 1/15 x 1/1 = 1/15, a Final Odds *against* god existing of *fifteen to one*: a god is the *least* likely explanation of our universe; not the most.

The response to this conundrum is to resort to some attempt to present evidence that is claimed to be unlikely *unless* a god was involved (and hopefully unlikely enough to overcome any prior odds against it). Most apologetics consists of such arguments, and these are as Bayesian as any other arguments are: the theist claims some evidence *e* is "less likely" on atheism than on theism, and therefore theism is more likely than atheism. Their own logic requires a Bayesian calculation: this disparity in the probabilities (the "expectedness" or "predictability") of the cited evidence (the Evidential Odds) must somehow produce a disparity in the probabilities of the conclusions (the Final Odds). Only Bayes' Theorem explains how this would do that. Which manner of argument one then discovers requires *assuming* the Prior Odds start out even. The rest of apologetics consists of resisting the consequences of contrary arguments (such as regarding the *low* prior probability of god-causes, as just analyzed; or regarding *contrary evidence* presented, such as in the case of the Argument from Evil, to be examined shortly).

---

[9] Stenger, *Has Science Found God?*; Fodor, *Unreasonable Faith*, 12–151; and Pearce, *Did God Create the Universe?*

The Fine-Tuning Argument

The most obvious example of "evidence that is claimed to be unlikely," after critics dispatch the Cosmological Argument, is the Fine-Tuning Argument, which states that a universe can only produce life capable of contemplating these questions if its fundamental "physical constants" are so "finely tuned" as to defy any explanation but intentional design. This is a Bayesian argument. There are two competing hypotheses: the life-producing quality of this universe is a lucky coincidence, or else it was intelligently designed. The theist proposes that, stated simply thus, since the "god" hypothesis predicts the observation ("fine-tuning") with near 100% certainty, while the "luck" hypothesis requires an extraordinarily improbable occurrence, the disparity in those two hypotheses (the Evidential Odds) is extraordinarily in favor of "god." Therefore, all else being equal (i.e., if the Prior Odds are 1/1), the Final Odds on the existence of god are enormous, and atheism is refuted. This is correct as to the logic of it, and Bayes' Theorem explains why, but it is incorrect as to its premises. Evidence is being left out; and when it is reintroduced, the conclusion *reverses*. Bayes' Theorem, once again, explains why.

To test two hypotheses against each other, one must assess all pertinent evidence *e*, everything each hypothesis predicts.[10] In this case the "luck" hypothesis requires an extraordinarily improbable event: biogenesis, i.e., that a self-replicating molecule would be randomly assembled in the universe by chance accident. The only way that can be probable is if there were an extraordinary number of random events of molecular mixing—like the lottery: any single win is improbable, but there are so many tickets bought that the odds that the lottery *will be won* are essentially 100%. And so we observe it to be: lotteries are routinely won. And in cosmology the only way this can be the case is if the universe is extraordinarily old, extraordinarily large, extraordinarily full of random molecular mixing, and yet also extraordinarily *lacking* places hospitable to life (since an accidentally assembled universe would produce those, as well, only by chance accident). But *that* is surprising on the "god" hypothesis; yet is 100% expected on atheism—in fact, this is the only kind of universe we could observe on atheism, because without gods, only such universes could produce observers to any credible probability. This means nearly all godless universes observed will be extraordinarily large,

---

[10] Sober, "The Design Argument" 117–48; Ikeda and Jefferys, "The Anthropic Principle" 150–66; Carrier, "Neither Life Nor the Universe," 279–304.

extraordinarily old, extraordinarily full of material, and extraordinarily inhospitable to life. For example, nearly all of this universe is a lethal radiation-filled vacuum; and almost all that is in it apart from that consists of stars and black holes, which are absolutely lethal to life; and next after that is almost all dead rocks and lethal atmospheres. In fact, almost nothing in this universe is a suitable place for life to arise and evolve. This is exactly what one expects to see—in fact, in all probability, what one would have to see—on atheism. But it is not at all what one expects to see on theism. So why would a god make the universe look exactly like a universe with no god in it? Any answer one gives to that question remains an unevidenced assumption to which an improbability attaches, an improbability that commutes to their conclusion, as previously demonstrated. Ockham's Razor strikes again.

Fine-tuning is, therefore, a property all godless universes will be observed to have (it is impossible to have atheists *other than* in a godlessly fine-tuned universe—since universes that cannot produce observers will never be observed), which means the probability we would observe fine-tuning on the "luck" hypothesis is 100%. Since theism can never make this evidence "more" likely than 100%, fine-tuning can never be evidence for theism. The evidence theists are leaving out (the vast size, age, content, and lethality of the universe) drops the probability of this universe being observed on the "god" hypothesis *below* its probability on atheism. God has no need of fine-tuning—he can make universes work without it—and without any absurd size, age, content, or lethality. Only godless universes require that. Fine-tuning is therefore evidence *for atheism*.

The only available response is to concede the point, and insist this only moves the question back to the Prior Odds, where atheists have to assume an extraordinarily lucky event: the one universe that just randomly came to be, just happened to be one of the rarest kinds—one that would produce observers. But logically, this supplies no actual rebuttal because the probabilities in Bayesian argument are always in ratio. What matters is not how improbable something is, but how much more or less probable it is than something else. And here the theist's contrary hypothesis is resting on *essentially the same improbability*: that we just happened to be so incredibly lucky as for there to be a god—a super-powered, disembodied mind of the greatest genius and knowledge and thus greatest informational complexity, the most improbable of entities—who also just happened to want to create a messy, deadly, absurdly large, old, and junk-filled universe that would eventually randomly produce a few people in it, a universe that would look, bizarrely, exactly like a universe would have to look if there were no god at all. Things appear to be a wash on this point: the atheist rests on no greater a chance accident here than the theist does. Fine-tuned god or fine-tuned universe—neither is more likely than the other.

Arguably the atheist is even proposing a much more likely accident. Though it is not necessary to demonstrate that here, for even at equal odds the point is secured; nevertheless, there are two respects in which this is the case. First, an infinite mind entails infinite specified complexity, as well as such improbably lucky facts as "disembodied minds are possible." Of all the "things" you can get by random chance, an infinitely complex god is the least likely of them, the more so if it requires an improbably convenient physics. By contrast, the mere fine-tuning of a few physical constants can produce an observer-generating universe to a much lower finite probability. Second, fine-tuning is more likely on atheism than theism by the same reasoning applied to biogenesis. Where atheism entails biogenesis is most likely to be observed if there is an enormous amount of molecular mixing (hence we expect, and behold, a vastly old, large, littered universe), atheism also entails fine-tuning is most likely to be observed if there is a multiverse, i.e., if our universe is just one of countless randomly configured universes. This is the lottery again: if there are countless randomly generated universes, the probability of a universe like ours approaches 100% no matter how finely tuned it is.

Atheism therefore predicts it is likely we would accumulate evidence supporting the existence of a multiverse; and lo, cosmological science is converging on exactly that conclusion: multiverses are the inevitable outcome of an extremely few simple physical facts, facts that observations currently make likely.[11] This is an unexpected outcome on theism (ergo, improbable) but a highly expected outcome on atheism (ergo, probable), which is another disparity entailing an Evidential Odds favoring atheism, not theism. For all the reasons outlined above, fine-tuning is stronger evidence for a multiverse than for a god. The one follows inevitably from a few simple facts now known to be likely; the other does not.

Every Other Argument

Every argument for god meets the same outcome.[12] Apart from always being rendered unsound on the basis of some equivocation fallacy, the Ontological Argument actually just reduces to testing competing hypotheses as

---

[11] See for example, Davies, "Multiverse Cosmological Models" 727–43; Carroll, *From Eternity to Here*; and Stewart, *God and Cosmology*.

[12] See Koterski and Oppy, *Theism and Atheism*; Murray, *Atheist's Primer*; Carrier, *Sense and Goodness*.

to what is most likely the necessary underlying substrate of everything; and insofar as any such thing is necessary, observational evidence more strongly supports simple godless substrates (e.g., spacetime) than extremely complex, ontologically baseless ones (e.g., bodiless super-spirits). Again, the argument proceeds only by omitting evidence, in this case of simpler alternatives that meet all necessary requirements. For example, you cannot have anything more fundamental than spacetime: that which "never exists" and "nowhere exists" does not exist; ergo, everything needs a place and time to exist; except places and times themselves: spacetime is therefore the only known entity capable of being self-existent. Why, then, do we need another? Ockham's Razor strikes.

The Argument from Religious Experience ("I experience my god; therefore, my god exists") similarly operates by the omission of evidence: all contrary religious experiences, across space and time. When one puts that evidence back in, one finds there are generally two competing hypotheses: that religious experience is a product of human psychology and culture (and thus will vary in accordance with human knowledge and cultural change) or actual contact or communication with a god (and thus will have remained consistent across the entire globe over tens of thousands of years). The psychocultural hypothesis predicts that the gods "contacted" will wildly differ in all their content (moral, existential, theological), that many religious experiences will even lack gods (Taoism, Buddhism, Scientology), and that these will all change across history and cultures. The "god" hypothesis does not predict any of that to be the case. The total evidence is therefore 100% expected if there is no god; but less than 100% expected if there is. Religious experience is therefore *evidence for atheism*, not theism.[13]

Likewise the Argument from Consciousness (that thought would be dependent on a complex, vulnerable, fallible, resource-wasting brain is required if there is no god, but nearly inexplicable if there is), the Argument from Miracles (as already noted with respect to the conveniently perfect disparity between the reliable and non-reliable observation databases, which is exactly what we expect on atheism, but not on theism), the Moral Argument (that morals would evolve over time to increasingly meet human social needs through human innovation, trial, and error is exactly what we expect on atheism, but not what we expect to observe on theism, which sooner predicts perfect morals communicated from the start, as well as a universe governed by moral laws, rather than a wholly indifferent amoral physics), the Argument from Meaning (that humans are mortal and must, and have only, found diverse

---

[13] This is most thoroughly demonstrated in Dennett, *Breaking the Spell*.

meaning in their lives on their own, is what we expect on atheism, and not on theism), and so on. Even the Argument from Evil is really a reversal of any Design Argument (of which the Fine Tuning Argument is just one instance), because it consists of reintroducing omitted evidence regarding the design of the world, and then applying Ockham's Razor to the overall result.[14] In every case, the theist is putting forward a Bayesian argument (some "evidence" they claim is more likely if a god exists is supposed to entail that the existence of a god is more likely), and in every case, reintroducing the evidence that the theist left out produces the opposite conclusion. This is the power of a Bayesian analysis of logical arguments.

Conclusion

A decent understanding of Bayes' Theorem can equip one to identify when an argument for any conclusion of fact is logically sound and why; or if not, why. This extends even to general principles, like "extraordinary claims require extraordinary evidence," arguments from silence, and Ockham's Razor. And brought to bear on arguments for god, it unravels each one: Bayesian reasoning explains why "excuse making" to "explain away" all the evidence rendering a god unlikely is logically invalid (by revealing the hidden premises about probability that such devices require ignoring); and how reintroducing all the evidence that theists leave out of any argument, reverses that same argument into a solid case against any respectable probability of the existence of a god. This renders Bayesian reasoning a powerful tool in the philosophy of religion, as it has proved to be in so many other fields.[15]

---

[14] See Sterba, *Good God Logically Possible*; Trakakis, *God Beyond Belief*; and Howard-Snyder, *Evidential Argument*.

[15] For more on that point see, Mcgrayne, *Theory That Would Not Die*; and Silver, *Signal and the Noise*.

BIBLIOGRAPHY

Bashour, Bana, and Hans Muller, eds. *Contemporary Philosophical Naturalism and Its Implications.* New York: Routledge, 2014.

Bovens, Luc, and Stephan Hartmann. *Bayesian Epistemology.* Oxford: Oxford University Press, 2004.

Carrier, Richard. "Christianity's Success Was Not Incredible." In *The End of Christianity*, edited by John Loftus, 53–74. Amherst, New York: Prometheus, 2011.

———. "Neither Life Nor the Universe Appear Intelligently Designed." In *The End of Christianity*, edited by John Loftus, 279–304. Amherst, New York: Prometheus, 2011.

———. *Proving History: Bayes's Theorem and the Quest for the Historical Jesus.* Amherst, New York: Prometheus, 2012.

———. *Sense and Goodness Without God: A Defense of Metaphysical Naturalism.* Bloomington, Indiana: AuthorHouse, 2005.

———. "Why the Resurrection is Unbelievable." In *The Christian Delusion: Why Faith Fails*, edited by John Loftus, 291–315. Amherst, New York: Prometheus, 2010.

Carroll, Sean. *The Big Picture: On the Origins of Life, Meaning, and the Universe Itself.* New York: Dutton, 2017.

———. *From Eternity to Here: The Quest for the Ultimate Theory of Time.* London: Oneworld.

Clark, Kelly James. *The Blackwell Companion to Naturalism.* Hoboken, New Jersey: Wiley-Blackwell, 2015.

Davies, Paul. "Multiverse Cosmological Models." *Modern Physics Letters A* 19, no. 10 (2004): 727–43.

Dennett, Daniel. *Breaking the Spell: Religion as a Natural Phenomenon.* New York: Penguin, 2007.

Fodor, James. *Unreasonable Faith: How William Lane Craig Overstates the Case for Christianity.* United States: Hypatia Press, 2018.

Howard-Snyder, Daniel. *The Evidential Argument from Evil.* Bloomington: Indiana University Press, 1996.

Hunter, Douglas. *Political-Military Applications of Bayesian Analysis: Methodological Issues.* Nashville, Tennessee: Westview, 1984.

Ikeda, Michael, and Bill Jefferys. "The Anthropic Principle Does Not Support Supernaturalism." In *The Improbability of God*, edited by Michael Martin and Paul Draper. Translated by Ricki Monnier, 150–66. Amherst, New York: Prometheus, 2006.

Jaynes, E.T. *Probability Theory: The Logic of Science.* NY: Cambridge University Press, 2003.

Koterski, Joseph, and Graham Oppy, eds. *Theism and Atheism: Opposing Arguments in Philosophy.* Farmington Hills, Michigan: Macmillan, 2019.

Levitin, Daniel. *A Field Guide to Lies: Critical Thinking with Statistics and the Scientific Method.* New York: Dutton, 2019.

Mcgrayne, Sharon Bertsch. *The Theory That Would Not Die: How Bayes' Rule Cracked the Enigma Code, Hunted down Russian Submarines, and Emerged Triumphant.* New Haven: Yale University Press, 2011.

Murray, Malcolm. *The Atheist's Primer.* Peterborough, Ontario: Broadview, 2010.

Pearce, Jonathan. *Did God Create the Universe from Nothing? Countering William Lane Craig's Kalam Cosmological Argument.* United Kingdom: Onus, 2016.

Silver, Nate. *The Signal and the Noise: Why So Many Predictions Fail—but Some Don't.* New York: Penguin, 2020.

Sober, Elliott. "The Design Argument." In *A Companion to Philosophy of Religion*, edited by Charles Taliaferro and Paul Draper. Translated by Philip Quinn, 117–48. Hoboken, New Jersey: Wiley-Blackwell, 2004.

Stenger, Victor. *Has Science Found God? The Latest Results in the Search for Purpose in the Universe.* Amherst, New York: Prometheus, 2002.

Sterba, James. *Is a Good God Logically Possible?* New York: Palgrave Macmillan, 2019.

Stewart, Robert, ed. *God and Cosmology: William Lane Craig and Sean Carroll in Dialogue.* Minneapolis: Fortress, 2016.

Trakakis, Nick. *The God Beyond Belief: In Defence of William Rowe's Evidential Argument from Evil.* Dordrecht: Springer, 2007.

Tucker, Aviezer. *Our Knowledge of the Past: A Philosophy of Historiography.* Cambridge: Cambridge University, 2004.

Weber, Patrick, Karin Binder, and Stefan Krauss. "Why Can Only 24% Solve Bayesian Reasoning Problems in Natural Frequencies: Frequency Phobia in Spite of Probability Blindness." *Frontiers in Psychology* 9 (2018): 18–33.

Zenker, Frank. *Bayesian Argumentation: The Practical Side of Probability.* London: Dordrecht, 2013.

ABOUT THE AUTHOR

Richard Carrier is the author of *Sense and Goodness without God* (AuthorHouse 2005), *On the Historicity of Jesus* (Sheffield-Phoenix 2014), *The Scientist in the Early Roman Empire* (Pitchstone 2017), and many other books, chapters, lectures, and articles, including peer-reviewed work in philosophy and the history of Christianity. As an independent scholar he teaches online courses in philosophy and history and regularly publishes articles on his namesake blog richardcarrier.info. He holds a B.A. in history with a minor in classical civilizations from U.C. Berkeley, and an M.A., M.Phil., and Ph.D. in ancient intellectual history from Columbia University. He is a fellow of the Westar Institute and a current member of the Society of Biblical Literature and the Global Center for Religious Research. He specializes in the modern philosophy of naturalism, the origins of Christianity, and the intellectual history of Greece and Rome, and is a veteran of the United States Coast Guard.

MORE FROM THE AUTHOR

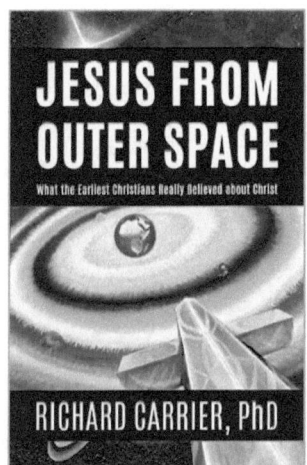

Jesus from Outer Space: What the Earliest Christians Really Believed about Christ
Pitchstone Publishing, 2020

Sense and Goodness Without God: A Defense of Metaphysical Naturalism
AuthorHouse, 2005

Epidemics and Religion:
From Angry Gods and Offended Ancestors to Hungry Ghosts and Hostile Demons

Louise Marshall,
University of Sydney

Abstract: *Throughout history, religious beliefs have been a primary way of understanding the experience of epidemic disease. This article offers a pan-historical and cross-cultural analysis of such interactions. The first section examines common structures and assumptions of religious explanatory models. These are characteristically two-fold, nominating both supernatural causal agents and particular human actions that have set these forces in motion. A society's identification of the behaviors that would prompt the infliction of mass suffering and death upon an entire people reveals a great deal about the values and world view of that culture. Most revolve around definitions of the sacred, which could be polluted, profaned or neglected by deliberate or inadvertent actions, and acceptable standards of moral behavior. Defensive strategies vary according to the nature of the supernatural agency held responsible, from one or more angry gods to offended ancestors, hungry ghosts or hostile demons. The final section investigates the extent to which religion may be helpful or harmful in shaping responses to epidemics, including the present global pandemic of Covid-19.*

Keywords: Religion, Epidemics, Plague, Covid-19, Pandemic

Throughout history, religious beliefs have been a primary way of understanding the experience of epidemic diseases. Religion is here defined as cultural practices and beliefs that have as their goal relationship and communication between human beings and those (usually) unseen spiritual entities or forces that are believed to affect their lives.[1] As anthropologists have noted, the dominant motif of a religion—its fundamental characteristics—is often revealed in the ways in which it explains misfortune and sickness and by the steps recommended to avert these.[2] Classifying such

---

[1] Westerlund, *African Indigenous Religions*, 2, quoting Brenner, "Histories of Religion in Africa," 164.
[2] Evans-Pritchard, *Nuer Religion*, 313; Westerlund, *African Indigenous Religions*, 4.

Socio-Historical Examination of Religion and Ministry
Volume 3, Issue 1, Summer 2021   shermjournal.org
© Louise Marshall
Permissions: editor@shermjournal.org
ISSN 2637-7519 (print), ISSN 2637-7500 (online)
https://doi.org/10.33929/sherm.2021.vol3.no1.05 (article)

beliefs as "primitive" or "civilized" according to the degree to which they approach or diverge from some external, imposed ideal (whether monotheism or modern scientific medicine) is less useful than recognizing the extent to which all religions offered a way of making sense of common human experiences of danger, suffering and disease.

In the case of epidemics, religious beliefs are forged in the furnace of catastrophic mass disease and high mortality, affecting not just one or two unfortunates but large numbers of sufferers at the same time. For many societies, this represents a qualitatively different situation from individual experience of sickness and health, generating different explanations and responses.[3] Because epidemics affect entire communities at a time, prescribed actions are usually public and collective, rather than private and individual, since the goal is to end the epidemic and restore health for the entire group.

Religion may offer more than one possible reading of events and may be integrated within or co-exist alongside other, more empirically inflected ideas of epidemic disease causation and cure. Ancient Assyria, for example, is known for its extensive medical corpus of naturalistic therapies, but Assyrian scholarly healers were also exorcists and priests who performed propitiatory rituals to soothe the angered gods and made no distinction between natural and supernatural causes of disease.[4] Similarly, religious and naturalistic interpretations and practices co-exist in Indian Ayurvedic medicine, Confucian China, medieval Islam, early modern Europe, and in many societies today.[5] Religion is thus not necessarily monolithic as an explanatory model, nor exclusive of others. Most often, people will find explanations that work for their particular set of imperatives. Being conscious of such diversity and pluralism of understandings allows us to recognize the robust creativity and resilience of human responses to epidemic disease across time and space.

The following discussion is not exhaustive, but aims to chart some of the principal ways in which religion has interacted with epidemic disease. The first section looks at common structures and key assumptions of religious explanatory models. The categories of heavenly beings held responsible are analyzed in turn. Since averting strategies only make sense in terms of the set of beliefs within which they were conceived, they will be discussed alongside

---

[3] For a stimulating analysis of epidemics as 'dramaturgic' events, see Rosenberg, "What is an Epidemic?," 1–17.

[4] Heeßel, "The Hands of the Gods," 120–30.

[5] Selin and Shapiro, *Medicine across Cultures*; Watts, *Disease and Medicine in World History*.

each other. The concluding section looks at how religion has influenced human behavior in the face of epidemics, both positively and negatively.

Understanding Causes:
A Two–Fold Model

The most important role that religion played in relation to epidemics was explaining what was happening in terms that made sense to that particular culture. Usually, such explanations were two-pronged, looking upwards to the supernatural realm and outwards (or perhaps better, inwards) to contemporary society. Epidemics were usually identified as let loose upon the world by supernatural forces: one or many gods, demons, or spirits of the dead. In most cases, these heavenly beings were not seen as acting randomly, but as responding to particular human actions that offended them. A society's identification of the behaviors that would prompt the infliction of mass suffering and death upon an entire people reveals a great deal about the values and world view of that culture. These vary considerably, but usually revolve around definitions of the sacred—which could be polluted, profaned, or neglected by deliberate or inadvertent actions—and of acceptable standards of moral behavior within the community.

For all cultures, explaining epidemic disease is less focused on addressing the disease symptoms of individual sufferers and much more about the cosmic disorder which such bodies show forth. Epidemic disease represents the world out of joint, a disastrous upset of the expected cosmic harmony. Religion aims to identify the causes, redress the problem, and restore good relations between heaven and earth. To do this, many drew on specially designated human intermediaries. These men and women—priests, chanters, oracles, diviners, seers, prophets, soothsayers, exorcists, and other specialists—were recognized as being gifted with special skills and status that enabled them to clarify the wishes of the supernatural powers and identify the human failings responsible. From them, too, would often come specific recommendations for remedial devotional and ritual action.

Divine Agency and Divine Cure

When epidemics are viewed as divine punishments for human error, the gods who send the disaster are also those who will lift it, if correctly approached. In heavenly pantheons, as in monotheism, the gods are inherently dualistic, both benevolent and punitive, the source of the scourge and the means of deliverance. In ancient Sumer, the underworld god Nergal was a benefactor of humanity and protector of kings, as well as a fearsome warrior god who unleashes war, pestilence and devastation upon the land.[6] His destructive powers are enthusiastically celebrated in a hymn in his honor from the second millennium BC,

> Lord of the Underworld, who acts swiftly in everything, whose terrifying anger smites the wicked, Nergal, single-handed crusher, who tortures the disobedient, fearsome terror of the Land, respected lord and hero…Nergal, you pour their blood down the wadis like rain. You afflict all the wicked peoples with woe, and deprive all of them of their lives.[7]

Such hymns were part of placatory rituals designed to mollify the angry gods and restore their good humour by heaping up their praises.[8]

This dualism is not unique to ancient Mesopotamia. Apollo of Greek mythology was the god of learning and the arts, as well as the death-dealing archer shooting plague arrows upon those who offended him. Yoruba divinities supervise all aspects of human existence, but punish with misfortune, disease, and epidemics.[9] The most feared is Shopona, powerful as a whirlwind, who attacks by sending smallpox, insanity, and other crippling diseases.[10] Judaism, Christianity, Islam, and monotheistic African religions, like those of the Nuer and the Masai, all recognized the supreme creator God as both author of their devastation and source of their liberation.[11] In India, Sitala has been venerated since the sixteenth century as the goddess of smallpox.[12] The heat of her anger causes the disease when she possesses the body, but if she is appeased and cooled by human propitiation, she will leave and the sufferer will recover. Today she is the major village deity in Bengal and elsewhere, annually celebrated as "the mother" of the village, who takes away the fear of smallpox.

---

[6] Often described by scholars as the god of inflicted death: Wiggermann, "Nergal," 215–26.
[7] Black et al., trans., *The Literature of Ancient Sumer*, 160.
[8] Cunningham, *Deliver Me from Evil*.
[9] Westerlund, *African Indigenous Religions*, 121–48.
[10] Westerlund, *African Indigenous Religions*, 128–31.
[11] Pritchard, *Nuer Religion*, 311–22; Westerlund, *African Indigenous Religions*, 65–83.
[12] Nicholas, "The Goddess Sitala," 21–44; Arnold, "Smallpox and Colonial Medicine," 45–65; Arnold, *Colonizing the Body*.

Arguing Your Case Before an Angry God:
The Plague Prayers of King Mursili

Some of the earliest and most vivid examples of prayers composed to request divine aid against an epidemic come from ancient Anatolia (the Asian part of modern Turkey), from the reign of the Hittite king Mursili II (ruled c. 1321–1295 BC).[13] Faced with a devastating twenty-year pestilence, the king appeals to the gods through the intermediary of a priest reciting the prayer, "O, Storm-god of Hatti, my lord! [O gods], my lords! Mursili, your servant, has sent me, saying: 'Go speak to the Storm-god of Hatti and to the gods, my lords.'" The prayer continues with a dramatic evocation of unending death, reproaching the gods for their harshness—even, one might say, for their irresponsibility—in allowing the plague to last so long.

> What is this that you have done? You have allowed a plague into Hatti, so that Hatti has been very badly oppressed by the plague. People kept dying in the time of my father, in the time of my brother, and since I have become priest of the gods, they keep on dying in my time.

The king comes to the gods as an urgent petitioner, seeking answers to a terrible situation, "Will the plague never be removed from Hatti? I cannot control the worry of my heart, I can no longer control the anguish of my soul."[14]

Like a defendant in a law case, Mursili uses every means he can to present his case favorably to the gods gathered in judgement.[15] He stresses his piety and devotion to the temples of all the gods, and his many attempts to ask them to lift the plague are so far unsuccessful.

> When I celebrated the festivals, I busied myself for all the gods. I did not pick out any single temple. I have repeatedly pled to all the gods concerning

---

[13] At least eight prayers are known, addressed to various gods individually and collectively, that have been recognized by scholars as "among the most beautiful compositions in Hittite literature." See Singer, *Hittite Prayers*, 47–69, and 48, with an excellent exposition of the genre in the Introduction, 1–18. I have chosen to concentrate on the longest and most famous of the group by virtue of its exemplarity and its highly dramatic and lyrical language: Singer, *Hittite Prayers*, 57–61.

[14] Singer, *Hittite Prayers*, 57.

[15] For Hittite prayers as the enactment of a case in a divine court, with the king as defendant, the offended god as prosecutor, the addressed god as advocate [these roles combined in this plague prayer], and the court of justice the assembly of the gods, see Singer, *Hittite Prayers*, 5ff.

the plague, and I have repeatedly made vows [to them], saying: 'Listen [to me O gods], my [lords, and send away] the plague from Hatti.'[16]

The king further points out that the epidemic is against the gods' own self-interest, since so many have died that there is no-one left alive to honour them.[17]

In the divine court, the accused must admit guilt. Consultation of oracles has revealed that Mursili's father angered the storm god by breaking a treaty oath (sworn on the gods) and failing to maintain certain rites. Though himself blameless, Mursili accepts that punishment of his father's sin has fallen on him. Moreover, since the king is the priestly representative of his people before the gods, royal offences implicate the whole society in their punishment.

> O Storm-god of Hatti, my lord! O gods, my lords! So it happens that people always sin. My father sinned as well and he transgressed the word of the Storm-god of Hatti, my lord. But I did not sin in any way. Nevertheless, it happens that the father's sin comes upon his son, and so the sin of my father came upon me too. I have just confessed it to the Storm-god of Hatti, my lord, and to the gods, my lords. It is so. We have done it. But because I have confessed the sin of my father, may the soul of the Storm-god of Hatti, my lord, and of the gods, my lords, be appeased again. May you again have pity on me, and send the plague away from Hatti.[18]

Confession disarms the angry judges, who are further appeased with the offering of gifts in the form of sacrifices and libations. The identified offences are rectified—the king repairs the broken oath and promises to restore the neglected rites.

---

[16] Singer, *Hittite Prayers*, 58.

[17] This reproach is included in other plague prayers by Mursili, most eloquently in that to the Sun-goddess of Arinna: "No one prepares for you the offering bread and libation anymore. The plowmen who used to work the fallow fields of the gods have died, so they do not work or reap the fields of the gods. The grinding women who used to make the offering breads for the gods have died, so they do not make the god's offering bread any longer. The cowherds and shepherds of the corrals and sheepfolds from which they used to select the sacrificial cattle and sheep are dead, so that the corrals and sheepfolds are neglected. So, it has come to pass that the offering bread, the libations, and the offering of animals have stopped" (Singer, *Hittite Prayers*, 49–54, at 52).

[18] Singer, *Hittite Prayers*, 59–60. For a stimulating comparative analysis of such cultural assumptions across Hittite, Israelite, and Greek texts, see Hanson, "When the King Crosses the Line," 11–25.

Finally, Mursili reminds the gods to be merciful, like a good patron with an erring dependent.

> [I say] to you [as follows]: The bird takes refuge in the cage, and the cage preserves its life. Or if something bothers some servant, and he makes a plea to his lord, his lord listens to him, [has pity] on him, and he sets right what was bothering him. Or if some servant has committed a sin, but he confesses the sin before his lord, his lord may do with him whatever he wishes; but, since he has confessed his sin before his lord, his lord's soul is appeased, and the lord will not call that servant to account…I am now continuing to plead to the Storm-god of Hatti, my lord. Save my life! And if perhaps people have been dying for this reason, then during the time that I set it right, let there be no more deaths among those makers of offering bread and libation pourers to the gods who are still left…O Storm-god of Hatti, my lord, save my life, and may the plague be removed from Hatti.[19]

As this prayer forcefully spells out, gods and humans exist in a hierarchical but reciprocal relationship, which imposes responsibilities on each party: the king to admit faults and rectify offences, the gods to be compassionate and receptive to pleas for help. The king has fulfilled his side of the bargain, and it is now time for the gods to do theirs.

Heavenly Book-keeping

Heavenly pantheons are envisaged in terms that make sense to a particular society. In China, from the twelfth century CE, the influence of Confucian ideals led to a belief in a hierarchically organised celestial bureaucracy, with a Ministry of Epidemics presided over by five powerful deities, the Commissioners of Epidemics.[20] These divine bureaucrats drew up heavenly balance sheets of good and evil deeds for every person on earth, rewarding meritorious acts with health and sending disease when the balance tipped too far towards the negative. Epidemics occurred when the score sheets of an entire community were so unfavorable as to be judged beyond saving. Like bureaucrats everywhere, the Commissioners themselves stayed in their offices and sent their assistants to earth to carry out their commands. A host of

---

[19] Singer, *Hittite Prayers*, 60.
[20] Benedict, *Bubonic Plague in Nineteenth-Century China*, 100–30.

plague gods (*wenshen*) acted as their emissaries, carrying out annual inspections of morals and inflicting epidemics on those deserving of punishment.

As the active causative agents, it is the *wenshen* who receive cultic veneration. Images of the plague gods were set up to receive homage and worship, and festivals in their honor were held around the time when they were believed to be making their annual tours of inspection, to persuade them to return to heaven without marking the community down in their black books. Similar festivals were also held when an epidemic broke out. Prayers and ceremonies of cleansing and purification culminated in a procession to drive out demons (who could be enlisted by the plague gods) and see the gods on their way. The gods' departure was visibly enacted by placing images of the *wenshen* on boats made of paper or grass that were then floated away or burnt.

What Makes the Gods Angry?

Crimes that stir up the gods vary according to cultural priorities. In the plays of the Greek poet Sophocles (496–406 BC), Oedipus' murder of his father, the king, and his marriage with his mother, though unwitting, polluted the land in the sight of the gods and cried out for vengeance (*Oedipus Tyrannus*). Only the suicide of the queen and Oedipus' own blood offering (he blinds himself) and banishment could begin to wipe the stain clean. Disrespect or profanation of a divinity's cult were equally fatal. In Homer's *Iliad* (1:1–475), Apollo inflicts an epidemic on the Greek army after their king, Agamemnon, captures the daughter of the priest of Apollo and refuses to ransom her back to her father. Yoruba deities were angered not by moral shortcomings, but by failure to properly maintain their cult, including neglect, disrespect, and breaking taboos.[21] Hindu and Buddhist ideas of reincarnation and inherited karma raised the possibility that epidemics could be heaven-sent punishments for unrighteousness or misdeeds in a previous life.[22]

Judaic understanding of the causes of epidemics was determined by Israel's sense of mission as God's chosen people.[23] Directed against Israel's enemies, pestilence was an aspect of God's unique sovereignty, his unlimited power over all creation, and his ability to trump the gods of any other faiths. Yet Yaweh could also turn this fearful weapon upon his own people. This was the burden, as well as the promise, of the covenant between nation and God, a

---

[21] Westerlund, *African Indigenous Religions*, 139.

[22] Zysk, "Does Ancient Indian Medicine Have a Theory of Contagion?," 87–89.

[23] Baruch, "The Relation between Sin and Disease," 295–302; Kee, *Medicine, Miracle and Magic in New Testament Times*, 12–16.

mutual agreement that promised divine favor and protection on condition that Israel faithfully obeys the divine commandments. The polarities of judgement and deliverance, destruction and sustenance, are thus central to the relationship between God and his people, "I will kill and I will make to live, I will strike, and I will heal, and there is none that can deliver out of my hand" (Deut. 32:39–41). The only hope is repentance of sin and cleaving once more to God, for he has promised compassion after judgement, rewards after suffering, the renewal of divine favor, and blessing upon a chastised and penitent nation.

This concept of a God, at once merciful and severe, who punishes his people for their own good, is also a central feature of Christian and Islamic understandings of epidemic disease. When plague broke out in the mid-third century CE, Christianity was a minority religion in a hostile Roman world. According to bishops Cyprian of Carthage (d. 258) and Eusebius of Caesarea (c. 260–c. 340), although the epidemic appeared to strike down pagan and Christian indiscriminately, the purposes and end results for each were very different.[24] For the enemies of Christ, the plague was a justly deserved punishment that led to eternal torment. But for Christians, the plague should be welcomed as a way of testing one's faith and making sure you followed Christ's injunctions to care for the poor and the sick. Christians who died were called to paradise and eternal rest, and those who died caring for others were equal to the martyrs in the way they testified to the faith at the cost of their own lives. Thus, a paradoxical interpretation of hope and mercy was wrested from a seemingly calamitous situation. Early Islamic teachers similarly viewed epidemic disease as differentially freighted according to belief: for infidels, plague was a punishment and a disaster, but for faithful Muslims, it was a mercy and a reward, a martyrdom sent by God that led directly to paradise.[25]

When Christianity became the state religion of the Roman empire, this kind of dialectic explanatory model was less appropriate. Instead, like the Israelites, Christians recognized God was punishing them for their sins, chastising them into better behavior. Hence the pronouncement of pope St Gregory the Great (c. 540–604) in a sermon preached in Rome during a plague in 590 CE: "May our sorrows open to us the way of conversion: may this punishment which we endure soften the hardness of our hearts."[26] Interior repentance and conversion of morals had to be proven by collective rituals performed under the divine gaze by a united and reformed community, "so that

---

[24] Cyprian, *Thasci Caecili Cypriani De Mortalitate*; Scourfield, "The *De Mortalitate* of Cyprian," 12–41; Eusebius, *Ecclesiastical History*, 21–22, 121–26, 220–23.

[25] Dols, *The Black Death*, 13, 21–25, 109–21.

[26] Gregory of Tours, *History of the Franks*, 426–28.

when he seeth how we chastise ourselves for our sins, the stern Judge may himself acquit us from the sentence of damnation prepared for us." Islamic authorities also at times interpreted plague as divine castigation of sins, such as adultery, prostitution, usury, or drinking alcohol, with a consequently greater emphasis on the reformation of morals, as well as individual prayer and collective processions.[27]

Spirits of the Dead:
Community Beyond the Grave

As agents of epidemic disease, the ancestor spirits of certain African religions share many characteristics with the gods: they watch over the living and expect to be honored with correct cultic veneration. Like the gods, they are both agents of affliction and sources of healing.[28] They are angered by neglect of their rites, breaches of taboo, and flouting of acceptable behavior. Like the relatives they once were, they can be difficult, exacting, and demanding, holding grudges until they are properly propitiated. Kongo *nikisi* spirits, the oldest and most powerful of a hierarchically ranked series of ancestor spirits, are each associated with a particular disease.[29] Epidemics are caused by Mayimbi spirits, particularly potent *nikisi* who belong to a family of "smashers."[30] Severe epidemics are the work of male Mayimbi, while less serious outbreaks are attributed to female Mayimbi spirits. These spirits must be invoked and propitiated by sacrifices, to appease their anger and give them the honor and respect they require.

Ancestor spirits may also be more constrained than gods by close-knit ties of kinship joining the living and the dead in community, with their sphere of abilities limited to their own living relatives. In societies with strong traditions of sacred kingship, even if disrupted or abolished by colonial rule, such as the Sukuma and the Kongo, only the spirits of deceased chiefs can cause an epidemic afflicting many families at once.[31] During their life, chiefs were religious representatives of the entire territory, responsible for the correct performance of rituals maintaining the health of the community, and this power continues after death.

---

[27] Dols, *The Black Death in the Middle East*, 114–15, 119–21, 236–54.
[28] Westerlund, *African Indigenous Religions*, 85–120.
[29] Westerlund, *African Indigenous Religions*, 109–11.
[30] Westerlund, *African Indigenous Religions*, 114.
[31] Westerlund, *African Indigenous Religions*, 93–94, 107.

Elsewhere, relations between the living and the dead are more fraught, as in the Chinese belief in hostile or hungry ghosts, vengeful spirits of the unquiet dead who had suffered premature or violent deaths.[32] Their bodies unclaimed, their rites neglected, they cannot return home, but roam the countryside, searching for victims. Alone, they inflict disease on individuals, but joined together in packs, they are even more dangerous, capable of causing epidemics. These spirits are the polar opposites of African ancestor spirits. Unconstrained by family ties, they represent an uncontrollable, potentially lethal supernatural force, defining these particular dead as more demonic than human.

Hostile Demons and How to Get Rid of Them

As supernatural agents of epidemic disease, gods and ancestors share the essential quality of moral duality: they might punish, but they will also heal. Humans enter into cultic relations with them as a way of keeping the lines of communication open so that disagreements can be resolved and harmony restored. But demons are another matter, fundamentally malevolent and chaotic. Different strategies are therefore required. Whereas gods and ancestors are praised and petitioned, demons are exorcised, battled, and even tricked. In Vedic India (c. 1700–800 BC) and China from at least the sixteenth century BC, all diseases, including epidemics, were thought to be caused by demons who attacked the body from outside and possessed it.[33] A Chinese dictionary from the second century CE defined epidemics as corvée (*yi*), in the sense of a harsh and inescapable impost or servitude, clarifying that "it refers to the corvée exacted by demons."[34] With incantations and prayers, Vedic and Chinese healers engaged in a ritual battle to expel demons from the body. Subsequently, in China, belief in the demonic origins of epidemics existed alongside or was combined with the heavenly bureaucracy discussed above. Demons might act on their own, but more often they were thought to be under the control of the *wenshen*, or plague gods.[35]

Demons sometimes appear in Christian belief as secondary supernatural agents of the plague.[36] Jinn armed with piercing lances occupy a

---

[32] Benedict, *Bubonic Plague in Nineteenth-Century China*, 110–12.
[33] Zysk, *Asceticism and Healing*, 3–20; Zysk, "Ancient Indian Medicine," 79–96; Kuriyama, "Epidemics, Weather and Contagion," 3–22.
[34] Kuriyama, "Epidemics, Weather and Contagion," 3.
[35] Benedict, *Bubonic Plague in Nineteenth-Century China*, 110.
[36] Marshall, "God's Executioners," 177–99.

similar place in some Islamic accounts of the Black Death and later epidemics.[37] However, if demons or jinn are allowed to harry humanity with epidemic disease, it is only because God has given them permission to do so. The evil spirits act not in their own right, but as part of the divine plan. Sometimes demons co-operate with angels in imposing punishment on sinful humanity.[38] Nevertheless, such a withdrawal of active divine agency from the task of chastising sinners leaves open the possibility for others, such as saints and holy people, to wrest control from the demons and provide protection from the plague.[39]

Heavenly Helpers

In addition to the supernatural beings who cause the plague, many religions provide for additional heavenly helpers. Bhaisajyaguru, the "medicine" Buddha, dispenses a range of healing benefits, including protection against epidemics.[40] Until the threat of smallpox declined in the modern era, several Shinto deities in Japan were petitioned for protection against it and other epidemics.[41] Both the Christian belief in a triune godhead and the cult of the saints offered many possibilities for playing one heavenly power against another.[42] Before an angry God the Father, Christians could appeal for relief to Christ the merciful Son. If Christ is enraged, then one might invoke his mother, the Virgin Mary, who is known to be especially forgiving of sinners and enjoys a mother's privilege in overriding or deflecting her son's destructive impulses. As the special friends of God, the saints were also well placed to intercede with the deity, acting as impassioned advocates before the throne of the divine judge.

---

[37] Dols, *The Black Death in the Middle East*, 115–18.

[38] Marshall, "God's Executioners"; Marshall, "The Collaboration from Hell," 19–45.

[39] St. Sebastian's intervention against the plague was first solicited against an epidemic spread by a demon and an angel working in concert; see Marshall, "The Collaboration from Hell." For Renaissance depictions of St. Nicholas of Tolentino wresting plague arrows from demons to save the city of Pisa, see Marshall, "La costruzione di un santo contro la peste: il caso di Nicola da Tolentino," 103–13. On the Virgin Mary as (selective) protector against demonically-launched plague attacks, see Marshall, "Manipulating the Sacred," 506–16 and fig. 12.

[40] Birnbaum, *The Healing Buddha*; Suzuki, *Medicine Master Buddha*.

[41] Ohnuki-Tierney, "Healing and Medicine," 3867–70.

[42] Marshall, "Manipulating the Sacred," 485–532; Marshall, "Plague Literature and Art," 522–30; Marshall, "Affected Bodies and Bodily Affect," 73–106. For the invention of the new plague saint Roch, both healer and victim of bubonic plague, see Marshall, "A New Plague Saint for Renaissance Italy," 543–49; Marshall, "A Plague Saint for Venice," 153–88; and Marshall, "St Roch and the Angel in Renaissance Art," 165–211.

Whether name saints, local patrons or specialist healing and plague saints, they could be relied upon to respond to their worshippers' appeal.

Conclusion:
Religion as Help and Hindrance

By providing an explanation of events judged meaningful and satisfactory by a particular society, and indicating concrete solutions believed to avert or change events, religion offers believers a way of making sense of the world, and thereby, perhaps, gaining some measure of control over it. During epidemics, religion often functions as a significant coping strategy. Such positive psychological effects have sometimes been insufficiently taken into account when historians have considered the psychological effects of past epidemics upon any given society.[43]

Many religions emphasize care of the sick as part of their work in the world, and have contributed significantly to the creation of institutions and personnel providing much-needed nursing and medical care for victims of epidemic disease.[44] In some instances, such as the practice of variolation as a part of the worship of the smallpox goddess Sitala in India, or the emphasis on cleansing and ritual purity, religious beliefs can have demonstrable positive therapeutic effects.[45] Conversely, religious rituals involving the coming together of many worshippers at a time, such as processions and pilgrimages, often facilitate the spread of epidemic disease.[46] In early modern Europe, clergy and believers who were convinced of the need to propitiate divine anger with penitential processions and keep churches open to all comers came into conflict with health boards and secular authorities determined to ban public gatherings and close churches to prevent widespread infection.[47] Similar scenarios featuring some religious leaders and communities unwilling to follow government-mandated health measures against infection have also played out

---

[43] As argued in relation to the Black Death and the second plague pandemic by Marshall, "Manipulating the Sacred." For this point in general, cf. Dein et al., "COVID-19, Mental Health and Religion," 4.

[44] Amundsen, *Medicine, Society and Faith*; Selin and Shapiro, *Medicine Across Cultures*; Zysk, *Asceticism and Healing*; Dols, *The Black Death in the Middle East*, 176–78; Crawshaw, *Plague Hospitals*; Cipolla, *Faith, Reason and the Plague*.

[45] Nicholas, "The Goddess Sitala," 27–29; Arnold, "Smallpox and Colonial Medicine," 50–51; Benedict, *Bubonic Plague in Nineteenth-Century China*, 120.

[46] For nineteenth-century India, see Nicholas, "The Goddess Sitala," 34–36.

[47] Palmer, "The Church, Leprosy and Plague," 95–99; Cipolla, *Faith, Reason and the Plague*; Slack, "Responses to Plague in Early Modern Europe," 443–45.

during the present global pandemic of COVID-19.[48] For the most part, however, faiths world-wide have adapted to the current emergency by moving religious services and devotional activities online, and have assisted in the delivery of urgently-needed community health and social services.[49] Yet, as the decision to drastically curtail but not cancel the 2020 hajj to Mecca indicates, navigating between the imperatives of religious belief and public health during a global pandemic remains a challenging task.[50]

Along with conquering armies, missionaries can be the cause of spreading epidemic diseases to previously unexposed populations they are attempting to convert. All too often, the resulting catastrophic mortality of Indigenous peoples in waves of epidemic diseases was seen by the conquering Europeans as divine judgement on the savage heathens.[51] This use of religious beliefs to justify stigmatization and persecution of minorities and outsiders — Jews, women, the poor, the lower classes, foreigners, racial minorities, practitioners of other religions, homosexuals, and queer people outside traditionally-defined gender or sexual norms—of whom the dominant group does not approve is the most troubling element of the encounter of religion and epidemics.[52] As the recent history of the AIDS epidemic demonstrated, such toxic conjunctions are not confined to the distant past.[53] Religiously-justified blaming and discrimination against stigmatized groups has occurred around the

---

[48] Wilson, "The Rightwing Christian Preachers"; Wildman et al., "Religion and the COVID-19 Pandemic," 115–17; Dein et al., "Covid-19, Mental Health and Religion," 1–9; Perry, Whitehead, and Grubbs, "Culture Wars and COVID-19 Conduct," 405–16.

[49] Wildman et al., "Religion and the COVID-19 Pandemic," 116; Dein et al., "Covid-19, Mental Health and Religion," 3–5; Marshall, "What Religion Can Offer."

[50] The pilgrimage was restricted to residents of Saudi Arabia, with 10,000 expected to take part: "Coronavirus: Scaled Back Hajj Pilgrimage Begins;" "Muslims Begin Down-sized Hajj Pilgrimage."

[51] Bray, *Armies of Pestilence*, 129; Crosby, *Ecological Imperialism*, 195–216; Chaplin, *Subject Matter*; Arnold, "Introduction: Disease, Medicine and Empire," 1–26; Watts, *Disease and Medicine*, 15–37.

[52] Nelkin and Gilman, "Placing Blame for Devastating Disease," 362–78; Rosenberg, "What is an Epidemic?," 5–9. For attacks on Jewish communities in Northern Europe in response to the advent of bubonic plague in 1348, see Ziegler, *The Black Death*, 87–98. For blaming and shaming across the confessional divide in the early modern era, see Slack, "Responses to Plague in Early Modern Europe," 436–39, 446–49. For nineteenth-century England and America, see Bray, *Armies of Pestilence*, 177, 183–84; Hays, *The Burdens of Disease. Epidemics and Human Response in Western History*, 130, 139–40.

[53] See the essays in Mack, "In Times of Plague," esp. Poirier, "AIDS and Traditions of Homophobia," 461–75, and Richards, "Human Rights, Public Health, and the Idea of a Moral Plague," 491–528; Rosenberg, "What is an Epidemic?," 1–17; Ron and Rogers, "AIDS in the United States," 41–58; Hays, *Burdens of Disease*, 301–6.

world and across multiple faiths during the present Coronavirus pandemic.[54] The global reach of such reports demonstrates that this is a key issue that cannot be ignored and requires a concerted response from all levels of society—as has indeed been urged in recent statements by international organizations such as UNICEF, Religions for Peace, and the United Nations Secretary General.[55] While the impact of COVID-19 continues to unfold around the world, what cannot be doubted is the role religion continues to play in shaping human perceptions of and responses to the traumatic experience of rapidly escalating global infection and mass mortality. To cite the apposite observations of the authors of a recent editorial on religion and COVID-19, across the spectrum of all possible reactions, whether negative or positive, harmful or helpful, it remains the case that "religious community-making tends to be an *intensifier of response*, strengthening resolve and motivating action....Human beings are complex and the way religion weaves itself through the lattice of human life is incredibly intricate."[56] In sum, religion cannot be ignored in any attempt to understand past, present, and future encounters with epidemic disease.

BIBLIOGRAPHY

Amundsen, Darrel. *Medicine, Society and Faith in the Ancient and Medieval Worlds.* Baltimore: Johns Hopkins University Press, 1996.
Arnold, David, ed. *Imperial Medicine and Indigenous Societies.* Manchester: Manchester University Press, 1988.
———."Introduction: Disease, Medicine and Empire." In Arnold, *Imperial Medicine*, 1–26.
———."Smallpox and Colonial Medicine in Nineteenth-Century India." In Arnold, *Imperial Medicine*, 45–65.
———. *Colonizing the Body: State Medicine and Epidemic Disease in Nineteenth-Century India.* Berkeley: University of California Press, 1993.

---

[54] "Israeli Rabbi: Coronavirus Outbreak is Divine Punishment"; Wildman et al., "Religion and the COVID-19 Pandemic"; Ellis-Petersen and Rahman, "Coronavirus Conspiracy Theories Targeting Muslims"; Mirza, "COVID-19 Fans Religious Discrimination in Pakistan"; Dein et al., "COVID-19, Mental Health and Religion," 5–6; Sarkar, "Religious Discrimination is Hindering the Covid Response"; Ghosh, "Modi's Covid-19 Policies"; "Religious Inequalities and the Impact of Covid-19."

[55] "Launch of Global Multi-Religion Faith-in-Action Covid-19 Initiative"; "UNICEF and Faith Groups Release New Guidance"; "Religious Hate Crimes, Racist Discourse Rising amid COVID-19."

[56] Wildman et al., "Religion and the COVID-19 Pandemic," 116.

Baruch, J. Z. "The Relation between Sin and Disease in the Old Testament." *Janus* 51 (1964): 295–302.

Benedict, Carol. *Bubonic Plague in Nineteenth-Century China.* Stanford: Stanford University Press, 1996.

Birnbaum, Raoul. *The Healing Buddha.* Boulder: Shambhala, 1979.

Black, Jeremy, Graham Cunningham, Eleanor Robson, and Gábor Zólyomi, trans. *The Literature of Ancient Sumer.* Oxford: Oxford University Press, 2004.

Bray, R. S. *Armies of Pestilence. The Effects of Pandemics on History.* Cambridge: Lutterworth, 1996.

Chaplin, Joyce E. *Subject Matter: Technology, the Body, and Science on the Anglo-Indian Frontier, 1500–1676.* Cambridge, MA.: Harvard University Press, 2001.

Cipolla, Carlo M. *Faith, Reason and the Plague in Seventeenth-Century Tuscany.* Translated by M. Kittel. London: Norton, 1979.

Conrad, Lawrence, and Dominik Wujastyk, eds. *Contagion. Perspectives from Pre-Modern Societies.* Aldershot: Ashgate, 2000.

"Coronavirus: Scaled Back Hajj Pilgrimage Begins in Saudi Arabia." *BBC News.* July 29, 2020. https://www.bbc.com/news/world-middle-east-53571886.

Crawshaw, Jane Stevens. *Plague Hospitals: Public Health for the City in Early Modern Venice.* Aldershot: Ashgate, 2012.

Crosby, Alfred W. *Ecological Imperialism: The Biological Expansion of Europe, 900–1900.* 2nd ed. Cambridge: Cambridge University Press, 2004.

Cyprian. *Thasci Caecili Cypriani De Mortalitate.* Translated by Mary Louise Hannan. Washington: Catholic University of America Press, 1933.

Dein, Simon, Kate Loewenthal, Christopher Alan Lewis, and Kenneth Pargament. "COVID-19, Mental Health and Religion: An Agenda for Future Research." *Mental Health, Religion & Culture* 23, no. 1 (2020): 1–9. https://doi.org/10.1080/13674676.2020.1768725.

Dols, Michael. *The Black Death in the Middle East.* Princeton: Princeton University Press, 1977.

Ellis-Petersen, Hannah, and Shaikh Azizur Rahman. "Coronavirus Conspiracy Theories Targeting Muslims Spread in India." *The Guardian.* April 13, 2020. https://www.theguardian.com/world/2020/apr/13/coronavirus-conspiracy-theories-targeting-muslims-spread-in-india.

Eusebius. *Ecclesiastical History*, vol. 2, *Books 6–10.* Translated by Roy J. Deferrari. The Fathers of the Church, 29. Washington: Catholic University of America Press, 1955.

Evans-Pritchard, E. E. *Nuer Religion.* Oxford: Oxford University Press, 1956.

Ghosh, Jayati. "Modi's Covid-19 Policies Make Clear that in India Some Lives Matter More Than Others." *The Guardian.* July 29, 2020. https://www.theguardian.com/commentisfree/2020/jul/29/modis-covid-19-policies-make-clear-that-in-india-some-lives-matter-more-than-others.

Gregory of Tours. *The History of the Franks*. Translated by O. M. Dalton. 2 vols. Oxford: Clarendon Press, 1927.

Hanson, Kenneth. "When the King Crosses the Line: Royal Deviance and Restitution in Levantine Ideologies." *Biblical Theology Bulletin* 26 (1996): 11–25.

Hays, J. N. *The Burdens of Disease. Epidemics and Human Response in Western History*. 2nd ed. New Brunswick: Rutgers University Press, 2009.

Heeßel, Nils P. "The Hands of the Gods: Disease Names, and Divine Anger." In *Disease in Babylonia*, edited by Irving L. Finkel and Markham G. Geller, 120–30. Leiden: Brill, 2007.

"Israeli Rabbi: Coronavirus Outbreak is Divine Punishment for Gay Pride Parades." *The Times of Israel*. March 8, 2020. https://www.timesofisrael.com/israeli-rabbi-blames-coronavirus-outbreak-on-gay-pride-parades/

Kee, Howard. *Medicine, Miracle and Magic in New Testament Times*. Cambridge: Cambridge University Press, 1986.

Kuriyama, Shigehisa. "Epidemics, Weather and Contagion in Traditional Chinese Medicine." In Conrad and Wujastyk, *Contagion*, 3–22.

"Launch of Global Multi-Religion Faith-in-Action Covid-19 Initiative. Faith and Positive Change for Children, Families and Communities." Joint Statement issued by UNICEF and Religions for Peace. April 7, 2020. https://www.unicef.org/press-releases/launch-global-multi-religious-faith-action-covid-19-initiative.

Mack, Arien, ed. "In Time of Plague: The History and Social Consequences of Lethal Epidemic Disease." Special issue, *Social Research* 55, no. 3 (Autumn 1988).

Marshall, Katherine. "What Religion Can Offer in the Response to COVID-19." *World Politics Review*. May 26, 2020. https://www.worldpoliticsreview.com/insights/28789/religion-and-covid-19-faith-during-a-pandemic

Marshall, Louise. "Manipulating the Sacred: Image and Plague in Renaissance Italy." *Renaissance Quarterly* 47 (1994): 485–532.

———. "La costruzione di un santo contro la peste: il caso di Nicola da Tolentino." In *San Nicola da Tolentino nell'arte. Corpus iconografico*, edited by Valentino Pace and Roberto Tollo. Vol. 1, *Dalle origini al Concilio di Trento*, 103–13. Milan: Motta, 2005.

———. "Plague Literature and Art, Early Modern European." In *Encyclopedia of Pestilence, Pandemics and Plagues*, edited by Joseph P. Byrne. Vol. 2, 522–30. Westport, Connecticut: Greenwood, 2008.

———. "A New Plague Saint for Renaissance Italy: Suffering and Sanctity in Narrative Cycles of Saint Roch." In *Crossing Cultures: Conflict, Migration, Convergence. Acts of the 32nd Congress of the International Committee of the History of Art*, edited by Jaynie Anderson, 543-49. Melbourne: Miegunyah Press, Melbourne University, 2009.

———. "A Plague Saint for Venice: Tintoretto at the Chiesa di San Rocco." *Artibus et Historiae* 66 (2012): 153-88.

———. "The Collaboration from Hell: A Plague Strike Force in S. Pietro in Vincoli, Rome." In *Religion, the Supernatural and Visual Culture in Early Modern Europe: An Album Amicorum for Charles Zika*, edited by Jennifer Spinks and Dagmar Eichberger, 19–45. Leiden: Brill, 2015.

———. "God's Executioners: Angels, Devils and the Plague in Giovanni Sercambi's Illustrated Chronicle." In *Disaster, Death and the Emotions in the Shadow of the Apocalypse, 1400–1700*, edited by Jennifer Spinks and Charles Zika, 177–99. London: Palgrave Macmillan, 2016.

———. "Affected Bodies and Bodily Affect: Visualising Emotion in Renaissance Plague Images." In *Performing Emotions in Early Europe*, edited by Philippa Maddern, Joanne McEwan, and Ann M. Scott, 73–106. Turnhout: Brepols, 2018.

———. "St. Roch and the Angel in Renaissance Art." *Studies in Iconography* 41 (2020): 165-211.

"Muslims Begin Down-sized Hajj Pilgrimage Amid Coronavirus Pandemic." *Al Jazeera*. July 29, 2020. https://www.aljazeera.com/news/2020/7/29/muslims-begin-downsized-hajj-pilgrimage-amid-coronavirus-pandemic.

Mirza, Jaffer Abbas. "COVID-19 Fans Religious Discrimination in Pakistan." *The Diplomat*. April 28, 2020. https://thediplomat.com/2020/04/covid-19-fans-religious-discrimination-in-pakistan/.

Nelkin, Dorothy, and Sander L. Gilman. "Placing Blame for Devastating Disease." In Mack, "In Time of Plague," 362–78.

Nicholas, Ralph W. "The Goddess Sitala and Epidemic Smallpox in Bengal." *The Journal of Asian Studies* 41, no. 1 (1981): 21–44.

Ohnuki-Tierney, Emiko. "Healing and Medicine: Healing and Medicine in Japan." In *The Encyclopedia of Religion*. 2nd ed., edited by Lindsay Jones. Vol. 6, 3867–70. Detroit: Macmillan Reference, 2005.

Palmer, Richard. "The Church, Leprosy and Plague in Medieval and Early Modern Europe." *Studies in Church History* 19 (1982): 79–99.

Perry, Samuel L., Andrew L. Whitehead, and Joshua B. Grubbs. "Culture Wars and COVID-19 Conduct: Christian Nationalism, Religiosity, and Americans' Behavior During the Coronavirus Pandemic." *Journal for the Scientific Study of Religion* 59, no. 3 (July): 405–16. http://dx.doi.org/10.1111/jssr.12677.

Poirier, Richard. "AIDS and Traditions of Homophobia." In Mack, "In Time of Plague," 461–75.

"Religious Hate Crimes, Racist Discourse Rising amid COVID-19, Secretary-General Warns in Observance Message, Urging Greater Inclusion, Respect for Diversity." Press Release, United Nations Secretary General Statements and Messages. August 20, 2020. https://www.un.org/press/en/2020/sgsm20214.doc.htm.

"Religious Inequalities and the Impact of Covid-19." Institute for Development Studies. September 27, 2020. https://www.ids.ac.uk/news/religious-inequalities-and-the-impact-of-covid-19/.

Ron, Aran, and David E. Rogers. "AIDS in the United States: Patient Care and Politics." *Daedalus* 118 (1989): 41–58.

Rosenberg, Charles E. "What is an Epidemic? AIDS in Historical Perspective." *Daedalus* 118 (1989): 1–17.

Richards, David A. J. "Human Rights, Public Health, and the Idea of a Moral Plague." In Mack, "In Time of Plague," 491–528.

Sarkar, Sonia. "Religious Discrimination is Hindering the Covid-19 Response." *BMJ* (June 2020). http://dx.doi.org/10.1136/bmj.m2280.

Scourfield, J. H. D. "The *De Mortalitate* of Cyprian: Consolation and Context." *Vigiliae Christianae* 50 (1996): 12–41.

Selin, Helaine, and Hugh Shapiro, eds. *Medicine Across Cultures. History and Practice of Medicine in Non-Western Cultures*. Dordrecht: Kluwer, 2003.

Singer, Itamar. *Hittite Prayers*. Atlanta: Society of Biblical Literature, 2002.

Slack, Paul. "Responses to Plague in Early Modern Europe: The Implications of Public Health." In Mack, "In Time of Plague," 433–53.

Suzuki, Yui. *Medicine Master Buddha: The Iconic Worship of Yakushi in Heian Japan*. Leiden: Brill, 2012.

"UNICEF and Faith Groups Release New Guidance on How to Support Communities in Times of COVID-19." Press release, UNICEF. July 30, 2020. https://www.unicef.org/press-releases/unicef-and-faith-groups-release-new-guidance-how-support-communities-times-covid-19.

Watts, Sheldon. *Disease and Medicine in World History*. London: Routledge, 2003.

Westerlund, David. *African Indigenous Religions and Disease Causation. From Spiritual Beings to Living Humans*. Leiden: Brill, 2006.

Wiggermann, F. A. M. "Nergal." In *Reallexikon der Assyriologie und Vorderasiatischen Archäologie*, edited by A. Bramanti, Erich Ebeling, and Michael P. Streck. Vol. 9, 215–26. Berlin: De Gruyter, 1998.

Wildman, Wesley J., Joseph Bulbulia, Richard Sosis, and Uffe Schjoedt. "Religion and the COVID-19 Pandemic." *Religion, Brain & Behavior* 10, no. 2 (April 2020): 115–17. http://dx.doi.org/10.1080/2153599x.2020.1749339.

Wilson, Jason. "The Rightwing Christian Preachers in Deep Denial over Covid-19's Danger." *The Guardian*. April 4, 2020. https://www.theguardian.com/us-news/2020/apr/04/america-rightwing-christian-preachers-virus-hoax.

Ziegler, Philip. *The Black Death*. New York: Harper and Row, 1969.

Zysk, Kenneth G. *Asceticism and Healing in Ancient India. Medicine in the Buddhist Monastery*. Oxford: Oxford University Press, 1991.

———. "Does Ancient Indian Medicine Have a Theory of Contagion?." In Conrad and Wujastyk, *Contagion*, 79–96.

ABOUT THE AUTHOR

Louise Marshall is an Honorary Senior Lecturer at the University of Sydney, Australia, where she taught medieval and Renaissance art for many years. Her primary field of research is Italian Renaissance plague images, on which she has published extensively and is preparing a book. Other research interests include late medieval and Renaissance devotional imagery, the history of emotions, and early representations of purgatory. Her research has been supported by the University of Sydney; the Vittorio Branca International Center for the Study of Italian Culture at the Fondazione Cini, Venice; the Australian Research Council Centre for the History of Emotions; the Renaissance Society of America; and the Gladys Krieble Delmas Foundation, UK.

ACKNOWLEDGEMENT

This is a revised and expanded version of an essay first published as "Religion and Epidemic Disease," in *Encyclopedia of Pestilence, Pandemics and Plagues*, ed. Joseph P. Byrne (Westport, Connecticut: Greenwood, 2008), 2:593–600; republished with permission of ABC-CLIO, LLC, conveyed through the Copyright Clearance Center, Inc.

MORE FROM THE AUTHOR

"St Roch and the Angel in Renaissance Art,"
Studies in Iconography 41 (2020): 165-211

"Affected Bodies and Bodily Affect: Visualising Emotion in Renaissance Plague Images," in *Performing Emotions in Early Europe*, Brepols, 2018

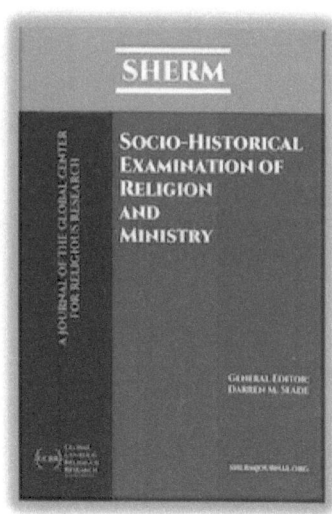

"Jesus is a Stranger Here":
The Healing Jesus Crusade and its Perception by the Muslim Community of Ede (Southwest Nigeria)

Raheem Oluwafunminiyi
University of Ilorin, Nigeria
&
Siyan Oyeweso
Osun State University, Osogbo, Nigeria

Abstract: This article examines the nature of religious interactions in the Muslim stronghold town of Ede in southwest Nigeria between the Muslim majority and the Christian minority. In particular, it examines the conflict that arose between Muslim and Christian groups in the town over the famous Christian programme, "Healing Jesus Crusade" in 2011. The programme represents the height of religious misunderstanding in Ede as the situation almost degenerated into open conflict between Muslims and Christians during this period. This article looks at the fundamental and immediate causes of the conflict, as well as the nature of the conflict, its implications for religious interactions in Ede, and the methods adopted in resolving the conflict. Based on oral interviews and the use of extant literature, this article contends that the crisis surrounding the "Healing Jesus Crusade" was a manifestation of the "aggressive" Christian evangelism in the Muslim-dominated town of Ede, and the "radical" reactions of the Muslim majority to maintain the status quo of the dominance of Islam in the town.

Keywords: Ede, Christianity, "Healing Jesus Crusade", Islam, Yoruba, Dag Heward-Mills

---

Introduction

The religious situation in the southwestern part of Nigeria, which is mainly inhabited by the Yoruba,[1] is particularly interesting for two reasons. First, the region has a significant mix of Muslims and Christians, as well as adherents of Yoruba traditional religions. Second, the region has a record of religious tolerance and mutual coexistence, and it has less religious conflagrations compared to the northern and eastern parts of the

---

[1] For the Yoruba, see Ogundiran, *The Yoruba*.

country where Islam and Christianity are the dominant religions, respectively.[2] The prevailing commonwealth of blood relations among the Yoruba people, which promotes communal and brotherly existence, has often been singled out as one of the major factors responsible for promoting these peaceful interactions.[3] The commonwealth of blood relations places a premium on family ties and values that must be kept over differences among members. It encourages cooperation and forbids rancor of any kind.[4] This has largely been responsible for peaceful coexistence in families where members profess diverse religious beliefs (Christianity, Islam, and African Traditional Religions).

Despite these relatively peaceful interactions, however, clashes among people of different religious faiths in Yorubaland are not unknown. Inter-religious clashes often break out due to aggressive evangelism by different religious groups in places considered as strongholds of rival religious groups. This has been observed in Yoruba towns and cities such as Epe, Iwo, Ede, and Ilorin, where Islam is dominant,[5] and in Abeokuta, Badagry, Ilesha, Ile-Ife and Ogbomosho, the strongholds of Christianity.[6]

Against this background, this article examines the nature of religious interactions in the Muslim town of Ede and the conflict that arose between Muslim and Christian groups in the town over the famous Christian program, "Healing Jesus Crusade." Held from 6–7 July 2011, the program reached the height of religious misunderstanding in Ede as it almost degenerated into open conflict between Muslims and Christians during the period. This article looks at the fundamental and immediate causes of the conflict, the nature of the conflict, its implications for religious interactions in Ede, and the methods that were adopted by concerned parties in resolving the conflict. The article is based on oral interviews conducted in 2012 and 2014 in Ede and complemented with the use of extant literature. It contends that the crisis surrounding the "Healing Jesus Crusade" was a manifestation of the "aggressive" Christian evangelism in the town of Ede and the "radical" reaction of the Muslim majority to maintain the status quo of the dominance of Islam in the town.

---

[2] Nolte, Ancarno and Jones, "Inter-religious Relations in Yorubaland," 27–64.
[3] See Asante, *The History of Africa*, 145.
[4] See Babalola, "Religious Harmony in Yorubaland."
[5] Gbadamosi, *The Growth of Islam*.
[6] For details on early Christian expansion in Yorubaland, see Ajayi, *Christian Missions in Nigeria*.

Ede as a Stronghold of Islam in Yorubaland

Ede is a Yoruba town in Osun State, southwest Nigeria. Historically, the town was founded as an Oyo[7] military outpost in the fifteenth century under the leadership of one Timi (the title of the paramount ruler of Ede), an Oyo warrior-prince and a fiery archer.[8] Ede today is very expansive as it covers several neighboring communities and a host of other towns. The town was predominantly inhabited by adherents of Yoruba traditional religions until the 1820s when Islam was introduced to the people by itinerant preachers from Nupe and Ilorin to its North.

Ede ranks among the few Yoruba towns where Islam enjoys prominence and considerable acceptance. Over the years, the Muslims of Ede have domesticated the Islamic culture, which is today apparent in everyday socioeconomic and religious lives. This can be seen in the presence or location of traditional Muslim compounds in the town such as *Ile Imale* (Muslim Compound), *Ile Talafia Imam* (Talafia Imam Compound), *Ile Daodu Lagunju* (Daodu Lagunju Compound), and *Ile Akajewole* (Akajewole Compound), among others, as well as the multitude of Qur'anic schools and mosques and the dominance of Islamic modes of dressing among males and females.[9] Due to these and other indices, Ede has long since become a reputed stronghold of Islam in Yorubaland, only to be rivalled by neighboring and distant towns such as Iwo, Ikirun, Ibadan, Iseyin, Ijebu, Epe and Badagry.

The implantation of Islam in Ede and its emergence as a stronghold of Islam in Yorubaland did not occur as mere accidents of history but, rather, as products of several years of efforts by pioneer Muslims in the town. A major historic factor in the development of Islam in Ede was the emergence of one Abibu Lagunju (1847–1900), the first Muslim Timi of Ede and one of the first Muslim traditional rulers in Yorubaland. Originally known as Sangolami Lagunju, he used his position as Timi to further the interests of Islam in Ede. He appointed the first Chief Imam for Ede named Nuhu Adekilekun and also played host to several itinerant Muslim scholars and preachers from the Arab World and from northern Nigeria who eventually settled in Ede. Furthermore, Timi Lagunju mandated his chiefs to put on turbans in the palace and ensured that his followers performed the five Muslim daily prayers and the Friday

---

[7] Oyo is the name of a very powerful empire that stretched across what is today's West Africa beginning from the seventeenth century until its fall around 1835. See Law, "A West African Cavalry State," 1–15.

[8] For details on early history of Ede, see Olunlade, *Ede*.

[9] See Dokun, *Islam in Ede*.

congregational prayers. The hallmark of Timi Lagunju's reign included the employment of Islamic law (Shari'ah) in the administration of justice in Ede.[10] His support for Islam thus ensured that by the first decade of the twentieth century, when Christianity was slowly finding its way into the town, Islam had emerged as the major religion among the people of Ede while a good number of its inhabitants held on to the traditional religions or practiced both religions in syncretic forms. Since the 1850s, Islam had supplanted the traditional Ogun (Yoruba deity of iron) and Sango (Yoruba deity of thunder) worship with which Ede was associated and which had become the major religion of the people.

In the second half of the nineteenth century, when European Christian missionaries began to penetrate several Yoruba towns and cities, they attested to the firm establishment of the Islamic faith in Ede. For instance, W. H. Clarke, the famous Baptist missionary who traversed the length and breadth of Yorubaland, visited Ede in 1875, during the reign of Timi Lagunju.[11] Recounting his experience, Clarke reported that Islam enjoyed royal patronage and was firmly rooted in the town. Clarke described Timi Lagunju as a "tolerant Muslim" and "young follower of the prophet."[12] He also made contact with a company of civil "Muhammedans," one of whom was a man from Hausaland who engaged in the silk trade. The high point of Clarke's visit and reception was that one of the elders who gave the vote of thanks on his departure was a Muhammedan.[13] Clarke's visit was significant for several reasons. First, it showed how tolerant and accommodating Ede Muslims were. Second, it served as a precedent for harmonious interface and interaction between social outsiders and insiders, and lastly, it laid the foundation for the development of the Baptist mission which later became the first Christian denomination in Ede.

In contemporary times, an important development in the consolidation of Islam in Ede is the multiplicity of Islamic sects, groups and organizations. Some of these groups belong to orthodox Islam, which sets out to ensure that Islam is practiced the way the Holy Prophet of Islam, Muhammad, did devoid of innovation.[14] Other sects are anti-orthodox in principle and practice. Some of the religious groups in Ede are the Ansar-ud-Deen Society, Ahmadiyya Muslim Jama'at, Zumuratul-Mu'minin Society, Nasrullahi-l-Fathi Society (NASFAT), Fatihul Quareeb, the Muslim Congress of Nigeria, the Muslim Students Society of Nigeria (MSSN), Ta'wunil Muslimeen, National Council

---

[10] Makinde, *The Institution of Shari'ah*, 69.
[11] Clarke, *Travels and Explorations*.
[12] Clarke, *Travels and Explorations*.
[13] Clarke *Travels and Explorations*.
[14] Balogun, "Challenges and Affirmations," 123–50.

of Muslim Youth (NACOMYO), Tabligh Jamaah, the Tijaniyyah and Quadriyyah Brotherhoods, and a host of other elitist Islamic religious societies.[15] These groups are united in their efforts to expand and consolidate Islam in Ede in the face of aggressive Christian evangelism. Even though their principles and operations differ on such issues as the conduct of social ceremonies like marriage, births and funerals, they have a common fundamental purpose of promoting and consolidating Islam in contemporary Ede. These Islamic groups are largely composed of the elites in the society who resist being misled by modernity and influences from other religions. Today, more than half of the indigenes and residents of Ede are Muslims.[16]

Growth and Development of Christianity in Ede since 1857

The Baptist Mission took the lead, among different Christian missionary groups, in the introduction, propagation, and spread of Christianity in Ede.[17] Although Clarke's visit to Ede in 1857 did not yield any immediate gain, the seed of evangelization and soul-winning had already been sown by that visit. The seed, however, germinated in the early twentieth century when what can be called "organized Christianity" commenced in the city. Central to this introduction of Christianity in Ede was one Jacob Oyeboade Akerele of Olosun Compound. Akerele was from a traditional religious background who left Ede for neighboring Ogbomoso early in his life around 1892.[18] By this period, Ogbomoso had already emerged as the foremost stronghold of Baptist missionaries in Yorubaland.[19] His guardians were staunch Baptists who provided him with the privilege of acquiring Western education. It stands to logical reason that the first obligations of his guardians were to convert him to Christianity and to make him acquire Western education.

With these two new acquisitions, Akerele returned to Ede, his hometown, and began a Christian evangelistic mission in 1900. As a literate in Western education, he caught the attention and affection of the reigning traditional ruler of Ede, Timi Oyelekan (1899–1924), who went ahead to appoint him as his scribe.[20] This situation afforded him the opportunity of being

---

[15] For details, see Adeniyi, "Growth and Development," 350–76.
[16] Nolte and Ogen, "Beyond Religious Tolerance," 1–30.
[17] Atanda, *Baptist Churches in Nigeria*.
[18] "First Baptist Church, Oke Apaso, Ede."
[19] Ajayi, "The Place of Ogbomoso," 16–38.
[20] First Baptist Church.

close to the traditional authority and gave him protection and freedom to preach, spread, and convert people without serious hindrances from adherents of other faiths. Interestingly, Akerele was highly organized in his approach to evangelism. He began to organize literary classes for young men and women in Ede and focused on how to read and write in the English language. He thus seized the opportunity to instruct and educate the children in Bible verses and messages. This, in effect, marked the beginning of Christian evangelism in the predominantly Muslim town of Ede. As a personal scribe to Timi, he received the royal blessing, and the hallmark of his evangelism was the establishment of the earliest Baptist Church in Ede. The church, with a thirty-member congregation drawn mainly from Muslims and Traditionalists, was situated in a place called Babasanya Compound on a portion of land provided by Timi Oyelekan.[21] The formal opening of the Church was a great occasion in Ede and considerable human and material supports were received from the Baptist mission in Ogbomoso. Incidentally, the lifespan of the church was short-lived as irreconcilable internal bickering created factions that pushed many converts to revert to their earlier religions. What is today regarded as the First Baptist Church at Apaso, Ede, was later established by the faction led by Akerele. In 1914, another faction led by Reverend Laniyi regrouped and joined the Apaso Church. With the Church becoming stronger, it started to establish new branches in different parts of the town and outlying villages.[22]

In subsequent years, other Christian denominations found their way into Ede. Examples include the Anglican Church Mission, which emerged on the religious scene in the town in about 1911.[23] As one of the five oldest European Christian missions that came to Nigeria under Henry Townsend in the 1840s,[24] the Anglican Mission began in Ede and eventually the first Anglican Church was built in 1920 with the first baptism conducted in the town on 16 August 1935. Another major Christian denomination in Ede is the Roman Catholic Church, established in Ede in 1921. Today, there are many Catholic Churches in Ede. Following the Catholic Church was the Africa Church Mission, which was introduced to Ede in 1926,[25] while the Christ Apostolic Church (CAC) arrived in Ede in 1939.[26] Another prominent Christian mission in Ede is the Seventh Day Adventist (SDA), which was introduced into Nigeria

---

[21] First Baptist Church.
[22] First Baptist Church.
[23] Anglican Diocese of Osun, *Outline History of Churches,* 78–94.
[24] Kwashi. "The Church of Nigeria," 165–83.
[25] Ojo, *History of African Church,* 1–7.
[26] Akande, *"Baba Abiye."*

in 1914.[27] The mission arrived in Ede in the early 1950s.[28] Also of note is the Celestial Church of Christ (CCC) which has, since its establishment, become a major player in Ede Christendom. The first Parish of CCC in Ede was established in 1968.[29] In 1969, the Church moved to its first site in Ede and has made tremendous progress in the town with significant achievements in membership and branches amid strong opposition. In contemporary Ede, there are numerous other Pentecostal Christian denominations with large followings. These include the Cherubim and Seraphim Church (C&S), Redeem Christian Church of God (RCCG), Deeper Life Christian Ministry, Mountain of Fire and Miracles Ministry (MFM) and a host of others.

The introduction and development of Christianity in Ede over the years has challenged the Islamic dominance in the town with far-reaching consequences for Muslim-Christian relations. While the Muslim majority in Ede struggles to maintain the status quo, the growing Christian communities in the town are also making frantic efforts to expand their base and influence in the Muslim-dominated town. Over the years, this has led to strains in religious coexistence, manifesting as religious conflicts, competitions, altercations, confrontations, and near-crises. However, the people of Ede have been able to manage religious conflicts and have not witnessed any serious open religious conflagrations in recent times.[30]

Issues in Christian-Muslim Relations in Ede before 2011

As indicated earlier, Ede is a town that has a shared population of Muslims, Christians, and Traditionalists. Over the years, Muslims have remained the majority, but there is a growing population of Christians in the town in addition to adherents of traditional religions. The introduction and growth of Christianity in Ede no doubt elicited inauspicious reactions especially from Muslims who suspected a serious challenge to their hitherto-established dominance. Although both Christians and Traditionalists view the predominance of Islam as a threat, they react to it in different ways. Muslims and Traditionalists often have a common agreement on certain practices believed to be accommodated by both religions. A case in point here is polygamy, a practice frowned upon in the Christian religion but endorsed by

---

[27] See Wogu, "Trailblazers of Adventism," 1–13.
[28] Ayodeji, *Christian Education*, 55.
[29] Personal communication with Prophet J. Segun Oniye.
[30] For details, see Peel, *Religious Encounter and the Making of the Yoruba*, 114–21.

Islam and traditional religions. This is, however, not unique to Ede but a general phenomenon in Yorubaland.

Given Islam's position of dominance, Christians began to compete more strongly with Muslims than with traditional practitioners. As Christian evangelism grew steadily and expanded in Ede, the Christians came up with the idea to establish schools, hospitals, maternity wards, and dispensaries. All these were used as direct and indirect instruments of evangelization, as Christians had the advantage of Western education. Given that the policy and the curriculum of the missionary schools tilted towards conversion to Christianity, many Ede Muslims refused to enroll their children and wards in these schools out of fear of losing them to Christianity. Indeed, many pupils from Muslim homes who enrolled at the Christian schools were successfully converted to Christianity. In response to this challenge, and to avoid further systematic conversion of their children, Muslims enrolled their children in Arabic and Islamic schools to acquire Qur'anic education and to learn a trade. Also, Islamic groups and individuals agreed to come together to establish private Muslim schools for the education of their children.

Christians began to witness a dramatic turn with the ascension of Timi John Adetoyese Laoye (1946–1975) as the traditional ruler of Ede. Timi Laoye, a convert to Christianity, was trained by the Baptist Church and thus did not hide his preference and support for Christianity, given the fact that he was the first Christian to be installed as Timi.[31] The Church in Ede did not leave things to chance and immediately availed itself of the royal patronage, support, and protection available to it under the Christian Timi. This is quite understandable, given that Ede, for much of its history, had been ruled by Muslim traditional rulers who made use of the Timi traditional institution to promote and entrench Islam. The installation of a Christian Timi was not pleasing to the Muslims in Ede, who did not want the disruption of the status quo. As the emergence of Timi Laoye made a difference to the fortunes of the Ede Christian community, it also contributed to Muslim-Christian rivalry.

The educational gap between the Muslims and Christians continued to widen when, in 1949, the Baptist Church established a Teachers' Training College to increase the number of teachers instructing in Ede. This gave the Christians an edge to produce more teachers in the town. In response to this, the Muslims organised a fundraiser to build a community school to eliminate the fear of conversion to Christianity. Yet upon completion of the community

---

[31] For details on Timi Laoye, see his autobiography, Laoye I, *The Story of My Installation*.

school in 1963, only Christians were qualified for the appointment and also available to teach. Timi Laoye employed most of the qualified Christian teachers at the community school, which soon created an atmosphere of resentment by the Muslims against him as the school in question was later named Baptist High School, Ede.[32] This further heightened and entrenched their fears about allowing their children to attend Christian schools or learn under Christian teachers.

In reaction to this challenge, a second fundraiser was organized, and the proceeds were used to build a new school that was named Ede Muslim Grammar School in 1974.[33] Despite the strained relationship between the Muslims and their Christian ruler, Timi Laoye encouraged the establishment of Muslim schools such as Bamigbaye Memorial School, which later changed to Tajudeen School. It should be noted, however, that the colonial takeover of control and regulation of schools in the twentieth century did not fundamentally alter the pro-Christian nature of the schools.[34] This situation continued well into the post-independence era after the Federal Military Government took full control of schools from the missionary organizations in Nigeria in the early 1970s, following the end of the Nigerian civil war.[35]

Since the 1970s, Islamic organizations and the Ede Muslim community have often demanded the inclusion of Islamic Studies in the school curricula for Muslim children. Consequently, most schools, particularly in Yorubaland, introduced Islamic Religious Knowledge (IRK) alongside Christian Religious Knowledge (CRK) in the curricula of government schools. Of particular interest here is the fact that religious instruction in Baptist schools has raised issues of conflict among Muslims and Christians in Ede. Most Christian schools in Ede did not want to teach IRK in their schools, the same way that most Islamic schools refused to offer CRK, even though these schools enroll Christian and Muslim pupils. Despite this, a few schools teach both the IRK and CRK subjects. While expressing frustration over the challenges facing the Baptist Mission in Ede, a respondent observed that "The imposition of the teaching of IRK on Baptist schools is a major challenge. The imposition of Hijab on students at Baptist schools is also a problem. Similarly, there is also the refusal to teach CRK in Muslim schools in Ede."[36]

---

[32] Dokun, *Islam in Ede.*
[33] Dokun, *Islam in Ede.*
[34] For the nature and impact of the government takeover of schools during the colonial period, see Fafunwa, *A History of Education in Nigeria.*
[35] Fafunwa, *A History of Education in Nigeria.*
[36] Personal communication with Reverend Z. A. Oke.

The most critical area of conflict between Muslims and Christians in Ede is the use and competition over public space for religious activities. While the Christians attempt to organize public religious activities as part of evangelism, the Muslim majority of the town sees this as a means to lure Muslim youths into Christianity and, in response, organizes counter-religious programs to mitigate the impact of such programs. It is within this context that the background, course, and consequences of the "Healing Jesus Crusade" episode in Ede in 2011 can be properly situated.

Dag Heward-Mills and the "Healing Jesus Crusade" in Ede

The "Healing Jesus Crusade" was a five-day public Christian programme held at Ede from 6–11 July 2011. It was organized by a renowned preacher and African Evangelist, Dag Heward-Mills, who was born in London to a Ghanaian father and a Swiss mother.[37] He founded the United Denominations of the Lighthouse Group of Churches, formerly Lighthouse Chapel International Church, in 1987, and later established the "Healing Jesus Crusade" in 2004, as a purely evangelistic arm of his Ministry. The early evangelism campaigns were focused on Ghana, but they soon moved throughout the West African sub-region to fulfill its global objectives of mass evangelism.[38]

As part of Dag Heward-Mills' "Healing Jesus Crusade" across the West African subregion, Ede was selected as the venue of the Nigerian crusade in 2011. The choice of Ede for the program was not unconnected with the fact that the town is a Muslim stronghold not only in Osun State but also in Nigeria as a whole. For the Muslim population of Ede, the "Healing Jesus Crusade" was perceived as a larger plan to "Christianize" major Muslim towns, Ede in particular. This assumption was linked to the success recorded in the establishment of Bowen University in the neighboring town of Iwo by the Baptist Mission in 2001. The establishment of the Redeemer's University in Ede by the Redeemed Christian Church of God (RCCG) in 2005 was also viewed by Ede Muslims as another attempt by Christians to break the town's Muslim stronghold.[39] All these created apprehensions for the Muslims, who feared that the growing influence of Christian groups in Ede may spell doom for Islamic ascendancy in the town.

---

[37] Our History, "Lighthouse Chapel International."
[38] Ede Crusade, "Dag Heward-Mills."
[39] Personal communication with Ibraheem Dende Tijani Adekilekun.

Crusade Preparations and Awareness

The United Denominations of the Lighthouse Group of Churches and the whole Christian Community in Nigeria were mobilized for visitation to Ede and, as a result, every Christian denomination was persuaded to fully and actively participate. Considering the magnitude of the crusade, six neighboring Local Government Areas which fall within a thirty-kilometer radius catchment area of Ede were mobilized as well. The preparations for the crusade commenced in May 2011, with a team of four men who travelled from Ghana on a fact-finding mission in Nigeria. The job of this team was to visit and identify possible crusade venues. Ede was one of the six venues visited and selected afterwards. Later, in the same month, another team of thirteen people led by the International Crusade Director left Ghana for Nigeria to prepare the six cities for the crusade.

This team was joined in Ede by the second group of five advance team members led by the Convoy Manager, eleven drivers, and sixteen Anagkazo Bible and Ministry Training Centre (ABMTC)[40] students on evangelistic mission. Publicity in anticipation of the crusade commenced immediately. The degree and quality of publicity and awareness about the crusade aptly demonstrated its international connections. The organizers made use of the electronic and print media to sensitize the people of Ede, in particular, and the whole of the country, in general. Television programs and advertisements were regularly aired while radio jingles and announcements heralding the preparations were echoed from time to time. The jingles and announcements were produced in the local pidgin English, English, and Yoruba languages for all categories of the targeted audience—a crowd of half a million people. The result was a surge in publicity across major radio and television platforms in the catchment area.[41]

Crusade paraphernalia like handbills, posters, banners, and billboards with messages and pictures of the Evangelist, Dag Heward-Mills, were mounted all over the town. Significantly, several cars mounted with public address systems, and Christian volunteers moved around Ede to inform the community about the forthcoming visitation. Almost every commercial vehicle had a bumper sticker with a different message about the crusade. The whole of Ede was dressed in crusade materials. All available roadside walls and shops were

---

[40] For details on the ABMTC, see History, "Anagkazo Bible Ministry Training Centre."

[41] The authors personally witnessed this surge in publicity throughout the period in Ede and its environs.

painted in yellow, the color of the crusade, with big inscriptions. This aggressive form of publicity is not unusual, given that the crusaders themselves acknowledged that four out of every five persons in Ede professed the Islamic faith. The crusaders understood one fact: even though the fundamental underlining objective was to win converts from a Muslim dominated population, this could not be achieved in an atmosphere devoid of peace and understanding. Thus, the crusaders invited the Timi, who they described as a God-fearing Muslim, to the crusade. Also, a high-powered delegation from the crusade organizers called on the Chief Imam of Ede for a courtesy visit.

Quite expectedly, the Muslim community in Ede immediately put up a hostile reaction towards the preparation of the crusade and, in particular, the various messages printed on the banners, posters, billboards, and stickers. To some Muslims, such counter-reaction was unnecessary. This brings us to the question of whether Jesus is a stranger to the Ede community or not. This question, as we shall examine subsequently, fundamentally informs the perception of the "Healing Jesus Crusade" in Ede by the Muslims. At the end of the program, while the conference organizers claimed that the crusade recorded several miracles, the Muslim community in Ede emphasized that none occurred. The official website of Evangelist Heward-Mills put the success and miracles recorded at the crusade in Ede in these words:

> When the great man of God arrived, the streets were lined up with people, many of whom were also dressed in the "Healing Jesus Crusade" colours, cheering, waving and hoping to catch a glimpse of him. He was warmly received by the pastors and kings of the land at two separate civic reception ceremonies, held in his honour. At the gatherings, He declared to the welcoming crowd that Jesus was going to do something good for them during ... the ... crusade. And true to the Evangelist's word, God visited the people of Ede, saving thousands of souls, delivering multitudes from the bondage of sin and healing many of their infirmities. Many phenomenal miracles were recorded including the miracle of a dead fetus coming back to life during the third night of the crusade. A young pregnant woman who was between 5 to 6 months pregnant had experienced the absence of movement of the baby (Fetus) in her womb. She became very worried and reported to a hospital where she was examined by doctors on two different occasions. The doctors upon examination could not detect a fetal heartbeat so the fetus was diagnosed as dead. When she heard about the crusade in town, she decided to believe God for a miracle so, on the third night of the crusade, she attended with a friend. During the time the Evangelist was

praying for the sick, she placed her hand on her belly and determined, in her own words, "to experience the miracle of Lazarus!" Suddenly, she began to feel kicks in her womb! She could not believe it. She ran forward with great joy and excitement to testify about what she had felt and what she believed it meant. The next day, she went again to the hospital to check if her miracle was ... real. The doctors examined her once again. She returned to the crusade again in the evening with an ultrasound scan report indicating that the baby who had been declared dead twice by the doctors, was now alive; A live fetus at 22 weeks with no abnormalities!!! This was the 2nd miracle of the dead being raised, in the life and ministry of Evangelist Dag Heward-Mills and he is still trusting God to see at least twenty of such miracles. Jesus is a Healing Jesus and He still works miracles today, for those who believe.[42]

To the Muslim Community in Ede, all these so-called miracles recorded during the crusade had been pre-planned by the organizers of the event, who aimed to deceive people and lure them into accepting Jesus and converting to Christianity. To them, it was a fraud.[43] Several Muslim respondents also claimed that most of the people who attended the crusades were not from Ede but non-residents brought by the organizers from different parts of the country who had been provided with free transport, food, clothes, and medical services.[44]

Is Jesus Christ Truly a Stranger to Ede People?

To the people of Ede, the idea that "Jesus is a stranger" is completely unfounded and has no basis, given the historical development of Christianity in the town. Ede may not be the first Yoruba town to identify with Christianity. The religion, however, reached Ede in the nineteenth century about the same period it was introduced to places like Ilesa and Ogbomoso where local adaptation was high and the majority of the indigenes professed Christianity. It can be argued that Jesus himself began to make his influence felt in the town for the first time in 1857 through the renowned Baptist missionary, W. H. Clarke. Timi Lagunju allowed Clarke to preach the Christian gospel to the chiefs and a company of civic Muslims. Clarke records that he was "pleased

---

[42] Ede Crusade, "Dag Heward-Mills."
[43] Personal communication with Ibraheem Dende Tijani Adekilekun.
[44] Personal communication with Nureni Lawal and Alhaji Adio. See also, Banaat, "In Ede."

with his (Lagunju) free and open toleration....His first proposal as to the length of my stay was nine days which honor I could but decline in staying four or five days as a maximum."[45]

Apart from this, subsequent developments in Christendom in Ede have shown a considerable presence and domestication of the gospel of Jesus Christ. The Baptists, in particular, made a significant representation of Jesus Christ for a very long period such that early Christian indigenes of Ede claim to know Jesus Christ through Baptist evangelism. Other missions that emerged subsequently can also attest to the same feat.

For the Ede Muslim community and, indeed, the Islamic organizations such as the Muslim Students Society of Nigeria (MSSN), the National Council of Muslim Youth (NACOMYO), Muslim Rights Concern (MURIC), Ta'wunil Muslimeen, and the Tabligh Jamaah, who are the contemporary vanguards of pristine Islam, all steadfastly ignore the percentage of Christian presence in Ede even though they recognize that they coexist in the town. More important still is the fact that there are some Muslims who have been converted to Christianity and still live with their Muslim relatives within the same compound. There is little or no antagonism towards these converts because of blood ties. The same reaction was experienced by the founder of CAC in Ede, Prophet Samson Oladeji Akande, being an indigene of Ede. Founders of other Churches who were not indigenes were not accorded the same treatment although they achieved quite a lot of success in Christian evangelism in Ede. There is a popular Yoruba proverb that says "a disobedient child is not left for the Tiger as prey." The import of this proverb is that no matter how unpleasant a situation is, there is always a way to manage or resolve it. This demonstrates the degree of Yoruba liberal disposition towards different religious affiliations.[46] By implication, this is a subtle way of acknowledging that Jesus is not a stranger in the Ede community. However, the Islamic superstructure which has been imposed on a permanent indigenous substructure is a healthy assurance of continuous dominance by the Muslims in the town.

The "Healing Jesus Crusade" was considered by the Muslim Community in Ede as a deliberate foreign intrusion from Ghana and as part of a larger plan to Christianize the strongholds of Islam in the Osun State, of which Ede is one. Furthermore, the suspicion of the Ede Muslim community was more provoked, given the mass mobilization and collaboration of various Pentecostal Churches around the catchment area of Ede, particularly the surrounding six

---

[45] Clarke, *Travels and Explorations*, 114.
[46] Peel, *Christianity, Islam and Orisa Religion.*

Local Government Areas. The large-scale use of institutional and traditional media (television and radio) associated with the exercise also led to great concern on the part of the Muslims. Finally, the deliberate choice of Ede as the site of the crusade was perceived as an attempt to disrupt the religious peace and tranquility long enjoyed in the town.

The reaction of the Ede Muslim community, and of radicals in particular, almost snowballed into a full-blown crisis. The Muslim community was taken by surprise over the choice of Ede as one of the hosts of the popular "Healing Jesus Crusade." These were incidentally perceived by the Muslims as a deliberate attempt by the Christian evangelists, both local and foreign, to renew and further a project of conversion, which hitherto was a herculean task, in the predominantly Muslim town of Ede. The particular incident that seemed to irritate the Muslim community was the invitation of one of the local Muslim clerics in connection with the crusade by the men of the State Security Service for interrogation. Though the cleric was released on the same day, the message that passed to the Muslims was that they were being witch-hunted. Furthermore, in an attempt to showcase and confirm the power of Jesus Christ and the Holy Spirit in terms of soul winning, miracles, and setting people free from all kinds of burden and bondages, evangelist Dag Heward-Mills publicly invited armed robbers to the five-day crusade. This act was viewed differently by the Muslims, who saw it as clear intimidation and a Christian conspiracy against the town. There was no doubt that Ede was already under siege and for them, their aggressive reaction became a matter of exigency.[47]

Counter Reaction and Near Crisis

The Ede Muslim community did not leave things to chance in their reaction to the perceived Christian encroachment on their domain. The Muslims felt challenged and, as a result, mounted a counter-publicity campaign to forestall any Christian incursion into their territory. Given the degree and extent of publicity over the "Healing Jesus Crusade," apart from feeling subjected to several public disturbances, it can also be argued that the Muslim community leaders became concerned about the crusade being a massive success. Thus, Muslims mobilized individuals, youth organizations, cleric compounds, and Muslim elites for counter-publicity. Electronic and print media were adopted by Muslims to carry out this mission. There was a massive display of posters, banners, billboards, stickers, and prompt distribution of handbills with

---

[47] Personal communication with Mutiu Lawal.

particular counter-messages addressing those already displayed by the Crusaders. This was in addition to the painting of physical structures such as walls, kiosks, the fronts of residential buildings, and those that are close to the streets. A prominent Muslim cleric in Ede reacted thus, "The Christians were the ones overstepping their boundary. How can you paint someone else's house because of a crusade? They even tried to put a banner in front of my house, but I protested. I can say all Muslims in the town protested not against the crusade itself but the method of publicity."[48]

As noted earlier, banners, billboards, stickers, and signposts with bold inscriptions were placed and mounted at strategic places and also at the nooks and crannies of Ede with messages: "Healing Jesus Crusade," "Only Jesus Can Save," and "Jesus Died Because Of You." Each of these banners was accompanied by the name of the international preacher, Dag Heward-Mills. Considering this as sacrilegious, the Muslims also mounted their banners and billboards side by side and in some cases, directly opposite the Christian banners with messages: "Allah Is The Healer! Don't Be Deceived..!"; "Islam Is The Truth"; "If Your Lord Is Dead, Allah Lives Forever."

Despite the high-level diplomacy with Islamic clergy and with pastors of all Christian denominations, the seeming peace and accommodating gesture exhibited by the Muslims turned sour. The Ede Christian community, especially the organizers of the crusade, viewed the Muslims' reaction as sheer insubordination and a grossly offensive act. The Christian organizers expressed their readiness to urgently address the situation in any way possible. There was palpable tension throughout Ede as Muslim youth began to mobilize in anticipation of a possible outbreak of confrontation. The dramatic rupture that ensued which almost escalated into open confrontation was, however, resolved by the combined team of the Timi traditional institution, Ede League of Imams and Alfas, community leaders, and Christian elders.

The role of the current Timi of Ede, Munirudeen Lawal (Laminisa I), in the resolution of the crisis was remarkable. The Timi traditional institution is rooted in Sango, as indicated earlier. The stool on which the Timi sits and Sango are inseparable and this fundamentally explains why Sango has been one of the major traditional festivals in the town.[49] This explanation is necessary to establish the fact that the Timi traditional institution is not to support or favor a particular religion over the other. The religious affiliation of whoever is on the throne does not come into play and it is not allowed to influence decisions on

---

[48] Personal communication with Alhaji Olagunju.
[49] Beier, "Sango Shrine of the Timi of Ede," 30–5.

matters of public interest. Timi Munirudeen Lawal passionately appealed to all warring factions to allow religious peace and tranquility for which the town of Ede is known. The monarch remarked that as a traditional ruler of the town, he is a father to the Muslims, the Christians, and the Traditionalists, and, therefore, called for calm and for all parties to tolerate one another.[50]

For the League of Imams and Alfas represented by the Chief Imam of Ede, the crisis was viewed as unnecessary. As a man with vast experience, the Chief Imam, Moshood Hussein Akajewole, decried the act of transgression on the part of any religion and reiterated the teaching of Islam on tolerance of other religions. He cited the portion of the Holy Qur'an which supports tolerance where Allah says "There is no compulsion in religion; indeed the right path has become distinct from the wrong path..." (Baq. 2:256) and where Allah commanded the Prophet Muhammed to inform the disbelievers to practice their religion while he also practiced the religion of Islam (Kaf. 109:6).[51] This confirmed the position of Islam on religious tolerance. The verses the Chief Imam cited were meant to give exhortation, particularly to the teeming Muslim youth of Ede. Members of the Tabligh Jamaah were also involved in quelling the protest. Explaining the role played in curtailing local anger and the protest from escalating, a Tabligh member notes that:

> All Muslims are one family. Anything a Muslim does is also done by the whole community. The protest against the crusade was the collective effort of the Ede Muslim community. We, the Tabligh Jamaah are not violent. Islam forbids Muslims from engaging in violent acts. However, there are Muslims who engage in violent acts. If we see such a person, we have to call that person and tell him to stop what he is doing.[52]

The Christian elders were made to realize that there had always been cordial relations between the adherents of the two religions. It was recalled during the resolution meeting that a Christian, Reverend D. T. Afolayan, was appointed in the past as the Financial Secretary of the Ede Central Mosque Building Committee to demonstrate the Muslims' gesture of religious accommodation.[53] According to the Chief Imam, he was a responsible indigene of Ede and a well-respected figure in all strata of religion such that his

---

[50] Personal communication with Timi of Ede, Munirudeen Adesola Lawal (Laminisa I).
[51] Personal communication with Mojeed Lawal and Rasheed Adio.
[52] Personal communication with Mikhali Abu Muslim.
[53] Personal communication with Moshood Hussein Akajewole.

appointment into such a strategic and sensitive religious position appeared to be a welcome development by Muslims. Both Muslims and Christians in Ede were urged to embrace such cordial relations and to make religious tolerance the bedrock of Ede in everyday socioreligious interactions. In the case of the community leaders, the peaceful coexistence of all the people of Ede was paramount. Imbued by the popular Yoruba proverb, "an indigene will not wish destruction upon his town," Ede community leaders rose and rallied themselves for the peaceful resolution of the crisis. Apart from ensuring that the crusade achieved its objectives, the town as a whole stood to benefit from the economic boost and international exposure. Thus, the leaders appealed to all parties involved to give peace a chance and to allow religious harmony and tranquility to prevail.

It can, however, be argued that the controversies that surrounded the "Healing Jesus Crusade" and the success of its management could be attributed to the fact that Ede people recognize the importance of peaceful coexistence and religious tolerance. Even though the activities of the organizers appeared provocative to Ede Muslims, the reactions of the Muslim youths and groups were also overzealous and unnecessary. It was in reaction to this, and the need for mutual understanding, that a leading and respected figure in Ede affirms that:

> There is no doubt that Ede is one room in terms of history, religions and culture. My late father was a devout Muslim while my mother who was of Igbo extraction was a Christian. I am a Muslim with Muslim and Christian wives but my children are all Muslims. My immediate younger brother, Dr Deji Adeleke, is a prominent member of the Seventh Day Adventist Church. His wife and children are all Christians. Our younger brothers and sisters chose the faith of their choice and consequently, there are several Muslim and practicing Christians in the family. All members of the family participate actively during the *Eid-el-Fitr* and *Eid-el-Kabir* festivals ditto for Christmas and New Year festivities. In our family and the larger Ede community, Islam, Christianity and traditional religions coexist peacefully.[54]

The point being made here is that the reality of the recent situation is that both Islam and Christianity are far-expanding in most Yoruba towns and cities. It must also be realized that Christian evangelism is being extended to places

---

[54] Personal communication with Senator Isiaka Adetunji Adeleke (now late).

hitherto considered as Muslim strongholds and vice-versa. This may be a great test for the much-acclaimed Yoruba religious tolerance in the future.

Conclusion

The article has discussed the nature of religious interactions in contemporary Ede, focusing on the conflicts which erupted between the Muslim majority and the Christian organizers of the event associated with the "Healing Jesus Crusade" of Evangelist Dag Heward-Mills held in Ede in July 2011. The article shows that the "Healing Jesus Crusade" was a key episode in the history of religious interactions and encounters in Ede. It was the climax of a near-religious crisis in the town which almost degenerated into a physical confrontation between some Muslim youth and organizers of the crusade. The crisis was, however, successfully managed by the prompt interventions of the Ede traditional council under the Timi, the Ede League of Imams and Alfas under the Chief Imam, opinion and community leaders, as well as leading Christian clergies in the town. This article concludes that the crisis surrounding the "Healing Jesus Crusade" was a manifestation of the "aggressive" Christian evangelism in the Muslim-dominated town of Ede and the "radical" reactions of its Muslim majority to maintain the status quo of the dominance of Islamic religion in the town.

BIBLIOGRAPHY

Adeniyi, M.O., "Growth and Development of Islamic Societies in Ede." In *Islam and Society in Osun State: Essays in Honour of Oba Raufu Olayiwola Adedeji II*, edited by Siyan Oyeweso. Abuja: Mega Press Limited, 2012.

Adetoyese, John Laoye I, *The Story of My Installation*. Ede: Afin Timi, 1956.

Ajayi, Ademola S. "The Place of Ogbomoso in Baptist Missionary Enterprise in Nigeria." *OGIRISI: A New Journal of African Studies* 8, no. 1 (2011): 16–38.

Ajayi, J.F. Ade. *Christian Missions in Nigeria, 1841–1891: The Making of a New Elite*. London: Longmans, 1965.

Akande, Funso. *"Baba Abiye": The Making of the Prophet: The Testimony of Prophet Samson Oladeji Akande*. Ede: Gospel Promotion Outreach, 2002.

Anglican Diocese of Osun, *Outline History of Churches in the Diocese of Osun Anglican Communion*. Osogbo: Safesight Publishers, 2007.

Asante, Molefi K. *The History of Africa: The Quest for Eternal Harmony*. New York: Routledge, 2015.

Atanda, Joseph A. *Baptist Churches in Nigeria, 1850–1950: Accounts of Their Foundation and Growth*. Edited. Ibadan: University of Ibadan Press, 1988.

Ayodeji, Adesegun A. *Christian Education in the Seventh-Day Adventist Church in Remo, Ogun State, Nigeria, 1959–2004*. PhD. Thesis, University of Ibadan, 2009.

Babalola, E.O. "Religious Harmony in Yorubaland: How Feasible?" In *Christian-Muslim Encounter in Modern Nigeria*. Edited by E. O. Babalola. Lagos: Eternal Communications Ltd., 2002.

Balogun, Adeyemi, "Challenges and Affirmations of Islamic Practice: The Tablighi Jamaat." In *Beyond Religious Tolerance: Muslim, Christian and Traditionalist Encounters in an African Town*. Edited by Insa Nolte, Koya Ogen and Rebecca Jones. Woodbridge: James Currey, 2017.

Banaat, A. "In Ede, Osun State, a fraud is underway in the name of Christianity." Nairaland.com. Accessed May 21, 2021. http://www.nairaland.com/707841/ede-osun-state-fraud-underway

Beier, Ulli. "Sango Shrine of the Timi of Ede." *Black Orpheus* 4, 1958: 30–35.

Clarke, William H. *Travels and Explorations in Yorubaland 1854–1858*. Edited by J. A. Atanda. Ibadan: Ibadan University Press, 1972.

Dokun, L.A. *Islam in Ede*. B A. Long Essay, University of Ibadan, 1974.

Ede Crusade. "Dag Heward-Mills." Daghewardmills.org. Accessed May 21, 2021. http://www.daghewardmills.org/healingjesuscrusade/index.php/campaign-reports/campaigns-in-2011/181-ede-crusade

"Evangelism In Africa. Healing Jesus Campaign with Dag Heward-Mills." Daghewardmills.org. Accessed May 21, 2021. http://www.daghewardmills.org/healingjesuscampaign/.

Fafunwa, Babs A. *A History of Education in Nigeria*. Ibadan: NPS Educational Publishers, 1974.

"First Baptist Church, Oke Apaso, Ede: A Century of Practical and Expansive Evangelism in Edeland, 1900–2000," A Centenary Brochure (undated).

Gbadamosi, Tajudeen G.O. *The Growth of Islam among the Yoruba, 1841–1908.* New Jersey: Humanities Press, 1978.

History. "Anagkazo Bible Ministry Training Centre." Anagkazobibleministrytrainingcentre.org. Accessed May 21, 2021. http://www.anagkazobibleministrytrainingcentre.org/about.html

Kwashi, Benjamin A. "The Church of Nigeria (Anglican Communion)." In *The Wiley-Blackwell Companion to the Anglican Communion*. Edited by Ian S. Markham, Barney J. Hawkins, Justyn Terry and Leslie N. Steffensen. West Sussex: John Wiley & Sons Limited, 2013.

Law, Robin. "A West African Cavalry State: The Kingdom of Oyo." *The Journal of African History* 16, no. 1 (1975): 1–15.

Makinde, Kola Abdul-Fatah. *The Institution of Shari'ah in Oyo and Osun States, Nigeria, 1890–2005.* PhD. Thesis, University of Ibadan, 2007.

Nolte, Insa and Ogen, Olukoya. "Beyond Religious Tolerance: Muslims, Christians and Traditionalists in a Yoruba Town." In *Beyond Religious Tolerance: Muslim, Christian and Traditionalist Encounters in an African Town*. Edited by I. Nolte, K. Ogen and R. Jones. Woodbridge: James Currey, 2017.

Nolte, Insa M., Ancarno, Clyde and Jones, Rebecca. "Inter-religious Relations in Yorubaland, Nigeria: Corpus Methods and Anthropological Survey Data." *Corpora* 13, Is. 1 (2018): 27–64.

Ogundiran, Akinwumi. *The Yoruba: A New History.* Indiana: Indiana University Press, 2020.

Ojo, Simeon A. *History of African Church in Ede, Osun State.* Ede: Monec Printers, (undated).

Olunlade, E. A. *Ede: A Short History.* Ibadan: Ministry of Education, 1961.

Our History. "Lighthouse Chapel International." Lighthousechapel.org. Accessed May 21, 2021. http://www.lighthousechapel.org/lci2/index\.php/home/our-history.

Peel, John D. Y. *Christianity, Islam and Orisa Religion: The Traditions in Comparison and Interaction.* California: University of California Press, 2016.

———. *Religious Encounter and the Making of the Yoruba.* Bloomington: Indiana University Press, 2000.

Raifu, Isiaka. "Interrogating Shariah Practice in Yoruba land, 1820–1918." *IOSR Journal of Humanities and Social Science* 21, Is. 12 (2016): 3–9.

Wogu, Chigemezi N. "Trailblazers of Adventism in Nigeria, 1900s–1930s." *Journal of Adventist Mission Studies* 15, no. 2 (2019): 1–13.

ABOUT THE AUTHORS

Raheem Oluwafunminiyi is a doctoral student in the Department of History and International Studies, University of Ilorin, Nigeria and Research Fellow at the Centre for Black Culture and International Understanding, Osogbo, Nigeria. His research interests intersect themes such as political and social history (Nigeria), Yoruba cultural history, and contemporary popular culture. He has published widely in learned journals and books in these areas. Raheem is currently researching the Yoruba context of holy wells in Ile-Ife and Ondo and the collections in the Ulli Beier Photographic Estate at the CBCIU, Osogbo. In 2021, he facilitated the shipment of ten complimentary copies of the book titled, *The Brutish Museums: The Benin Bronzes, Colonial Violence and Cultural Restitution*, from Professor Dan Hicks, renowned archaeologist and anthropologist, based at the University of Oxford. The books were in turn donated to selected cultural and tertiary institutions based in Osun State, Nigeria.

Siyan Oyeweso is a Professor of History at the Osun State University, Osogbo, Nigeria. He was a Visiting Professor and Executive Director at the Centre for Black Culture and International Understanding in Osogbo, Nigeria. Oyeweso is a Fellow and Life Member of the Historical Society of Nigeria, Fellow at the Nigerian Academy of Letters, and is a member of several other professional associations. His research interests include Islam in Yorubaland, Higher Education, culture and history of Nigeria, Nigeria's intellectual history, and the Nigerian Civil War. He is widely published in several national and international journals.

MORE FROM THE AUTHOR

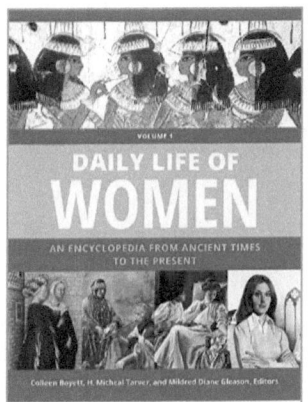

"Waka Musicians," in *Daily Life of Women: An Encyclopedia from Ancient Times to the Present*
ABC-CLIO, 2020

Oyo: History, Tradition and Royalty
University of Ibadan Press, 2001

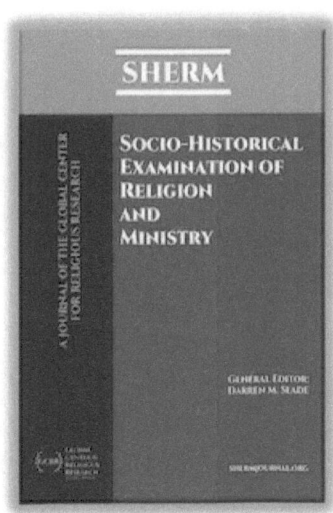

'Emet:
The Paradox of Death and Afterlife

Zev Garber,
Los Angeles Valley College

Abstract: *This article by Garber represents Jewish thoughts on death and dying that were presented at the 28th Annual Symposium on Jewish Civilization sponsored by the Philip M. and Ethel Klutznick Chair in Jewish Civilization, Creighton University, and other sponsors, and delivered at the University of Nebraska Omaha. Conference title, "'Olam Ha-Zeh v-`Olam Ha-Ba': This World and the World to Come in Jewish Belief and Practice." The section on "Jewish Martyrdom" is mainly influenced by thoughts expressed in Chapter 2 in Garber and Zuckerman,* Double Takes: Thinking and Rethinking Issues of Modern Judaism in Ancient Contexts.

Keywords: Adamology, Burial Service, Death, Kiddush Ha-Chayim, Kiddush Ha-Shem, Olam Ha-Ba

---

My article will cover the following topics: (1) Adamology, the human being, body and soul; (2) Death: Halakha and tradition; (3) conceptual language differences dealing with life, death, afterlife; (4) *Kiddush HaShem* (martyrdom celebrated) and *Kiddush Ha-Ḥayim* (choosing life); and (5) burial service. Finally, I will argue that the psychology of death and mourning are rooted in the philosophy of *"emet"* the portal to the Academy on High. Kaddish matters.

In an address delivered at the Lehrhaus in Frankfort-on-the-Main in 1934, Martin Buber (1878–1965) observed that Judaism teaches neither adoration (heathenism) nor conquest (Christianity) of cosmic forces but their sanctification and, consequently, their glorification. Not the earth above humanity nor humanity above the earth, but humanity and the ecosystem in equilibrium. Correspondently, cognizant life and death issues play out on Earth. Ever since Sinai, Torah teaches "to till (it) and keep (it)" Earth in terms of an intertwined word-pair: *Adam* (generic mankind) and *Adamah* (earth), which are birthed brought into being by YHWH (the timeless and infinite Master of All), whose ineffable Name breathes the "breath of life" (see Gen 2:7). In creative imagination, human life is evanescent, a breath of *ruaḥ Elokim* (wind/spirit of

---

Socio-Historical Examination of Religion and Ministry
Volume 3, Issue 1, Summer 2021   shermjournal.org
© Zev Garber
Permissions: editor@shermjournal.org
ISSN 2637-7519 (print), ISSN 2637-7500 (online)
https://doi.org/10.33929/sherm.2021.vol3.no1.07 (article)

God; Gen 1:2). The human being lives between the pillars of life and death, and s/he contemplates the afterlife. The purpose of this essay is to provide a Jewish understanding of life, death, and the afterlife.

Adamology:
The Human Being, Body and Soul

The Torah narrates that Man is created in the image of God (Gen 1:27; 2:7) and Talmud Torah extracts that Man's being is of body (*guf*) and soul, sacred components that are united to work, care, respect, and restore Earth and all therein (Gen 2:15). Soul-talk in the Bible is restricted to terminology. *Nefesh* is the life animating principle connoting human, animal, and fowl life (*nefesh hayyah*; see Gen 2:7, 19). Body and material desires are motivated by *nefesh*, positive and negative (e.g., *nefesh rasha* ["soul of the wicked,"], Prov 21:10). Interestingly, "blood" is the medium of the *nefesh*, so expressed in "the life (*nefesh*) of the flesh is in the blood (Lev 17:11). In biblical context, *ruah* suggests a) nature's element "wind" ("a wind from God sweeping over the water" (Gen 1:2b); and b) "breath" ("The Lord said, 'My breath shall not abide in man forever, since he too is flesh" (Gen 6:3a). Essentially, *ruah* is portrayed as emanating from God and returns to God who bestowed it (Qoh 12:7).

The verb *yṣr* ("form") is the verb of creation designated in the second Creation story (Gen 2) albeit with an alternate spelling. Two *yuds* in the creation of Man: "Then the Lord God formed (*va-yiytser*) Man of the dust of the Earth (ground). He blew into his nostrils the breath of life, and Man became a living being *nefesh hayyah*" (Gen 2:7). One *yud* in the formation of animals: "And the Lord God formed (*va-Yitser*) out of earth all the wild beasts and all the birds of the sky, and brought them to man to see what he would call them; and whatever the man called each living being (*nefesh hayyah*), that would be his living name" (Gen 2:19). Grammar aside, rabbinic hermeneutics view the double *yuds* as symbolic of the doubled *yetser* that man not animals is endowed: "*yetser ha-tov* and *yetser ha-ra*", inclinations to act ethically and morally, choosing good or evil, respectively.

A lesser-known rabbinic interpretation is that the Lord God formed (*yatsar*) Man to live in life (Earth) and afterlife (Heaven). *Neshamah* is first associated with *nishmat hayyim* ("breath of life," Gen 2:7. op. cit) and shares with *nefesh, ruah,* and *yetser* total identity with the *guf* in life and death. Ultimately, *neshamah* is the sole word for soul everlasting, enclosed in the *guf* but not separate and independent at death. The test of nasal breath leaving the body at death is the severance of the *neshama* from the *guf* and represents classic Jewish law's final outward sign that life has expired.

The rabbinic view of body and soul is mutual coexistence, working as a unit in the private and public space, ideally, doing meaningful acts of *kedushah* and *tikkun* ("holiness" and "repair"). Several illustrations follow in the verse,

> Just as the Holy One of Blessing fills the world, so does the soul (*neshamah*) fill the body. Just as the Holy One of Blessing sees but cannot be seen, so does the soul see but cannot be seen... Just as the Holy One of Blessing is pure, so is the soul pure. (*b. Ber* 10a)

Man is made in the image of God, teaching that the *guf* is sacred and treated as sacred since it houses the soul specially created for it during the week of *beriat olam* ("creation of the world"). A more viable position is presented by the influential Halakhist and biblical translator, Saadia Gaon ben Joseph (882–942) who is conversant in Greco-Arabic philosophy. He argues that the soul is created at the same moment as the body, albeit of a different material element (*Emunot ve-Deot*, ch.6). Finally, the lesson of the second century Rabbi Yehudah Hanasi counters Emperor Antoninus' assertion that the soul and body alone are not capable of performing bad acts by advancing that the body and soul can only do so when in harmony. This is illustrated by the lame guard and blind guard working together, not individually, to steal fruit from a high tree (*b.Sanh* 91b). Likewise, divine reward and punishment are meted out after the soul returns to the body at Resurrection since the body and soul in unity are responsible for intent and deeds *ba`olam ha-zeh u-va-ba-olam ha-ba* (in the "current world and afterlife").

The language related to body-soul unity, coexistence and separation, is philosophic, midrashic, and liturgical. The eternity of the soul since creation is axiomatic, but the state of the soul at the death of the body differs from no change to full-course alteration. Maimonides' (1135–1204) philosophic view of God and the soul is Aristotelian. He describes a number of faculties of the soul, all of which are related to the relationship of a living person to his or her material environment, perceptions, memories, creativity, and desires. The compartments of the soul are finite in relation to a person's perceptions, memories, desires and so on. At death these faculties expire with the body, but lifetime learning and philosophy soulfully inscribed are not erased by the *malakh ha-mavet* ("Angel of Death"). Daily liturgy reenacts the death passage in daily ritual. For example, in a state of sleep, the body-soul are temporarily separated and so mourning-like rituals are proscribed, such as the washing of hands (as in the presence of the dead) and recitation of special prayers before and after sleep. Sleep is "one-sixteenth of death" (y. *Ber.* 1a). Waking, therefore, is like a miniature rebirth. On the waking of the body, the *modeh 'ani* is recited: "I thank you, living and eternal King, for giving me back *nishmati* ("my soul") in mercy. Great is Your faithfulness." In sum, life is a gift of God, acknowledged every day, a spiritual pep pill to prepare for the daily blessings and challenges of a new day.

Tradition teaches that body-soul unity is beneficial, cooperative, and reciprocal. *Guf* decomposition and the existential state of the *neshama* preeminence is important, but not the *ikkar*, the principle concern. Rather, the modus operandi is the *Taryag Mitsvot*, the 613 Commandments (positive and negative) that singularly and collectively sanctify the person and the world. Soul knocking, conscience responding, and body acting enable and enact the holy, redemptive work instructive by the Torah of Moses.[1]

State of Death:
Views from Bible, Rabbis, Tradition, Contemporary

Judaism in the biblical era views individual immortality in three stages. One: biological immortality, "Be fruitful and multiply" (Gen 1:28; 9:1), living on through one's children. Two: name immortality, being remembered for a blessing due to a life lived by justice, mercy, and charity in the fullest adherence to the commandments and teachings of the Torah narrative, teaching, and theology. Three: group immortality, the continuity of the peoplehood surpasses personal death. Dead people are consigned to a common space called Sheol and live a shadowy existence while living in dust of the earth (see Dan 12:2; Ps 30:10; Job 17:16, and on). Biblical references to the resurrection of the dead in the Bible are primarily from the Persian period.[2]

---

[1] The philosophical foundation of Judaism is minimal on belief and maximal on behavior. The Sinaitic revelation is mainly divine legislation, not doctrine. Rabbinic tradition lists the total number of Torah commandments as 613 (known as *TaRYaG*, a mnemonic formed by translating the numbers into their corresponding Hebrew letters; thus, T=400, R=200, Y=10, G=3). The Talmud states, "613 commandments (*mitsvot*) were revealed to Moses at Sinai, 365 being prohibitions equal in number to solar days, and 248 being mandates corresponding in number to the limbs of the human body" (*b .Mak.* 23b). Another source sees the 365 prohibitions corresponding to the supposedly 365 veins in the body, thereby, drawing a connection between the performance of *mitsvot* and the life of an individual.

[2] See www.mechon-mamre.org. Copy of the Hebrew-English Bible (JPS 1917) is available online.

Isaiah 26: 19

Verse in context is a rejection of life without meaning leading to a doomsday predicament: "The dead live not, the shades rise not" (v. 14). Interpreted as an antiphonal poem proclaiming the resurrection of the dead, it engages God and celebrates the miracle of resurrected new life. As dew revives vegetation, supernatural *tal* ("dew") resurrects the dead. Personal resurrection is read into these lines. However, more seemingly is the restoration of the nation Israel as noted in the verse:

יט יִחְיוּ מֵתֶיךָ, נְבֵלָתִי יְקוּמוּן; הָקִיצוּ וְרַנְּנוּ שֹׁכְנֵי עָפָר, כִּי טַל אוֹרֹת טַלֶּךָ, וָאָרֶץ, רְפָאִים תַּפִּיל. **19** Your dead shall live (*God addresses Israel*), my dead bodies shall arise (*assertion of the people*)—wake and sing, ye that dwell in the dust (*resurrected people engages in new song and spiritual vitality*)—for Thy *dew* is as the dew of light, and the earth shall bring to life the shades (*divine revitalization of the thin and shadowy personalities of the dead*).

Daniel 12:1–3

The end of the era of Antiochus IV (175–164 BCE) is related in Daniel 11. This is followed by reward for the righteous then and forevermore (Tradition). Archangel Michael, the angelic defender of Israel (see Dan 10:13, 21), in a time of dire need (the Antiochus era), sustains the remaining loyal people. At the same time, divine justice rewards/resurrects the martyred righteous dead whose love of God was paid by the ultimate sacrifice. They join their living kin in a restored homeland. Celestial rewards await the *maskilim* ("enlightened," interpreted as the spiritual leaders), who turn many to acts of righteousness, they will shine as a stellar fixture in the heavenly abode:

א וּבָעֵת הַהִיא יַעֲמֹד מִיכָאֵל הַשַּׂר הַגָּדוֹל, הָעֹמֵד עַל-בְּנֵי עַמֶּךָ, וְהָיְתָה עֵת צָרָה, אֲשֶׁר לֹא-נִהְיְתָה מִהְיוֹת גּוֹי עַד הָעֵת הַהִיא; וּבָעֵת הַהִיא יִמָּלֵט עַמְּךָ, כָּל-הַנִּמְצָא כָּתוּב בַּסֵּפֶר.	1 And at that time shall Michael stand up, the great prince who stands for the children of thy people; and there shall be a time of trouble, such as never was since there was a nation even to that same time; and at that time thy people shall be delivered, every one that shall be found written in the book.
ב וְרַבִּים, מִיְּשֵׁנֵי אַדְמַת-עָפָר יָקִיצוּ; אֵלֶּה לְחַיֵּי עוֹלָם, וְאֵלֶּה לַחֲרָפוֹת לְדִרְאוֹן עוֹלָם.	2 And many of them that sleep in the dust of the earth shall awake, some to everlasting life, and some to reproaches and everlasting abhorrence.
ג וְהַמַּשְׂכִּלִים--יַזְהִרוּ, כְּזֹהַר הָרָקִיעַ; וּמַצְדִּיקֵי, הָרַבִּים, כַּכּוֹכָבִים, לְעוֹלָם וָעֶד.	3 And they that are wise shall shine as the brightness of the firmament; and they that turn the many to righteousness as the stars for ever and ever.

Qoh 9:5–6

In Second Temple Judaism, a mixed message of soul redemption is conveyed. To the Psalmist, the soul of the righteous may be redeemed (Ps 49:13–15); and to the Qohelet, there is the total rejection of life after death sets in:

ה כִּי הַחַיִּים יוֹדְעִים, שֶׁיָּמֻתוּ; וְהַמֵּתִים אֵינָם יוֹדְעִים מְאוּמָה, וְאֵין-עוֹד לָהֶם שָׂכָר--כִּי נִשְׁכַּח, זִכְרָם.	5 For the living know that they shall die; but the dead know not anything, neither have they any more a reward; for the memory of them is forgotten.
ו גַּם אַהֲבָתָם גַּם-שִׂנְאָתָם גַּם-קִנְאָתָם, כְּבָר אָבָדָה; וְחֵלֶק אֵין-לָהֶם עוֹד לְעוֹלָם, בְּכֹל אֲשֶׁר-נַעֲשָׂה תַּחַת הַשָּׁמֶשׁ.	6 As well their love, as their hatred and their envy, is long ago perished; neither have they any more a portion forever in anything that is done under the sun.

Additionally, a sophisticated future day of judgment for all peoples and nations developed in the Second Temple period apocalyptic literature. A day in which ephemeral souls are reconnected with dead bodies, resurrected and judged by God, evaluated by one's earthly behavior. Pre-sorting, compartmentation, and direction of souls prior to and about Judgment Day is extant in Jewish Pseudepigrapha literature (1 En. 22; 4 Ezra 7), Greek philosophy (Plato, *Republic* 10.614–615), and New Testament sources depicting judgment of sinners, etc. All sources suggest that the differentiated afterlife is determined by pre-mortem behavior than by post-mortem fatality.

The salvation of every Israelite/Jew is intrinsically linked with the salvation of Israel and guided by Torah teachings, the spread of justice and righteousness a necessary requisite in the coming of the Messianic Age for the living and the restored dead (*guf,* mortal/material body). The rabbinic world to come is not the Messianic era and so the principle is immortality of the soul or resurrection of the soul not component matter. So, the teachings of Maimonides and Judah Halevi (1075–1141). Nonetheless, Talmudic sources explicitly state that the dead will be resurrected wearing their clothes (b. *Ketub* 111b) and that the righteous whom God will resurrect will not return to their dust (*b. Sanh* 72a), pointing to a belief in bodily resurrection. So, the teachings of Naḥmanides (1194–c.1270), Ḥasdai Crescas (c.1340–c.1410), and his pupil, Joseph Albo (c.1380–1435).

Rabbinic tradition envisions a refined and ethereal recomposed new body reunited with the soul of the deceased. The reunion of eternal soul and afterlife body is done by God at a future moment chosen by him. The mystery of the Afterlife defies logical thought and reconstruction. It is normally explained in similar cadences as the mystery of birth and ultimately doctrinaire beriat `olam ("creation of the world"). How do you explain existence from non-existence and previous states of existence? You do not. "We will consider the matter when they come to life again?" (*b. Nid* 70b).

The doctrine of the physical resurrection of the dead coupled with the immortality of the soul are extant in contemporary practice and belief of Orthodox Judaism. In contrast, Non-Orthodox Judaism believes in the immortality of the soul rather than the resurrection of the dead.

Torah and Afterlife:
The Enigma of *Kiddush HaShem*[3]

In common religious usage, Torah is the unity of total revelation, the Written Torah (*Torah sheh-biktav*) and related authoritative rabbinical

---

[3] Several thoughts expressed in this section are extracted from Garber, "Holocaust, the Practice of Judaism during," 420–34.

commentary, the Oral Torah (*Torah sheh-b'al-peh*). Torah is a system derived from contact between the human and the divine that instructs by means of narratives, aphorisms, laws, commandments, and statutes which provide rules of life for individuals, nature and society. The verse, "Moses charged us with the teaching (Torah) as the heritage of the congregation of Jacob" (Deut 33:4) suggests the inalienable importance of Torah to Israel: Torah is to be transmitted from age to age, and this transmission has become the major factor for the unity of the Jewish people throughout their wanderings. In the traditionalist view of the Written Torah of Moses, our teacher is eternal ("I believe with perfect faith that this [written] Torah will not be changed, and that there never will be any other Torah from the creator, blessed be His name"; ninth principle of the "Creed of Maimonides"). The Oral Torah is the application of the written Torah to forever-changing historic situations, which continues to uncover new levels of depth and meaning, thereby making new facets of Judaism visible and available in each generation. However, the Reformers (such as Solomon Ludwig Steinheim, 1790–1866) contend that not every word of the Torah is equally binding or meaningful and so they permit a "selective acceptance" of biblical revelation. The classic statement on the role of Torah in the lives of Reform and Orthodox Jews can be understood from their interpretation of the *mattan Torah*: a) the Dual Torah of Sinai is given at one time, at one place and every Israelite receives the Torah in his and her own way and time (Traditionalists and the eternal Torah); and b) the voice of God is heard in every generation, i.e., revelation is the divine word of God to man but not given at one time nor at one place (Liberals and progressive revelation).

Qualitatively and quantitatively, the Nazis' near-complete destruction of the European Jewry represents the worst threat to Judaism's self-definition: a people made in the image of Torah, commanded by God to bring humankind closer to the prophetic ideal of the parenthood of God and the peoplehood of humanity. How Judaism, the religion of the ghettos, on the gallows and in the gas chambers responded to the commandment, "Choose life, that you may live, you and your seed" (Deut 30:19), may be approached in three ways: 1) Kiddush ha-Shem, here meaning, "to die for the sanctification of the Name" and the problem of baptized Jews; 2) preserving life and taking life, and under what circumstances; and 3) the sanctification of life by death. Many Talmudic and modern authorities maintain that a Jew murdered solely on the charge of being a Jew is forgiven of all sins, private and public by divine compassion. The millions of murdered Jewish victims, whose governments by decree did not protect them, thereby rendering them "stateless," are rewarded on earth by the posthumous citizenship granted to them by the State of Israel (Act of Knesset,

1953), and in heaven by the bliss of the world-to-come. The Six Million are revered as the exemplar of the meaning and glory of *Kiddush ha-Shem*. But does this include the thousands of "baptized Jews" among them? What to do with Edith Stein, for example, who was born Jewish, converted to Catholicism in 1922, entered a convent in Cologne in 1933, spoke of her *Life in a Jewish Family* (1933), protested vehemently the Nazi policy against the Jews, and was gassed at Auschwitz in August 1942? At the mass for her beatification (a step below sainthood) in Cologne on May 1, 1987, Pope John Paul II described

> Edith's life (as) formed by an unremitting search for truth, educated by the benediction of the Cross (and) died as a daughter of Israel, "for the glorification of the most holy name of God," and at the same time as Sister Teresa Benedicta of the Cross.[4]

Church authorities believe that Edith Stein was "simply one more Jew to be murdered with bureaucratic efficiency"; they maintain that "one who is born Jewish does not cease to be a Jew, albeit an apostate Jew, simply by conversion to another faith, even Christianity"; and may not her sin of apostasy be considered null and void in light of her victimization and martyrdom?

Perhaps, but this does not nullify her act of apostasy, an affront to the *locus classicus of Kiddush ha-Shem*: "You shall keep my commandments and do them: I am the Lord. You shall not profane my holy name; but I will be hallowed among the children of Israel; I am the Lord who hallows you" (Lev. 22:31–32). Judaism's regard for human life (*pikku'aḥ nefesh*) permits under circumstances of pain or death violations of most commandments. However, under no circumstances may the three cardinal sins be willingly entertained: idolatry (apostasy), unchastity (incest, adultery), and murder (*b.San.* 74a). The dispensation of sins brought about by acts of Jewish martyrdom embrace "normal" transgressions (Sabbath ordinances, dietary laws, rites of passage, etc.) and do not contain the serious offenses against man and God. On the latter, some authorities permit forced apostasy in private, i.e., less than ten Jews (male and/or female), in order to save one's life. But Edith Stein's choice of Christianity was not coerced nor did she celebrate her conversion privately. In a prayer, she confessed to her savior, "that it is his cross, which now be imposed on the Jewish people." By the most lenient stretch of Jewish compassion, Edith Stein, an individual, is a martyred Jewish victim; ironically, the Church's beatification makes her a blessed symbol of the cross thereby declaring she was

---

[4] Garber, *Shoah*, 86.

(and is not) a Jew. Unlike other living "baptized" Jews from the Shoah, who are potential returnees to Judaism, Sister Theresa's faith as a Christian and fate as a martyr were sealed by Auschwitz and Vatican.[5]

Preserving life is a core teaching of Judaism. The Torah contains no specific injunction against suicide. In the verse, "And surely your blood of your lives will I require it" (Gen 9:5a)—a thought contained in an expanded verse(s) on the prohibition of homicide—the Sages taught that suicide was wrong and punishable by divine decree, which entailed burial outside the sacred precincts of the cemetery, and suspension of mourning laws and customs. This strong edict to discourage Jews who might surrender their lives in violation of Jewish law, caused additional grief and embarrassment for the family of the deceased. To mitigate this problem, the Sages ruled that suicide must be voluntary and premeditated, *me'abbed 'atsmo lada'at* ("one who destroys himself knowingly"). The rabbinical presumption is that a person who kills oneself—axiomatic in cases of child suicide—does so without the necessary premeditation. The *locus classicus* is the suicide of King Saul, who was in great mental distress "lest these uncircumcised (Philistines) come and thrust me through, and make a mock of me...Therefore, King Saul took his sword, and fell upon it" (1 Sam 3:14). His death by his own sword is used by many rabbis as a precedent for not stigmatizing a person who in a situation of anguish, stress and despair, takes their own life.[6]

Therefore, in normal times, acts of suicide may be deemed blameworthy, in stressful times—Masada, the aftermath of the Bar-Kochba rebellion, the Crusades, Inquisition pogroms—killing oneself or letting oneself be killed for the "sanctification of God's Name" is seen by many as praiseworthy. Maimonides, who codified Jewish attitudes toward martyrdom, taught that if a Jew is made to transgress Halakah in public or in time of great religious persecution, one is expected to suffer death rather than transgress (Mishneh Torah, Yesode ha-Torah V.3). On the other hand, Maimonides made it clear that a person who unnecessarily suffers death—e.g., in circumstances under which Jewish law should be set aside in the interest of saving life—is ordinary suicide. But medieval French and German commentators opposed this decision. They felt that all people who sacrificed themselves—even when not strictly required are worthy of admiration and respect. This disagreement

---

[5] For more on Edith Stein, see Garber, "Edith Stein," 79–96 and "The Problem of Edith Stein," 1–7.

[6] A brief summary of martyrdom and suicide for the "sanctification of the Name" is found in Zimmels, *The Echo of the Nazi Holocaust in Rabbinic Literature*, 82–86 and in Rosenbaum, *The Holocaust and Halakha*, 35–40.

concerning the appropriateness of suicide is reflected in Shoah response concerning matters of life and death during such a humiliating time of personal anguish, degradation, and torture. Rabbi H.J. Zimmels' opinion is illustrative:

> A different outlook on suicide in general can be found in the era of the Nazi Holocaust. Humiliation, fear of torture and starvation produced two dramatically opposed feelings among the Jews living under the Nazi heel. These feelings had great consequences in their attitude to life.
> One was pessimism, resignation, despair and abandonment of any hope for the future, leading to suicide. The other was optimism, a strong will to survive and to bear patiently all sufferings and hope for a change for the better. The former view was shared mainly by the Jews of Germany and Austria, while the latter attitude can be found among Jews of Poland and other Eastern territories.[7]

It would appear that most responsa from the ashes agree: one may not commit suicide to avoid Nazi imprisonment and suffering, both mental and physical. The sage of inspiration is R. Hananya ben Teradyon (*b. Abod. Zar.* 18a) who did not speed up his death by burning: "It is best that He who has given life should also take it away; no one may hasten his own death" (from the *elah ezkerah* ["These (martyrs) I will remember"], Yom Kippur *musap* prayer). In a similar vein, R. Ephraim Oshry of Kovno rejected a Jewish request for suicide on a day that some 10,000 men, women, and children were taken away to be slaughtered. He argued that any action towards suicide "is *a ḥillul ha-Shem* ("profanation of God's Name") because it shows that the Jews do not trust in God to save them."[8] Oshry goes on to say with admiration that in the "ghetto of Kovno" there were no cases of suicide save in three instances. All the other inmates of the ghetto believed with perfect faith that God would not forsake His people." At the same time (1941), in another place, the diarist Chaim A. Kaplan concurs that suicide is not an option for the broken Jews of Poland:

> We are left naked, but as long as this secret power is still within us we do not give up hope. And the strength of this power lies in the indigenous nature of Polish Jewry, which is rooted in our eternal tradition that commands us to live.[9]

---

[7] Zimmels, *The Echo of the Nazi Holocaust in Rabbinic Literature*, 83.
[8] Oshry, *Sheilos u-teshuvos mi-ma'amakim, Response from the Holocaust*, 32–33.
[9] Garber, "Holocaust, The Practice of Judaism During," 431.

The litany of Jewish persecution and destruction over the centuries has contributed to the importance of *Kiddush ha-Shem* in the Jewish tradition. The Talmudic dictum, *yehareg ve'lo ya'avor* ("be killed and do not transgress") has been the spine of a martyred Jewish people whose limbs were torn in nearly every clime and time. In the medieval period, the Sephardim responded to acts of isolation, vilification and expulsion brought on by a policy of outward adaptation to the host culture and belief and inward turning to Judaism with messianism. Ashkenazim, on the other hand, demonstrated a very strong belief in *tehiyyat ha-metim* ("resurrection of the dead") as a way to combat relentless terror and forced apostasy.[10] Whole communities of Ashkenazim embraced martyrdom. Accounts of righteous martyrs of the past became part of everyday teaching and veneration of Central and Eastern European Jews. Indeed, a central focus on the mitsvah of martyrdom and its blessing ("Blessed art thou, O Lord our God, King of the universe who has commanded us to sanctify his name publicly") are found in the *shenei lukhot ha-berit* (known by the acronym, "Shelah") by the Prague-born and Polish educated halakhist and kabbalist R. Isaiah ben Abraham ha-Levi Horowitz (1565?–1630) and published in Amsterdam in 1649.

Nevertheless, the piestic, quiestic and pacifistic way to heaven represented by the traditional approach to martyrdom was challenged by individual religious Zionist rabbis and Hasidic rebbes alike who responded to the unparalleled horrors of the Shoah by the advocacy of spontaneous, as well as planned, acts of sanctifying life (*kiddush ha-hayyim*) even to death. The pattern of spiritual resistance falls into three categories, each responding to different stimuli but united by the enemy's determined goal of total annihilation of the Jewish people:

---

[10] This may explain why the *u-netaneh tokep* ("Let us tell how utterly holy this day is..."), is associated with Rabbi Amnon's hesitancy on personal martyrdom, and the *eleh ezkerah* are of central importance in the Ashkenazi Yom Kippur service. Though the latter's,

This has befallen us; we narrate it with a heart full of grief. Thou who art in heaven, heed our supplication; thou, O 'Lord, are a merciful and gracious God. Gracious one, look down from heaven: see the blood of the saintly martyrs, and remove all stains of guilt. O 'God, thou are the sovereign who does sit on the throne of mercy. We have sinned against you, our God; forgive us, O 'our creator...

may well originate with the memory of the ten rabbis killed by Hadrian for the unpunished sins of Joseph's brothers who sold him in slavery, the prayer's psychological appeal was shaped by Jewish martyrdom in the medieval lands of Ashkenaz. By the Sephardim, the Kol Nidre prayer acquired intense significance, since the cancellation of personal vows (Talmudic period) was interpreted to include the renunciation of vows to forswear Judaism and adopt Christianity in the period of persecution in Spain, Portugal and elsewhere.

1. Remember that in past religious persecutions, the enemy demanded the soul of the Jew, who responded by offering one's martyred body. The Nazis demand the body of the Jew and it is the Jew's obligation to fight and resist in order to preserve life. (Rabbis' Isaac Nissenbaum and Menahem Zemba, Warsaw Ghetto).
2. Observe Jewish belief, faith, rites of passage, and sacred calendar, however minimal and symbolic, for they contribute to reconstruction (*tikkun*) in the midst of destruction (Shoah). (R. Kaloni Kalmush Shapiro, Piaseczno).
3. Return to Zion and by rebuilding the Land of Promise the souls in burnt bodies can be restored to life by a people reborn (R. Issachar Schlomo Teechthal, Budapest).

To the religionist, the *Kiddush ha-Shem* ("Sanctification of the Name") is the noblest expression of service to Israel by dying for the sake of God's name. "The keeper of Israel that neither slumbers nor sleeps" (Ps 121:4) is implored to save Israel, and in so doing, "give glory unto thy name" (Ps 115:1). God is inseparably linked with the destiny of Israel; and in the face of unremitting tragedy, when many nameless sanctify his name, He is besieged to manifest his name—holiness, righteousness, mercy—by demonstrating his saving power in behalf of his chosen people before all nations. What concerns the ethnicist-modernist-secularist, however, is that the traditionalist values of passivism, pietism and quietism open the door for Jewish powerlessness and helplessness in the face of destruction. It is not submission to the "yoke of heaven," but a fist against heavenly and earthly decrees that encourages Jewish martyrdom. In short, the proclamation of the Zionist and Bundist youth of the ghettos of Poland, Galicia, Lithuania, Belorussia, and elsewhere: avenge the death of the *kedoshim* ("saintly ones") martyrs and be not *tson tibhah* ("sheep for the slaughter," Ps 44:23), but fighters of honor.

O nations, acclaim His people!
For He will avenge the blood of His servants,
—vengeance on His foes
And cleanse the Land for His people.
    (Deut. 32:43)
O guardian of a unique nation, guard
the remnant of a unique nation, and
suffer them not to perish
who proclaim the unity of the Name,

saying, The Lord is our God, The Lord is one.
(Daily Prayer Book, supplication prayer)
The Lord, he is God, The Lord, He is God
(1Kgs 18:39)
(Repeated seven times at the conclusion of the Yom Kippur service, and is part of the declaration of Jewish faith recited at death.)

The Burial Service

Five fundamental teachings of Judaism are emphasized in the traditional burial service called *tsidduk ha-din* ("The Justification of the Judgment"):

- The service acknowledges resignation to the judgment and justice of God. It affirms the absolute justice, righteousness, and mercy of God. It is inspired by the farewell Song of Moses (Deut 32:1–44), subsequent to his own death, which contrasts Israel's faithlessness and wayward ways with God's mercifulness and forgiveness. Retributive justice and divine compassion contrast the calamities of life. God, source of life and death (v. 34), is referenced multiple times in this chapter as the Rock (shelter, security, Sinai); "The Rock, His work is perfect, for all His ways are judgment; a God of faithfulness and without injustice, just and right is He" (v. 4). God is proclaimed as the true and blessed righteous Judge (*barukh dayyan ha'emet*) of all those whose judgments are righteous and true. Verses of adoration (Jer 32:9) and resignation (Ps 92:16) climatically proclaim, "the Lord gave, and the Lord has taken away; blessed be the Name of the Lord" (Job 1:21). The quizzical Jobian parable of earthly suffering seeding rightful actions seemingly unrewarded permeates *tsidduk ha-din* issues.
- Death proclaims the end of the bodily existence (*guf*) but the *neshama* (ethereal "soul")—the spark of God's essence—is untainted, immortal, and individual. That is to say, self-existence beyond the grave is protected by but not absorbed into the Divine Being.
- *Dayyan* and *Yom Ha-Din*. Torah Judaism teaches that the Supreme Being is a God of Justice and that Man is endowed with free will in the area of ethics and ethical decision making. Thus, every soul appears before the Judge of All on Judgment Day. Celestial levels of reward and punishment are meted out in accordance with actions done or not done by one's earthly actions. Though the descriptive form of reward and punishment is neither seeable nor comprehensible, commendable

actions are inspired by the prophetic declaration, "It has been told to you, O' Man, what is good, and what does the lord require of you: Do justly (acts of social justice), love mercy (self-acts of loving kindness to another), and walk humbly (modestly, decency, purity) with your God" (Micah 6:8). In Jewish teaching, God is the authority ("it has been told to you") for the observance of the moral law that he demands of all people ("O' Man").

- *Teḥiyyat Ha-Metim*. The doctrine of the *Resurrection of the Dead* belongs to the genre of non-rational but not anti-rational Jewish thought patterns that emanate from the explanatory act of God's creation of Heaven and Earth from nothingness (*creato ex nihilo*). The Resurrection article is not belief alone. It is defended by citing parallels with the state of pre-birth cognizance and the re-birth of plant-life following Winter's internment. Further, the decomposed dead body is not recomposed but a new *guf* serving as the depository of the previous earthly state of existence (sum total of deeds, thoughts, actions, habits, memory). In sum, death is not a voyage to nothingness but a World-to-Come related personality with its soul's existence in the pre-death earthly existence. Indeed, the Hebrew *olam ha-ba* (literally, "the World-that-is-Coming") conveys co-existing parallel dimensions.
- *Yemei Ha-Mashiaḥ*. In the biblical and rabbinic ages, indeed throughout Jewish thought, individuality is bounded to group identity and eternity. Thus *Goy* (Nation) *Yisrael* and `*am Yisrael* (People Israel) designated a national society. Later terminology, Jews and Judaism, embraces peoplehood and religion. With the addition of Land, the Isaiah spin of the Messianic Age embraces the Jewish quaternary of God-People-Land-Torah.

Isaiah Chapter 2 יְשַׁעְיָהוּ

א הַדָּבָר אֲשֶׁר חָזָה, יְשַׁעְיָהוּ בֶּן-אָמוֹץ, עַל-יְהוּדָה, וִירוּשָׁלִָם.

1 The word that Isaiah the son of Amoz saw concerning Judah and Jerusalem.

ב וְהָיָה בְּאַחֲרִית הַיָּמִים, נָכוֹן יִהְיֶה הַר בֵּית-יְהוָה בְּרֹאשׁ הֶהָרִים, וְנִשָּׂא, מִגְּבָעוֹת; וְנָהֲרוּ אֵלָיו, כָּל-הַגּוֹיִם.

2 And it shall come to pass in the end of days, that the mountain of the LORD'S house shall be established as the top of the mountains, and shall be exalted above the hills; and all nations shall flow unto it.

ג וְהָלְכוּ עַמִּים רַבִּים, וְאָמְרוּ לְכוּ וְנַעֲלֶה אֶל-הַר-יְהוָה אֶל-בֵּית אֱלֹהֵי יַעֲקֹב, וְיֹרֵנוּ מִדְּרָכָיו, וְנֵלְכָה בְּאֹרְחֹתָיו: כִּי מִצִּיּוֹן תֵּצֵא תוֹרָה, וּדְבַר-יְהוָה מִירוּשָׁלִָם.

3 And many peoples shall go and say: 'Come ye, and let us go up to the mountain of the LORD, to the house of the God of Jacob; and He will teach us of His ways, and we will walk in His paths.' For out of Zion shall go forth the law, and the word of the LORD from Jerusalem.

ד וְשָׁפַט בֵּין הַגּוֹיִם, וְהוֹכִיחַ לְעַמִּים רַבִּים; וְכִתְּתוּ חַרְבוֹתָם לְאִתִּים, וַחֲנִיתוֹתֵיהֶם לְמַזְמֵרוֹת--לֹא-יִשָּׂא גוֹי אֶל-גּוֹי חֶרֶב, וְלֹא-יִלְמְדוּ עוֹד מִלְחָמָה.

4 And He shall judge between the nations, and shall decide for many peoples; and they shall beat their swords into plowshares, and their spears into pruninghooks; nation shall not lift up sword against nation, neither shall they learn war any more.

ה בֵּית, יַעֲקֹב--לְכוּ וְנֵלְכָה, בְּאוֹר יְהוָה.

5 O house of Jacob, come ye, and let us walk in the light of the LORD.

The nationalism of the biblical and rabbinic ages combined with "The Lord shall reign for ever and ever" (Exod 15:18) and "the Lord shall be king over all the earth: in that day shall the Lord be one, and His name one" (Zech 14:9) speaks of a two-tier message related to the Messianic Age. First, no more universal war and the return, resettlement, and regeneration of the Jewish people to and on its biblical land. Second, the vindication and ingathering of Israel will sound the triumph of justice and the final consummation of the divine plan for humanity to live humanely in harmony with the flagship of the Messianic Kingdom, to walk in the light of the Lord.

Summary and Conclusion

Rabbinic Judgement

Teachings and views concerning life beyond the grave are multifaceted in rabbinic literature. Take *olam ha-ba*, for example. The phrase encompasses two acts on the stage of Adamology. Act One, the time-limited Messianic era, represents a world of no (more) world war, justice, peace and prosperity reign; further, the people of Israel live on in their own historic homeland under the rule of the *melekh ha-mashiaḥ* (King Messiah). Act Two is the last stage of Man's odyssey: the resurrection and final judgment of the dead. Rabbinic opinion differs on "life" after burial. Universalists argue that the *niftar/ah* "sleeps" till they rise again at the general resurrection of the dead. Another school argues that the truly righteous and repentant enter the blessed world to come when death occurs and the dastardly wicked (including *śone' Yisrael*) may go directly to *geihinnom* (Gehenna). A place or state of torment or suffering. Hell. Residency in this dark, secret netherworld ranges from short to long periods of time, with possible annihilation at the end, or at one's earthly death.

Martyrdom or Not Martyrdom

(A) Voluntary Martyrdom

Even if one successfully separates what Lucy S. Dawidowicz calls "the documentary wheat from the epistaphic chaffe" (*The War Against the Jews*, 1975), there is basic value in the latter. Dawidowicz maintains that the most widespread example of historical falsification in Holocaust historical myths is the story of the ninety-three Beit Ya'akov Maidens who chose mass suicide over the degradation of a German brothel. Their alleged last will and testament is a letter in their name written by their teacher, Chaya Feldman. One of the suicides, which states a religious affirmation, "It is good to live for God, but it is also good to die for Him," and ends with a request, "Say Kaddish for us, your ninety-three children." The question as to the fact or fiction of the epistle is not the only issue; what is significant is the contribution made by this simple and sublime thought to the "faith knowledge" of *Kiddush ha-Shem*.[11]

(B) Inflicted Martyrdom

---

[11] See Garber, "The Ninety-Three Beit Ya'akov Martyrs," 97–118.

Rabbi Akiba's death by laceration is included in the *Eleh Ezkerah* ("The Ten Martyrs") *musap* prayer which is primarily recited in Ashkenazi services on Yom Kippur day. Contrary to the Talmudic view, the liturgical Ten Martyrs were executed on the same day. There are two reasons given for the execution. One: they founded schools of learning that ran contrary to imperial verdict during the reign of Hadrian; or two: they were slaughtered to atone for the sins of Joseph's ten brothers who sold him on Yom Kippur Day (as per the Book of Jubilees). Both explanations provide ethical and moral challenges. That is to say, slaughtered for the spread of Torah and proxy punishment, nay, execution.[12] More excruciating is Akiba's contented *'Eḥad'* in lieu of spitting at the executioner (saving life), as observed in b. *Ber* 61b:

...כשהוציאו לר' עקיבא להריגה זמן קרית שמע היתה והיו מסרקין את בשרו במסרק של ברזל, והיה מקבל עליו מלכות שמים באהבה. אמרו לו תלמידיו ר' עד כאן?

...When R. Akiva was taken out for execution, it was the hour for the recital of the 'Shema', and they were combing his flesh with an iron comb, and he was accepting upon himself the kingship of heaven with love. His disciples said to him: Our teacher, even to this point?

אמ' להן כל ימי הייתי מצטער על פסוק זה בכל נפשך אפילו נוטל את נפשך ואמרתי מתי יבוא לידי ואקיימנה, עכשיו בא לידי ולא אקיימנה?

He said to them: All my days I have been troubled over this verse, 'with all thy soul', [which I interpret,] 'even if He takes thy soul', and I said: When shall I have the opportunity of fulfilling this? Now that I have the opportunity shall I not fulfill it?

ולא הספיק לגמור את הדבר עד שיצתה נשמתו באחד.

And he did not have a chance to complete it (*ha-davar*) until his soul left his body while reciting the word *'Eḥad'*.[13]

---

[12] "The fathers shall not be put to death for the children, neither shall the children be put to death for the fathers; every man shall be put to death for his own sin" (Deut 24:16).

[13] This Talmudic citation is taken from sefaria.org.

(B) Not By Martyrdom

Hundreds of testimonies bear witness to facing extermination in Hitler's inferno. The Ḥasidic response during the European *Ḥurban* is unusual. The Kabbalistic-Hasidic Urglaube regarding the symbolic interaction of God and man, in which the actions of *etaruta delelata* (the lower world) have an impact on *etaruta deleʻela* (the upper world), imbued the activist and quietist schools of Hasidic responses to the trauma of *di milhomeh yohrn*. Pesah Schindler[14] makes a compelling case for the single-mindedness of most Ḥasidim, who defiantly opposed the Nazis' evil decrees but, in the end, joyfully accepted the divine decree. Among Schinder's findings, the Ḥasidim God's presence in history was not diminished by the Shoah, though his justice, compassion, goodness, and kindness appeared hidden to man's finite knowledge; suffering and personal sacrifice (*meserat nefesh*) were sustained on the strength of faith in the covenantal interrelationship between God and Israel and trust in his ultimate defeat of evil; the phenomenon of redemption was architectonic--rebuke, destruction, exile and redemption; in the context of Tsadik and Ḥasid, thwarting the Nazi evil did not obliterate its reality, but diminished its power by nature of a cosmic or myth perspective; the Rebbe played an altruistic role as a source of hithazqut ("encouragement") during the terrible trauma; and finally, the Hasidic victims of the *Ḥurban* engaged in multiple acts of sanctifying God's name not by martyrdom but by obligatory and voluntary acts of holiness in the service of God and man.

The Hasidic response to the Shoah is about the nature of empathy, about how faith and Halakha prepared a grief-stricken community for a life of woe and calamity. Ḥasidim maintains classical Orthodox beliefs rooted in spontaneous religious experience and by placing the Shoah in a Kabbalistic frame, they responded to the *Endlösung* in accordance with meaningful, clearly defined Hasidic tenets.

Take for example, the relationship of *Tsadikim* to their Ḥasidim. In a time of gathering insanity, the cadre of pious rabbeim collectively acted as a kind of sponge for misery, absorbing pain and cruelty before it overcame everything. By insisting that sanity could be restored in the world only after the natural order of things was restored by some established ceremony or rite (e.g., fraternal meal, *niggun*-laden prayers, strict adherence to the holy time and space, rules of passage, etc.), the *Tsaddik* played a major role in diminishing

---

[14] Schindler, *Hasidic Responses to the Holocaust.*

despair (*ye'ush*), which in turn enabled the Ḥasid to better cope with extreme circumstances. In an existentialist way, *Tsadik* and Ḥasid believed that their actions transcended ordinary events laced with danger (e.g., survival at the expense of abuse of one's fellow) and helped to rediscover dignity and self-respect, necessary ingredients for the total salvation of Israel and the world.

Once the seat of the central institution of Jewish self-government in Poland and a major center of Torah instruction represented by the Yeshiva of Lublin, the city of Lublin was the site of the first detention camp (*Reservat*) erected by the Nazis on Polish soil. Here, it is said, in the face of murderous and sadistic acts by the Nazis, a Hasidic ditty in *teshuvah* ("penance") evolved into a crying chant that gave succor to the sad fate of the Jews of Lublin.

> Lomir zich iberbeiten, avinu shebashamayim
> Lomir zich iberbeiten, iberbeiten, iberbeiten -
> "Let us be reconciled, our Heavenly Father,
> Let us be reconciled, let us make up"
> Mir velen zey iberleben, iberleben, avinu
> Mir velen zey iberleben, iberleben, iberleben -
> "We shall outlive them, our heavenly Father, We shall outlive them, outlive them, outlive them."

Truly, a statement of *hutzpah* and *ahavat Yisrael* (respectfully, courage bordering on the reckless and love of the Jewish people).

Kaddish: *Tikkun Olam*

What is the Jewish response to death? The laws of mourning require the mourner to behave as if they are dead. No normal activity (positive religious requirements, work, study, food preparation, excessive personal hygiene and grooming, conjugal relations, etc.) is permitted during the period of *Shivah*, the seven days following death. The mourner is touched by the anti-life and his/her activities reflect this sense of incompleteness. The mourner returns to religious requirements and social amenities by degrees. Paradoxically, the mourner and the mourned are united in the mourning observances; that is to say, by observing the absence of life, the mourner is sensitized to the value and quality of life.

I will share a personal observation: The liturgical symbol for "life" in the period of mourning is the Kaddish, is recited for eleven months in the case of a parent's death. The prayer talks not of death but of the task of building God's kingdom on earth, of restoring the world. Its doxology is an affirmation of the unity of the generations in their dedication to sanctify his name in life. As my father said the Kaddish for his parents, I said it for him, and one day my children will say it for me, the message is poignantly clear: for the Jew, the finality of death is overcome in the eternity of Israel and guided by the principle, "to love the Lord your God, to hearken to His voice, and to cleave unto Him, for that is your life and the length of your days" (Deut 30:20). My first Kaddish was recited in Jerusalem, Israel on the land which the Lord swore unto the patriarchs, to give them; a land in which my father and mother in their retirement chose to live and die.

My introduction to the Kaddish brought to mind a rabbinic lesson. In an ancient collection of rabbinic homilies, *Likkutei Rachman*, as interpreted by the Israel Nobel Laureate, S.Y. Agnon (1888–1970) we learn a reason for the recitation of the Kaddish:

> We recite the Kaddish after the death of a human being because the Almighty is praised thereby…When a king of flesh and blood looses one of his soldiers, his army is diminished, but since he has thousands of soldiers, his sense of loss is very light. Not so with the Holy One, Blessed be He: even though a single individual dies, the Kaddish is recited and the Name of the Holy One is praised.[15]

An individual is unique in the eyes of God. There never was, is, or will be another like them. We are told that it is not God's desire that anyone shall die (Ezek 18:32). And when a human being dies there is none to be set in his or her place.

When individuals recite the Kaddish, they offer God consolation for his loss. *Yitgadal, v-Yitkadash, Shemeh Rabba*: "may the power of the name be magnified, and may no lessening of power (brought upon by death of a person, who is made in the image of God) come to him who is blessed and sanctified." It is a somber and awesome thought, this ancient belief: saying that the Kaddish is not only an act of repairing the cohesion of the family (group), which has been profoundly shaken by death, but simultaneously, it is a task of restoring cosmic order (*tikkun olam*). In death as in life, Man is seeking God and God is seeking Man. So speaketh *eMeT*".[16]

---

[15] For more on this Agnon analogy, see Lamm, *The Jewish Way in Death and Mourning*, 149–50.

[16] *'emet'* is Hebrew for "truth." The tri-radical word, *'alep-mem-taw'*— is fascinating. The first radical is silent and the second and third letters spell "death." Popularly speaking, in death life truth is festered.

Appendix

Yehudi Boded: Lone Jew

Select pre-burial words from Daniel Israelson z"l and my description of his burial. Together they speak of the simplicity, grav(e)ity, longevity, and collectivity of a Jewish torah (teaching) of death. Kein yehi ratson!

Daniel Israelson's post-mortem wishes requested full *Halakhic* observance related to wash, dress, and burial. He requested the simplest Jewish burial, stating no-post mortem autopsy, embalming, cremation, and, for internment, the simplest pine coffin with bare interior and exterior lining, marking, etc. No flowers, song, icons, pictures, music or wine were required. Only verses from Tanack and HaSiddur HaShalem (Orthodox) were to be recited. However, an indelible design of the Magen David was to be placed on the lid of the casket to identify him with the faith of Israel. He strongly insisted that the proclamation of the Sh'ma, the primal affirmation of Jewish faith in the oneness of God, be stated. Additionally, his identity with the decimated Jewry and an Israel reborn was affirmed in his own words.

> Prayers and verses should also include the Six Million who perished in Auschwitz and other death camps whose Voice spoke out of the fire of the crematoria with the commandment, "Zakhor! Always remember, never forget!" to keep their memory alive and blessed all the number of our days.

> Prayers and verses should include the Jewish Homeland, the modern State of Israel, to keep its people, their families and children safe from harm, to protect the security of its borders, and to insure and guarantee the perpetuity of Israel's sovereignty to be known and recognized as the official Jewish Homeland by all nations of the world, and that peace be granted for all of Erets Yisrael.

I buried my student on 26 'Av (18 August, 2017), *erev parshat Re'eh*. An exceptionally talented, gifted, brilliant Daniel (Danny) Israelson (b. Reed) z"l, born 1944, *Ger Tsedek*, died alone. By his wishes, burial rites were followed in accordance with laws relating to purification (Taharah), shrouds, prayer shawl, Shomer, and traditional funeral service at the grave site. Two living nieces did not attend. Classmates from the mid-seventies are scattered wide and far. No one knew nor attended. The caretaker informed me of his passing, and I checked and double checked with Eden Mortuary (Mission Hills, CA) to ensure that the deceased's wishes were honored. They were. The liturgical words ("Surely goodness and mercy shall follow me all the days of my life; and I will dwell in the house of the Lord forever," (Ps 23:6); "HaShem will protect you from every evil; He will guard your soul. HaShem will guard your going out and coming in, from this time and forever," Psalm 121: 7–8) were inspirational. My eulogy focused on the opening words of *parshat Re'eh* recited in synagogues (Aug 19): "Behold I set before you this day a blessing and curse" (Deut 11:26) connected with "All this word which I command you, you shall observe to do; you shall not add thereto, nor diminish from it" (Deut 13:1) and wrapped in the thrice command of the prayer shawl fringes that Danni wore in life and now in his state of eternal sleep, See, Remember, Do (Number 15:39). ציצית (ṣiṣit, fringe) is spelled ציצת in Numbers 15 thus recording the numerical value of 590: צ (90) י(10) צ(90) ת(400) = 590 Add 13 (5 knots, 8 strings featured on the fringe) and the final total is 603 NOT 613 (signifying the 613 Commandments). There is a missing *Yud* written above the line, floating as it were. In my *dvar levayah*, I envisioned the floating *Yud* as the *neshama* of Danni z"l hoovering the *kever* before the burial. The deceased wrapped in *tachrichim* (burial shrouds) and covered with torn *tallit* (prayer shawl) due to a missing ṣiṣit ("The dead praise not the Lord," Ps 115:17) placed in a plain wooden coffin. Holy earth from Mount Olives in and on the coffin now entrusted to Mother Earth. Respect of the decease, El Malei prayer, and commitment of the living, Kaddish doxology, recited. Together, Earth and Heaven bear witness to the flight of the *neshamah* of Daniel ben Avraham u-ven Sara z"l to the designated Geniza, resting peacefully for his call on Judgment Day. May we remember the passing of Danni z"l and death of all Lone Jews in the words of Tradition: "May the Almighty comfort you (sic) among the other mourners of Zion and Jerusalem."

BIBLIOGRAPHY

Garber, Zev. "Edith Stein: Jewish Perspectives on Her Martyrdom." In *Shoah, the Paradigmatic Genocide: Essays in Exegesis and Eisegesis*, 79–96. Lanham, MD: University Press of America, 1994.

———. "Holocaust, The Practice of Judaism During," in J. Neusner, A.J. Avery-Peck, W.S. Green, eds., *The Encyclopedia of Judaism*, vol. 1. New York: Continuum, 1999.

———. "The Ninety-Three Beit Ya`akov Martyrs: Towards the Making of a Historiosophy." In *Shoah, the Paradigmatic Genocide: Essays in Exegesis and Eisegesis*, 97–118. Lanham, MD: University Press of America, 1994.

———. "The Problem of Edith Stein: Jewess and Catholic Saint." In *Women and the Holocaust: Narrative and Representation*, edited by Esther Fuchs, 1–7. Lanham, MD: University Press of America, 1999.

———. *Shoah, The Paradigmatic Genocide: Essays in Exegesis and Eisegesis.* Lanham, MD: University Press of America, 1994.

Lamm, Maurice, *The Jewish Way in Death and Mourning*. New York: Jonathan David Publishers, 2000.

Oshry, Ephraim. *Sheilos u-teshuvos mi-ma'amakim, Responsa from the Holocaust.* New York: Judaica Press, 1983.

Rosenbaum, Irving J. *The Holocaust and Halakhah*. New York, 1976.

Schindler, Pesach, *Hasidic Responses to the Holocaust in Light of Hasidic Thought*. Hoboken, 1990.

Zimmels, H. J., *The Echo of the Nazi Holocaust in Rabbinic* Literature. Republic of Ireland, 1975.

ABOUT THE AUTHOR

Zev Garber is Emeritus Professor and Chair of Jewish Studies and Philosophy at Los Angeles Valley College, and is Co-Head of Global Jewish Studies, GCRR. He has served as President of the National Association of Professors of Hebrew, Editor Emeritus of *Shofar*, and is Editor of *Iggeret*. He has authored hundreds of articles and reviews, and his publications include 15 books, including his most recent co-written volume, *Judaism and Jesus* (Cambridge Scholars, 2020). Zev Garber is emeritus professor and chair of Jewish studies and philosophy at Los Angeles Valley College, and is editor emeritus of *Shofar*. He has served as president of the National Association of Professors of Hebrew, and is editor of *Iggeret*. He has authored hundreds of articles and reviews, and his publications include sixteen books, including his most recent cowritten volume, *Judaism and Jesus* (Cambridge Scholars, 2020), and coedited volume, *The Annotated Passover Haggadah* (GCRR Press, 2021).

MORE FROM THE AUTHOR

The Annotated Passover Haggadah
GCRR Press, 2021

Judaism and Jesus
Cambridge, 2020

Want to be part of the world's *premier society* for global religious researchers?

Join the GCRR ACADEMIC SOCIETY...

...and join the tens of thousands of scholars, educators and students researching religion around the globe.

SIGNIFICANTLY LOWER MEMBERSHIP COSTS				**PRIORITY PEER-REVIEW AND PUBLISHING**
FREE DIGITAL SUBSCRIPTION TO SHERM ACADEMIC JOURNAL	 	 	 	**"RESIDENT SCHOLAR" POSITION ELIGIBILITY**

GLOBAL CENTER *for* RELIGIOUS RESEARCH
ACADEMIC INSTITUTE

WHERE RELIGIOUS STUDENTS, SCHOLARS AND SPECIALISTS **FLOURISH**

WWW.GCRR.ORG

Crime and Sin in Early Medieval England

Hannah Purtymun,
University of Edinburgh

Abstract: Early medieval society had complex views of crime and sin. In early medieval English society, concepts of crime and sin overlapped to a certain extant in terms of what "wrongs" were under either religious or secular jurisdiction, or which fell under both. An in-depth analysis of the definition of crime versus sin in early medieval English society has not yet been undertaken, a feat that is attempted in this article in the context of one of the worst crimes and sins: homicide. It is found that a crime can be defined as any act that is performed against the protection of the king, while a sin is any action that falls within the confines of the capital sins or can be considered either an affront to God or detrimental to the soul.

Keywords: Crime, Sin, Penitential, Early Medieval, England, Ireland, Law Codes, Homicide

---

From the seventh to the eighth century, society in early Anglo-Saxon England was beginning to integrate the Christianity of Ireland and the continent into their religious practices, laws and everyday lives. This integration was especially prevalent in regard to the treatment of crime and sin within society, and especially to the treatment of homicide. Homicide is prevalent in all secular and religious texts from the early medieval period; however, it is especially prevalent in all secular law codes and penitential texts, as well. It has even been argued that "As medieval laws changed to accommodate the social shifts regarding violence and crime...murder became more consistently regulated, recorded and adjudicated."[1] Due to the prevalence of homicide within these texts, it can be argued that homicide was a common crime, as well as sin, in the early Middle Ages. The seventh and eighth centuries were periods of rapid expansion for the Christian Church, especially within the British Isles, which influenced the formation of both religious texts and law codes. Penitential religious texts and secular law codes are the most prominent examples that provide insight into this treatment of crime and sin in early medieval English society. These texts allow for the examination of monetary and spiritual punishment in regard to both the crime and sin of homicide.

---

[1] Tracy, *Medieval and Early Modern Murder*, 5.

Socio-Historical Examination of Religion and Ministry
Volume 3, Issue 1, Summer 2021 shermjournal.org
© Hannah Purtymun
Permissions: editor@shermjournal.org
ISSN 2637-7519 (print), ISSN 2637-7500 (online)
https://doi.org/10.33929/sherm.2021.vol3.no1.08 (article)

The secular law codes of early medieval England include the laws of Aethelberht, Hloþhere and Eadric, Wihtred and Ine. These law codes were written between 600 and 695. While the codes themselves include a variety of crimes which provide important insight into what crimes were under secular jurisdiction, they also include their corresponding punishments which provides a more in-depth understanding of what crimes were considered the most severe in the early medieval period. The severity of the crime can be measured by the corresponding punitive fine implemented as a "punishment" for the crime. However, how secular law codes functioned in practice, specifically in terms of jurisdiction, has not yet been studied in depth in terms of homicide, but is something that will be examined in the following work.

Secular laws codes in the early medieval period functioned, just as in the modern world, as, "something that states create and administer so as to maintain a fundamentally non-violent moral order."[2] However, early medieval law codes functioned differently in that the punishment for a crime was almost always monetary and never explicit imprisonment; at least not in the early Anglo-Saxon law codes of the seventh century. This was generally because in the world of early medieval England "...the most serious sin was disloyalty to [the] king or lord;"[3] punitive fines were, thus, paid to the benefit of the king, as well as to the victim, depending on the crime. Secular law codes were also interconnected with ecclesiastical law to a certain extent in that their jurisdiction was sometimes overlapping, as were their functions; a phenomenon that will be explored more in depth.

The other significant type of early medieval text that was influenced by the spread of Christianity and dealt with concepts of sin were penitentials. These texts were, "handbooks for confessors...[which] contained long lists of possible kinds of sin together with the appropriate penance to make up for them."[4] Within these handbooks the lists of sin included many different homicidal variations, along with the spiritual penance or "punishment" for the sin. Penitentials originated in Ireland in the late fifth and early sixth centuries and then spread to England and the European continent during the early seventh century. These handbooks of penance were used in early medieval Ireland and England in a pastoral context, most frequently within monastic communities, but also within lay communities. While penitentials were prescriptive because a corresponding penance was listed for a particular sin, penance was often up to the interpretation and discretion of the confessor. This is also emphasized by

---

[2] Lambert, *Law and Order in Anglo-Saxon England*, 2.
[3] Thomson, *A History of Sin*, 123.
[4] Meens, *Penance in Medieval Europe, 600–1200*, 3.

the fact that there was a shift from public to private penance during the sixth century, meaning that confessors were able to tailor spiritual "punishment" for the particular sins that were committed. However, it remains unknown how these penitential texts functioned in practice during the early medieval period. Secular law codes and penitential texts provide "punishments" for the different variations of homicide.

During the early Middle Ages, specifically during the seventh and eighth centuries, secular and religious law codes were beginning to take form in England and Ireland for the first time since Christianity began to spread into the British Isles. Secular law codes and penitentials provided the structure to hold individuals accountable for their actions. While secular law codes were created to both prevent and punish what were considered to be "crimes" in the early medieval period, penitentials were created in order to provide a way for both clerics and laypeople to atone for their "sins." Whereas ecclesiastical law was created as a way for, "the church to sustain itself politically as an institution, and to wield social authority in collaboration, rather than by asserting dominance over, the laity."[5] However, the way these codes actually functioned in terms of their interaction and their role in society has been the subject of much historiographical debate.

Some scholars believe that during the early medieval period, secular law codes and penitentials were formed in mimicry of or parallel to each other, while others believe that they were formed separately but became increasingly intertwined throughout the period. Stefan Jurasinki is of the latter school of thought and argues that ecclesiastical law and secular law were intertwined as,

> Ecclesiastical law was at the time a category broad enough to encompass matters having nothing to do with the pastoral care of penitents [which] was an effect both of the gaps in the secular law and the tendency of Latin penitentials to claim for themselves the territory of secular jurisdiction.[6]

According to R.H. Helmholz, there was no canonical principle in the early Anglo-Saxon Church that required secular and religious law to be separate, which may explain the way these law codes seem to be interconnected.[7] Janet Nelson believes that "Penitentials straddle liturgy and law,"[8] providing another interpretation into the interconnectedness of all three

---

[5] Nelson, "Law and Its Applications," 299–326.
[6] Jurasinski, *The Old English Penitentials and Anglo-Saxon Law*, 34.
[7] Helmholz, *The Oxford History of the Laws of England*, 34.
[8] Nelson, "Law and Its Applications," 310.

types of ethical codes. Nelson's interpretation is supported by Rob Meens as he has examined the relationship between ecclesiastical law and penitentials and found that "Penitentials had been appended to canon law collections...while canons from such collections had been incorporated into penitentials and the other way around."[9]

Looking forward to the tenth century in Anglo-Saxon England, Nicole Marafioti has found that Archbishop Wulfstan of York in his *De medicamento animarum* believed similarly in this interconnectedness between ecclesiastical and secular law, as well as that the two ethical codes were formed parallel to each other. Wulfstan believed, "that good earthly law must operate in both secular and ecclesiastical spheres, with the best legislators shaping their decrees to conform with divine will."[10] While Wulfstan's statement comes almost three centuries after the creation of the first written law in early medieval England, it can be argued that a similar ideology was implemented within early medieval English society. In their seminal work, *The History of English Law,* Pollock and Maitland take a similar approach. This is demonstrated in their disclaimer at the beginning of their chapter on Anglo-Saxon law,

> This book is concerned with Anglo-Saxon legal antiquities, but only so far as they are connected with, and tend to throw light upon, the subsequent history of the laws of England...Much of our information about the Anglo-Saxon laws and customs is so fragmentary and obscure that the only hope of understanding it is to work back to it from the fuller evidence of Norman and even later time.[11]

This approach to use what is well known in historical study to shed light on areas that are less well known is one that is used frequently in early medieval period studies.

In the world of early medieval England, secular law was not physically documented until the first decades of the seventh century. Previous law codes in England were most likely similar or even identical to the first written laws; the biggest difference being that these codes were only transmitted orally. King Aethelberht of Kent was the first Anglo-Saxon to establish a law code, "according to the example of the Romans," i.e., written, as was recorded by the Venerable Bede in his *Ecclesiastical History of the English People* during the

---

[9] Meens, "Remedies for Sin," 407.
[10] Marafioti, "Secular and Ecclesiastical Justice in Late Anglo-Saxon England," 780.
[11] Pollock and Maitland, *The History of English Law Before the Time of Edward I*, 24.

eighth century.[12] Aethelberht reigned over Kent from 589 until his death in 616. It was during this near thirty-year period hat Aethelberht established written law codes. According to Lisi Oliver, it is Aethelberht's own conversion to Christianity that promoted the physical documentation of these laws.[13] It has also been considered by Patrick Wormald that St. Augustine, and therefore his Christian beliefs, may have influenced the decision of the Anglo-Saxon king to write down the laws themselves.[14]

Aethelberht's law code was similar in structure and content to the early Anglo-Saxon and Irish penitentials, the largest difference being the form of the "punishment" was monetary instead of spiritual penance. These structural similarities may betray the relationship between secular and religious law codes. For example, Aethleberht's twenty-fourth law states: "If a person kills someone, let him pay an ordinary person price, 100 shillings."[15] In contrast, the section of the Penitential of Theodore entitled "Of Manslaughter," the fourth canon states: "If a layman slays another with malice aforethought, if he will not lay aside his arms, he shall do penance for seven years; without flesh and wine, three years."[16] The structure and content of these two ethical codes are almost identical; the format being the wrong followed by the punishment. Yet again, the largest difference is the form of "punishment" or justice that is to be enacted. Due to the timeline of when these codes were written, it can be argued that penitential works may have influenced law codes, not the other way around. Aethelberht's law code was written sometime between his conversion to Christianity in 597 and his death in 616, while the earliest recorded penitential was the Penitential of Finnian written in Ireland between 525 and 550.[17] Other penitentials, such as the penitentials of Cummean and Columbanus, were written around the same time as Aethelberht's law code. However, a direct relationship between these penitentials and the early Anglo-Saxon law codes, specifically Aethelberht's, cannot be traced. Due to Aethelberht's recent conversion to Christianity in relation to when his law codes were formed, it can be argued that religious ideals and works, either penitentials or ecclesiastical law, would have influenced his law codes.

Just as there was a difference between the justice enacted in law codes versus ecclesiastical penitentials, there was also a difference between the

---

[12] Lambert, *Law and Order in Anglo-Saxon England,* 30–31.
[13] Oliver, *The Beginnings of English Law,* 16.
[14] Oliver, *The Beginnings of English Law,* 17.
[15] Oliver, *The Beginnings of English Law,* 67.
[16] Gamer and McNeill, *Medieval Handbooks of Penance,* 187.
[17] Gamer and McNeill, *Medieval Handbooks of Penance,* 86.

concepts of crime and sin, otherwise known as earthly wrongdoing and spiritual wrongdoing. However, crime and sin in early medieval England were not concepts as easily differentiated as they are today. Using the same method as other early medieval period scholars, information from a later period can be used to shed light on the beliefs of the seventh and eighth centuries. Marafioti found that,

> Criminal and sinful offenses were frequently addressed together in legislation of the late tenth and early eleventh centuries, and this has been taken to mean that the two were conflated—in the minds of lawmakers, at least—into a broad category of "wrong."[18]

If this same belief system of the tenth and eleventh centuries is implemented onto the study of earlier Anglo-Saxon law codes and penitentials, then the way the two forms of societal codes interact can be better explained. However, these two terms, crime and sin, can be defined more in depth for the early medieval period.

If crime and sin are defined using early medieval Anglo-Saxon and Irish sources, specifically law codes and penitentials written before the ninth century, then the two concepts can be argued to be interrelated but separate. There are relatively large differences in what is considered a crime in law codes and what is considered a sin in penitential texts with some overlap between the two. Using penitentials, a sin is any action that falls within the confines of the capital sins, or the "seven deadly sins," as well as any action that can be considered an affront to either God or the soul, which is why the categories of "heresy" and the "eucharist" are included in the penitential categories. The early Anglo-Saxon law codes, specifically those of Aethelberht, Hloþhere and Eadric, Wihtred, and Ine, seemed to consider a crime to be any act that is performed against the protection of the king. This is demonstrated in the concept of *wergeld* as "...payable for violating the king's law...and in general as a price of a life forfeit to the king for what damaged his people."[19] The "wrongs" that are addressed in both types of sources fall under both ecclesiastical and secular jurisdiction because they can be considered both a crime and sin; they are crimes against the king and sins against God and the soul.

Since crime and sin were connected in that they were both categories of people's actions that needed to be remedied in regard to either the legal

---

[18] Marafioti, "Secular and Ecclesiastical Justice in Late Anglo-Saxon England," 776.
[19] Wormald, *Legal Culture in the Early Medieval West*, 341.

system or their souls, especially in terms of wrongs such as homicide, law codes and penitentials could be implemented throughout the hierarchy of early medieval England to establish an overarching code of ethical behavior within society. Law codes and penitentials were used for this ethical code of behavior as they were more directly applicable to the laity than ecclesiastical law, which was formed and implemented at the top of the hierarchy. In early medieval England, society was divided up into a hierarchical system, as were their law codes. However, the early medieval English legal structure is much more complex than a traditional hierarchical structure. As Tom Lambert explains,

> On one end there are stateless societies, characterized by the (horizontal) 'kin-based' justice associated with feuding; on the other there were states, characterized by a (vertical) 'top-down' approach to crime and punishment, in which (vertical) bonds of lordship were dominant and (horizontal) kinship structures of marginal importance.[20]

Both "kin-based" and "top-down" approaches to justice were incorporated into the structure of Anglo-Saxon law codes. For example, Aethelberht's law codes were organized into the "top-down" structure with offences against the church and king at the top and offences against slaves at the bottom.[21] However, Aethelberht's laws also provided instances of "kin-based" approaches to law. In the second part of his twenty-fourth law code it states, "If the killer departs from the land, let his kinsmen pay a half person-price."[22] The early Irish legal system functioned much the same way, implementing both approaches to justice. However, the early Irish ecclesiastical and secular law, in this case the Old Irish canon law, also incorporated varying forms of justice for the types of crime committed in terms of their position within the hierarchy,

> There are three types of crime which a person commits: a crime which is of lesser value than himself for which he pays for his own property; a crime which is of equal value to himself for which he goes [into slavery]; a crime which is of greater value than he is for which he is killed and a fine paid by his kindred.[23]

---

[20] Lambert, *Law and order in Anglo-Saxon England,* 6.
[21] Oliver, *The Beginnings of English Law,* 36.
[22] Oliver, *The Beginnings of English Law,* 67.
[23] Fergus, *A Guide to Early Irish Law,* 216.

How this type of legal structure functioned in practice is, however, up for debate.

The concept of confession and penance, or the remission of sins, in the seventh and eighth centuries in Anglo-Saxon England was influenced by earlier penitential texts and traditions which originated in Ireland during the sixth century. These penitential practices developed for the laity out of monastic traditions beginning with the writings of Finnian in the mid-sixth century and St. Columbanus in the early seventh century.[24] In the mid-seventh century, another penitential work came into being, authored this time by the Irish religious figure Cummean.[25] The penitential varieties which originated in Ireland permeated into Anglo-Saxon England over the course of the seventh century. While these penitentials were used throughout England, they also influenced penitentials created by Anglo-Saxon authors, such as the Penitential of Theodore, written by Theodore of Canterbury in the mid to late seventh century. It is from these original Irish and Anglo-Saxon sources that penitential practices seem to have spread to continental Europe.[26]

Penitential books were written as handbooks of penance for confessors during the early medieval period. Books of penance were increasingly used in a pastoral context after the shift from public to private penance in the fifth and sixth centuries.[27] Due to the ecclesiastical nature of penitentials, they were more commonly used in a monastic setting than for members of the laity when they first came into being in England and Ireland. While scholars know that "Penance was a major theme in ecclesiastical life in the fifth and sixth centuries…"[28] whether penitential books were actually used and how they were used in terms of the laity has been the subject of much historiographical debate. Due to the prevalence of penitential copies that survive from the period shortly after the creation of the concept of private penance, it can be inferred that books of penance were used in regard to the laity in the early Middle Ages; however, to what extent they were used is still unknown.

Penitentials were structured in much the same way as early medieval law codes. While law codes were organized within a hierarchical structure, penitentials were organized by the type of sin and then by the type of sinner, either a member of the clergy or a layman. These books of penance were

---

[24] Meens, *Penance in Medieval Europe, 600–1200*, 54.
[25] Meens, *Penance in Medieval Europe, 600–1200*, 58. A consensus has not yet been reached on his actual position within the church.
[26] Meens, *Penance in Medieval Europe, 600–1200*, 70.
[27] Meens, "The Nature and Frequency of Early Medieval Penance," 43.
[28] Meens, *Penance in Medieval Europe, 600–1200*, 71.

structured as such in order to provide easier usage to confessors in their pastoral duties. For example, the Penitential of Cummean is divided up into eleven subsections of types of sin, all of which apply to both clergy and laymen. The Penitential of Theodore, however, is divided up into two books with fifteen subsections in one and fourteen in the other, within which different types of penance for clergy and penance for laymen are specified. The similarity in structure between secular law codes and penitentials is important to the understanding of the development of the two ethical codes. Since the two types of code are formatted so similarly, the theory that the two were formed parallel to each other, i.e., taking each other into account, is more plausible.

According to Helmholz, "the medieval ecclesiastical courts regularly exercised jurisdiction over secular crimes like theft and murder. The secular courts apparently did not have a monopoly on the trial of criminals,"[29] which he argues is because "The ecclesiastical courts dealt only with those crimes that were the subject of publicly held suspicion."[30] These crimes publicly held under suspicion correlate with some of the capital sins of Christianity such as murder, adultery, false testimony, theft, and in some cases abortion.[31] However, Lambert examines the concepts of theft and murder, both crimes held under public suspicion, and finds a theory contrary to that of Helmholz. Lambert finds that the difference between the treatment of theft and homicide is due to, "a fundamental division between two categories of royal jurisdiction."[32] More specifically, these two categories of jurisdiction are defined as prohibitive justice and protective justice; prohibitive justice being for those crimes punishable by death and protective justice being for everything else.[33] It is because of these two royal jurisdictions that Lambert does not consider the impact of ecclesiastical law. According to Lambert, a crime can only be considered a crime and not a sin if it is persecuted by royal law, otherwise it is solely a sin. In terms of homicide in early medieval England, both arguments seem flawed.

Homicide can be used as an example of a crime that could also be considered a sin in the early medieval period in order to demonstrate the process of jurisdiction. The prosecution of homicide functioned as a series of complex decisions made by the people involved with the 'wrong' itself within the hierarchical system of both religious and secular law. Since homicide is present

---

[29] Helmholz, "Crime, Compurgation and the Courts of the Medieval Church," 2.
[30] Helmholz, "Crime, Compurgation and the Courts of the Medieval Church," 15.
[31] Meens, *Penance in Medieval Europe, 600–1200,* 26.
[32] Lambert, "Theft, Homicide and Crime in Late Anglo-Saxon Law," 5.
[33] Lambert, "Theft, Homicide and Crime in Late Anglo-Saxon Law," 40.

in both ecclesiastical and secular law codes, homicide must be examined in terms of who was involved in the decision-making process in both sets of codes. If a murder took place in Anglo-Saxon England by an ordinary freeman against another freeman, which jurisdiction it was under, either secular or ecclesiastical, would come down to a decision by the victim's family. The victim's family may have chosen secular law to persecute the criminal under royal standards because in this case, there would be a punitive monetary outcome paid to the victim's family. This is because under ecclesiastical law, in penitential varieties, the punishment is spiritual rather than monetary; the victim's family may not feel that justice was enacted as there are no reparations made to them, only to God. The laws of Hloþhere and Eadric, written during the late seventh century, support this view as they are only concerned, "with scenarios in which one party has affronted another and ought to pay compensation."[34]

A similar situation is present in Ireland during the early medieval period in terms of how homicide was persecuted. However, according to the Old Irish laws, which originated in the seventh and eighth centuries, "The most serious offence against another person is to deprive him of his life."[35] Since homicide was considered the most serious offence in Ireland, it was primarily persecuted by secular law. The decision surrounding jurisdiction was largely a kinship or familial driven process, as it was in early medieval England. When a murderer was persecuted in early medieval Ireland, the form of "punishment" implemented was largely monetary. As Fergus Kelly explains,

> It seems that two main types of fine are normally paid to the victim's kin. The first is the fixed penalty for homicide which amounts to 7 *cumals* for every freeman, irrespective of rank...The other main fine is based on the honour-price of the victim's kin and is distributed among both his paternal and maternal kin.[36]

These two types of fines for the crime of homicide demonstrate the way secular law in Ireland was a way for the victim's families to receive reparations and for the Irish legal system to enforce their ideals of justice.

If secular law in both early medieval England and Ireland was focused on getting justice for the victim's family, as well as enforcing justice within society, ecclesiastical law, such as that found in penitentials, was focused on repairing the criminal or sinner's relationship with God. While this was

---

[34] Oliver, *The Beginnings of English Law*, 71.
[35] Kelly, *A Guide to Early Irish Law*, 125.
[36] Kelly, *A Guide to Early Irish Law*, 126.

important to the salvation of the sinner, it was also considered to be an important component of the communities' salvation as well. Rob Meens explains this almost symbiotic relationship more in detail:

> Sin was an individual matter because it affected the relation between God and the sinner, but it was also a communal one affecting the relation between God and community and sinner and community, thereby creating a triangular relationship between God, sinner and the Christian community.[37]

Even if secular law had been enforced and the murderer had paid his punitive dues, there was still this triangular relationship to take into account, which is why homicide fell under both ecclesiastical and secular jurisdiction. This theory is, however, contrary to the earlier decision-making process of the victim's family members contributing to the type of prosecution enacted. If the two law codes were not interconnected, justice would not be fully enacted in an early medieval sense. This may also be why the penance for homicide is so prevalent in all penitential varieties from this period. However, it is also possible, as Levi Roach has argued that "Anglo-Saxon law-codes show an increasing concern for the ecclesiastical well-being of the kingdom in this period, bearing witness to a new effort to craft a Christian society."[38] The way penitentials and secular law were implemented in practice is more complex in terms of homicide than the other 'wrongs' which fell under both jurisdictions due to the variation in types of homicide and the social status of the victim and perpetrator.

BIBLIOGRAPHY

Gamer, Helena M., and John T. McNeill. *Medieval Handbooks of Penance: A Translation of the Principal Libri Poenitentiales and Selections from Related Documents*. Second Octagon Printing. ed. Records of Civilization; 29. New York: Octagon Books, 1979.

Helmholz, R. H. "Crime, Compurgation and the Courts of the Medieval Church." *Law and History Review* 1, no. 1 (1983): 1–26.

———. *The Oxford History of the Laws of England: The Canon Law and Ecclesiastical Jurisdiction from 597 to the 1640s*. Oxford: Oxford University Press, 2004.

---

[37] Meens, *Penance in Medieval Europe, 600–1200*, 14.
[38] Roach, "Penance, Submission and Deditio," 346.

Jurasinski, Stefan. *The Old English Penitentials and Anglo-Saxon Law*. New York: Cambridge University Press, 2015.

Kelly, Fergus. *A Guide to Early Irish Law*. Dublin: Dublin Institute for Advanced Studies, 2005.

Lambert, Tom. *Law and Order in Anglo-Saxon England*. Oxford: Oxford University Press, 2017.

———. "Theft, Homicide and Crime in Late Anglo-Saxon Law." *Past & Present*, no. 214 (2012): 3–43.

Marafioti, Nicole. "Secular and Ecclesiastical Justice in Late Anglo-Saxon England," *Speculum* 94, no. 3 (2019): 774–805.

Meens, Rob. "The Nature and Frequency of Early Medieval Penance." *Handling Sin: Confession in the Middle Ages* (2013): 43–62.

———. "Remedies for sin." *The Cambridge History of Christianity: Volume 3 Early Medieval Christianities, c.600–c.1100* (2008): 399–415.

———. *Penance in Medieval Europe, 600–1200*. Cambridge: Cambridge University Press, 2014.

Nelson, Janet L. "Law and Its Applications." *The Cambridge History of Christianity* 3, (2008): 299–326.

Oliver, Lisi. *The Beginnings of English Law*. Buffalo: University of Toronto Press, 2002.

Pollock, Frederick, and Frederic William Maitland. *The History of English Law before the Time of Edward I*. 2nd ed. New York: Legal Classics Library, 1982.

Roach, Levi. "Penance, Submission and Deditio: Religious Influences on Dispute Settlement in Later Anglo-Saxon England (871–1066)." *Anglo-Saxon England* 41 (2012): 343–71.

Sharpe, Richard. *Life of St. Columba*. London: Penguin, 1995.

Thomson, Oliver. *A History of Sin*. Edinburgh: Canongate Press, 1993.

Tracy, Larissa. *Medieval and Early Modern Murder: Legal, Literary and Historical Contexts*. Suffolk: Boydell & Brewer, 2018.

Wormald, Patrick. *Legal Culture in the Early Medieval West: Law as Text, Image and Experience*. London: Hambledon Press, 1999.

ABOUT THE AUTHOR

Hannah Purtymun: Hannah Purtymun graduated in 2018 from Colorado State University with dual bachelor's degrees in Economics and International Studies. In 2019, she completed her master's degree in Medieval History from the University of Edinburgh and is a former president of the Late Antique and Medieval Postgraduate Society. She is currently working as a Grant Coordinator and Data Analyst for Heartland Grant Solutions in Colorado, as well as an Associate Editor for the Global Center for Religious Research. She has also been published in the *Journal of Business Diversity*.

The World's Premier Research Institute and Publishing House

JOIN THE GCRR ACADEMIC SOCIETY

And be part of tens of thousands of scholars, educators and students researching religion from around the globe.

SIGNIFICANTLY LOWER MEMBERSHIP COSTS	  	**PRIORITY PEER-REVIEW AND PUBLISHING**
FREE DIGITAL SUBSCRIPTION TO SHERM ACADEMIC JOURNAL		**PAID "RESIDENT SCHOLAR" POSITIONS AVAILABLE**

GLOBAL CENTER for RELIGIOUS RESEARCH
ACADEMIC INSTITUTE

WHERE RELIGIOUS STUDENTS, SCHOLARS AND SPECIALISTS **FLOURISH**

GCRR.ORG/JOINGCRR

Book Review:
Faith After Doubt
By Brian D. McLaren

Deena M. Lin,
California State University, East Bay

Abstract: *In* Faith After Doubt, *Brian McLaren formulates doubt as a means to enhance and enrich religious faith. In progressive fashion, doubt is reclaimed as a means to develop faith, such that believers can aim towards a greater solidarity with others and practice revolutionary love. By providing a nuanced analysis of faith, McLaren takes a phased approach where believers experience increased levels of wisdom and spiritual depth as they engage in different levels of doubt. This text may offer assistance to those who have been discouraged and fearful of entertaining doubt in their spiritual lives. Through invoking a healthy skepticism of inherited doctrines passed down by dogmatic Christianity, individuals are provided a means to further develop their faith as opposed to becoming disjointed from it. Much of this text constructs a progressive future for Christianity in an effort to ensure its relevance and continued survival. Beyond the complex analysis given to faith and doubt in this work, it is lacking a robust means to ensure that Christians will enact the revolutionary love McLaren aims to achieve. To impart such a vision of love requires practicing radical hospitality towards the most vulnerable, and believers cannot remain complicit to a toxic form of orthodoxy. Pursuing social justice aims necessitates an activist faith that critically probes dogmatic theology; and by making allowances for the faith commitments of all believers irrespective of consequence, this project remains a tepid means to further a truly progressive evolution of Christianity.*

Keywords: Faith, Doubt, Progressive Christianity, Theology, Brian McLaren

---

Religious doubt has been a thorny topic among Christian piety throughout history. According to Brian McLaren, doubt can cause much confusion for believers because it involves a kind of "double-vision or internal *division*," whereby they see through the eyes of faith and skepticism simultaneously.[1] In a religion that prides itself on creeds and doctrinal statements as a means to cultivate a solidarity of faith, doubt has been something

---
[1] McLaren, *Faith After Doubt*, 8.

which church authorities have not only shied away from but have gone further to preach about its sinful nature. *Faith After Doubt* provides a reimagining of doubt such that it may no longer be perceived as threatening to faith but, instead, can be understood as a means to strengthen and enrich the spiritual lives of believers. McLaren provides insight into various phases of faith, revealing the complexity of this notion, as well as the wisdom to be gained by those open to questioning the norms and assumptions of church doctrines and authority figures. Much can be gained by delving into this text, especially if one finds themselves disillusioned with status quo Christianity to the point where they are beginning to question ecclesiastical norms.

McLaren does not want doubt to be a source of shame among religious believers, and he entices readers to further study the practices and theologies of their congregations to ensure that their values line up with their faith commitments. To enact the revolutionary love he calls for in this text requires doubt to be a welcome component to faith for all individuals. He will argue that rather than be feared, doubt should be seen as a necessary means to question some of the policies of exclusion practiced among conservative communities. I will argue that to achieve the progressive vision of faith McLaren argues for requires doubt to be practiced among gatekeepers of toxic orthodoxy as well. In a society fraught with social disparities and divisiveness, now is not the time to employ a strategy of allowance towards those furthering these social ills. To exercise revolutionary love, Christianity must evolve out of its bystander-status, and there must be a call made to all believers, regardless of station, such that a new radical hospitality may be enacted towards the most vulnerable among us.

Faith After Doubt follows suit with much of McLaren's earlier work by primarily addressing readers who find themselves disconnected from the dogmatic mantras and conservative commitments coming out of mainline congregations in America. He is a recovering evangelical of sorts, having left the pastorate to teach with fellow progressives at the Center for Action and Contemplation. The thesis of his text further supports his liberal theological aims and is in accordance with the progressive mantras of his fellow colleagues at the Center who are doing work in a similar vein.

McLaren speaks not only to the disillusioned believer, but also those who have been so discouraged by mainline Christianity that they exiled themselves from it altogether. American congregations are facing a real existential crisis at the moment as most are experiencing dwindling numbers. According to McLaren, some individuals leave their congregations because they have begun questioning the Bible and the doctrines enforced by their church communities, others find the practices which alienate their faith community from others as no longer tenable, and some have lost trust in the institution as a whole.[2] Doubt has been experienced among folks in all these camps, and because congregations have often treated it as a threat to faith, many believers fear that they may lose their faith altogether if they give in to it. This is not a healthy coping strategy for believers; and rather than being perceived as detrimental to belief, McLaren argues that doubt may be used to probe the doctrines we have inherited, and critically challenge troubling dogma as we grow and mature in other areas of our lives.

Doubt is formulated as a precursor for transformation in our spiritual development, and McLaren argues that we can only broaden our faith through examining the underlying assumptions and doctrinal norms of ecclesial theologies and practices. Exercising self-examination in this way often makes us feel uncomfortable and alienated from others who seem content in their stage of faith development. When we experience doubt, it can feel as if we enter into a cloud of unknowing where darkness ensues because we recognize unanswered questions and different perspectives we failed to consider when we were locked into standard theological frames of recognition and intelligibility. McLaren does an excellent job detailing how doubt can make us feel like we are grieving a former self, or perhaps feel pain because we have lost a sense of belonging to the theology and faith groups we once communed with. Pain is often experienced in conjunction with growth because what we believe to be darkness is really shedding light on the unfamiliar. It is by exploring ideas we had previously been closed off to that we may gain a greater depth of faith and self-awareness.

Faith is treated with complexity in *Faith After Doubt*, and McLaren defines it as a major contributor to our sense of well-being. He states that it is "a matter of head, heart, and gut; of meaning, belonging, and survival; of intellect, intuition, and instinct. It is a whole-brain or whole-self proposal."[3] Through this lens, we can begin to understand that when doubt seeps in, the instinctive, intuitive, and intellectual aspects of our brains engage in an effort to return us to our place of intellectual comfort and security. There are many contributing factors that cause us to feel that the belief systems we have grown up with are true to who we are, and this stems from the fact that they have served as a major apparatus for meaning-making and a sense of belonging. When we start to question the assumptions and institutions that have been integral to our worldview, our instincts emerge to self-correct us into submission in an effort

---

[2] McLaren, *Faith After Doubt*, xv.
[3] McLaren, *Faith After Doubt*, 17.

to ensure our survival.[4] For these reasons, doubt can cause a real feeling of existential angst for us, where we may feel like we could lose everything—or everyone—if we allow it to take over. Posing a critical lens on the status quo of religion can cause some believers to experience a sense of panic and enter into crisis-mode when they begin to evaluate their inherited doctrines and belief systems. Doubting with vigor presses one to entertain alternative intellectual paradigms; and by doing so, we can feel a sense of alienation among our faith communities. Certainly, throughout the history of Christianity, those who have voiced their concerns with existing theological perspectives and practices have often been shunned or labeled heretical for bravely questioning orthodoxy. Doubt should not be defined as a means to deteriorate faith, and McLaren wants believers and gatekeepers alike to recognize it as an integral means to replenish faith commitments, such that Christianity may evolve into the future.

       Doubt functions as an apparatus for transforming faith in this text where faith may develop to phases beyond simply adhering to creeds or belief statements. If severed from doubt, the faith one adheres to is characterized by simply remaining loyal to the prescribed rules of status quo orthodoxy without question. McLaren provides an understanding of faith as manifested in stages which individuals experience as they enter into heightened levels of doubt. Crises of faith are required in order for one to expand in their spiritual commitments. These moments push us beyond our expectations so that we may entertain possibilities we failed to consider in a prior stage. One may see faith development as akin to how trees grow. To grow requires building on a previous layer such that more complex faith commitments may be given more spaciousness and have room to expand. McLaren describes that every new stage in the faith process "feels like a step up, because developmentally, at least, it is."[5] In order to enter a new phase of faith, one must critically engage with the accepted norms in their current stage. It is natural for one to feel disillusioned or stressed in this process because—perhaps for the first time—they are feeling squeezed by the limitations of status quo faith.

       Engaging with novelty can incite believers to probe inherited norms such that they may transition into a new phase of faith. McLaren elucidates four stages of faith, which increase in depth and complexity as one enters a new level of development. Most Christians are in Stage One, where simplicity is emphasized and believers focus on dualistic notions of right and wrong, invoking an us-versus-them attitude. When one finds fault with this level of

---

[4] McLaren, *Faith After Doubt,* 17.
[5] McLaren, *Faith After Doubt,* 60.

faith, such that they critically engage with its simplistic dogma in order to invoke a more complex faith, this is when individuals enter the second stage. This next level is one of independence, where one comes to recognize that Stage One faith is one version, but that need not be the only modality of faith. Stage Two faith sees faith with more nuance, where it is based on certain presuppositions which do not have to be universally accepted. Many believers find Stage Two an acceptable stopping point for their faith, but there are some who exercise their analytical minds even further, and embrace an even greater perplexity.

An individual enters Stage Three when they are suspicious of all institutions and authority figures, even those with a more complex faith at the second stage. When in Stage Three, believers are constantly expecting the worst when it comes to community organizations or religious institutions because they are fully aware of the ways that these enterprises can further social injustice. At this stage, one understands that truth is relative and largely based on self-interest. As such, they must remain critical of the policies and practices of religious authorities to reveal any inherent assumptions that may continue marginalizing the most vulnerable. McLaren mentions that the danger of Stage Three faith is that such a level of skepticism lends individuals to being averse to religious communities in general, and it can lead them to give up their faith altogether or regress back to an earlier stage in an effort to gain a sense of belonging, which is a human need we all have. An alternative to these two courses of action is possible, and this involves one traversing beyond constant skepticism.

It seems that McLaren is hoping that Stage Four may be the means by which Christianity may survive its current challenges. Transitioning to the last phase of faith requires an individual to be comfortable with contradiction and paradox, and they pause the constant probing of norms that was practiced in Stage Three. Stage Four involves exercising humility, such that one may begin to recognize that skepticism alone cannot provide them with any real sense of fulfillment or spiritual belonging. Progressing beyond Stage Three requires one to embrace the notion that mystery will always be present in some form. Taking guidance from the mystics, individuals in the fourth stage practice contemplative, non-dualistic awareness and exercise a faith beyond making righteous judgements to invoke "non-discriminatory, revolutionary love."[6] In this final stage doubt becomes a means by which individuals may exist in greater solidarity with our fellow beings, whether they be human or otherwise,

---

[6] McLaren, *Faith After Doubt*, 101.

and practice radical hospitality towards the stranger, as Christ did in his own time.

Throughout his phased approach to faith development, McLaren encourages believers to interpret doubt as necessary for one to deepen and enrich their spiritual lives. Such an understanding of faith as strengthened and reinvigorated by doubt is a refreshing change of pace for Christians. I believe many questioning souls may find his thesis comforting in our current context. To take such a positive spin on what has been fearfully misinterpreted as dangerous is welcome among the ever-increasing number of Christians who have become disheartened by their faith communities. Such feelings of disillusionment are understandable given the practices enacted by many conservative congregations to support political demagogues and their policies of exclusion. McLaren's emphasis on radical love may allow for Christians of this advanced faith to be more aligned with Christ-centered theologies, which is something many progressives will definitely be in support of.

The first nine chapters of the book offers much depth and nuance to the concepts of faith and doubt. McLaren's Christianity is not a religion that simply clings to dogmatic belief, which some may argue is fed by implicit bias, but can be reimagined as imparting faith as akin to a working hypothesis. Perhaps engaging greater doubt in this way is a nod to how William James envisioned it in "The Will to Believe."[7] McLaren admits in Chapter Nine that his phased analysis of faith may make some Christians uncomfortable and stresses that one need not fear if this is the case. He claims that his accounting of faith should not be deemed rigid or judgmental because these stages are best understood as a "general pattern" of faith and nothing more.[8] Even though McLaren takes a developmental approach to faith in the prior chapters of his text, it is a bit disappointing that he does not advocate for Stage Four faith as a goal for all Christians. This is because the aim of Stage Four is harmony (with individuals in other phases of faith), and it also includes Stage Three skepticism, which recognizes how dogmas become supported and systematized such that social injustice often follows.

In an effort to remain in solidarity with earlier-stage believers, McLaren shies away from wholeheartedly claiming Stage Four as a much-needed call for constructive change in American Christianity. Taking such a muted position

---

[7] McLaren's phased approach to faith in this text is quite different from James, but the notion that one must work out one's faith through being informed by their life experiences certainly resonates with the themes imparted in this work. See James, "The Will to Believe," 584–585.

[8] McLaren, *Faith After Doubt,* 106.

late in the text is strange given so much of it defines doubt as beneficial because it develops faith beyond mere simplicity and dualistic right-versus-wrong thinking. Doubt functions as a means to enrich faith, to reach new levels of depth and complexity. To suggest that Stage Four faith should not reign supreme, or to be fearful of characterizing early-stage believers as lacking critical self-reflection, really does his project a disservice.

McLaren argues that individuals in Stage One and Stage Two are limited in scope because they are too involved in us-versus-them dichotomies and defending their beliefs. In such early phases individuals are not concerned about welcoming a plurality of perspectives. Such believers are content to confine religion to indoctrinated systems of belief and antiquated institutional regimes, which have so often been used to fortify sexist, homophobic, racist, and xenophobic apparatuses of legitimacy. Of course, this is not to say that first and second stage believers are necessarily beholden to hostile orthodoxies, but McLaren certainly claims that believers who do not doubt are also those who fail to critically examine the religious, economic, and political norms of their church communities. Importantly, individuals must be open to examining the policies legitimized by dominant orthodoxy in order to enter into later stages of faith. By practicing such reflection on status-quo practices within their congregations, later stage believers are also those who are more aware of how churches can become servants to—and perpetuators of—the privileged.

Christian privilege has been viewed by many postmodern scholars to appear as a metanarrative that keeps white, heteronormative, cis men empowered. The benefit of advancing Stage Four faith as a goal for all believers is that it is a faith requiring critical Stage Three faith as integral to spiritual wellness. It is quite clear that not all Christians or theologies are healthy to adhere to; in fact, the reasons why so many are leaving the church is because of the heavy levels of toxicity latent within them. Christianity may have a healthy future if practitioners are brave enough to call out existing imbalances of power and seek to remedy them. McLaren provides a few examples of progressive communities who are doing this work as beacons of hope because they are willing to call out injustices of the past and present. It only makes sense for him to encourage his readers towards embarking in a more developed faith that is not afraid to call out problematic theologies as failing to impart the core Christian tenant of "revolutionary love."

In the Afterword, McLaren states again that Stage Four spirituality should not be understood as the best version or end goal of faith. He tells a story about his parents and others in older generations who remain content with doubting less and living within early-stage faith. Those wishing to stay in these zones of earlier faith should not be judged. Perhaps he does this out of fear that making a bolder stance would further divide progressives and conservatives, but such reluctance on his part is unfortunate. Throughout his phased approach, McLaren expands on the previous stages to enact a more enriching faith. Traditionalists may continue believing doubt and criticism to be a source of shame or deterioration of faith, but McLaren should remain consistent with the bulk of this project and boldly declare that early-stage faith is unhealthy.

The danger of making allowances for simplistic faith is that Christians will continue their sheep-like loyalty to theologies that may be oppressive towards marginalized communities. As McLaren argues, doubt is integral to spiritual health such that a greater solidarity with the most vulnerable may be enacted. Indeed, this is what it means to enact the revolutionary love he calls for in his work. Progressive Christianity requires a redefining of faith where it needs to engage with doubt. It also requires an activist element where Christians are compelled to call out unjust practices of the old guard that are detrimental to the future of religious faith, if not human life and the existence of the planet.

Prizing solidarity and harmony with others is a constructive aim for religion, but welcoming all types in an effort to remain impartial to the variety of faith that exists threatens the overall viability of the revolutionary love McLaren is aiming towards. As mentioned in his text, those who abide in Stage One faith are the same Christians who preserve theologies of exclusion and are out to enforce binaries that uphold one race, nation, gender, sexual orientation, or religion as more holy or akin to God's will than others. Certainly not all congregations advocate violence or a dismissal of those who do not adhere to their rules, but it cannot be denied that some do condone it either on a physical, psychological, or political level. It would be nice to see McLaren adhere to progressive values throughout. The consequence of allowing places of slippage under the guise of solidarity with all believers unfortunately welcomes toxic dogma back into the fold.

When describing the contemplative element of Stage Four faith, McLaren claims that it is not just praying and meditating on God's word, but it also requires active engagement in the world where one makes efforts to stop wrongdoing and further social justice. When defining the notion of revolutionary love, he utilizes Scripture, and this should also be presented as a means to take a deeper bite into gatekeepers who are dissuading their congregants to embrace a similar vision. Much of the book attempts to provide a revolutionary direction to Christianity so that it may progress towards a Stage Four faith that is about harmony and social justice. By not incorporating an activist element in his text, McLaren unfortunately may inadvertently remain complicit to toxic Christianity. There is so much in this text that could provide a critical apparatus whereby believers may be encouraged to move beyond early-stage dogmatic belief. In leaving out a full disclosure of how faith goes awry in tangible ways, many Christians may continue to support toxic leaders and ideologies that are not aligned with Christ's message. Such inaction leaves his project too abstract to further compassion where it is very much needed.

There is much complexity given to the concepts of doubt and faith in *Faith After Doubt*. By failing to want Stage Four faith and his vision of revolutionary love to reign supreme, as a vision for all Christians to aspire towards, McLaren's vision potentially lands flat. It is not enough to redefine faith and show how it can develop if we allow doubt and greater intellectual humility to enter in. A progressive faith must also call out the harmful practices of early-stage believers and gatekeepers of toxic orthodoxy. If we continue to make allowances for any version of Christianity, regardless of the injustice it gives credence to, such complicity makes us passively supportive of its supremacy. As McLaren mentions, quoting Richard Rohr, now is the time to "reorder" Christianity and free it from its chains to power (as opposed to love and care).[9] When we fail to speak to the specific troubles Christianity is facing, and what causes individuals to doubt to the point where they give up their faith altogether, this further allows religious authorities and their congregants to continue sitting on thrones of privilege with their boots on the necks of the most vulnerable.

---

[9] See McLaren, *Faith After Doubt*, 161.

BIBLIOGRAPHY

James, William. "The Will to Believe." In *Philosophy of Religion: An Anthology.* 7th ed, edited by Michael Rea and Louis P. Pojman. 578–587. Stamford, CT: Cengage, 2015.

McLaren, Brian D. *Faith After Doubt: Why Your Beliefs Stopped Working and What to Do About It.* New York, NY: St. Martins, 2021.

ABOUT THE AUTHOR

Deena M. Lin is a lecturer in philosophy and religious studies at California State University, East Bay and San Francisco State University, where she teaches courses in comparative religion and philosophy. She received her Ph.D. in Philosophy of Religion and Theology from Claremont Graduate University, and her research interests are in philosophical theology, poststructuralist thought, mystical theology, and identity politics. She co-edited *Butler on Whitehead: On the Occasion* with Roland Faber and Michael Halewood (Lexington Books, 2012). She has also published various articles and chapters in edited volumes on Judith Butler, Alfred North Whitehead, Rosi Braidotti, and others in the areas of philosophy, philosophy of religion, and theology.

MORE FROM THE AUTHOR

Butler on Whitehead: On the Occasion
Lexington Books, 2012

Whitehead and Continental Philosophy in the Twenty-First Century
Lexington Books, 2019

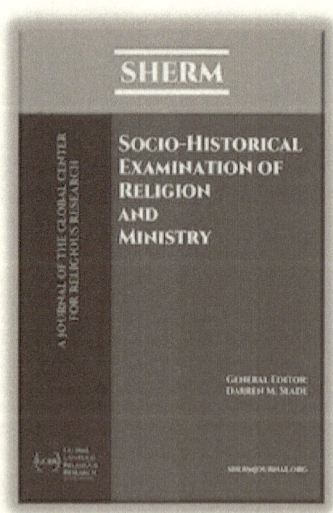

BIBLIOGRAPHY

James, William. "The Will to Believe." In *Philosophy of Religion: An Anthology*. 7th ed, edited by Michael Rea and Louis P. Pojman. 578–587. Stamford, CT: Cengage, 2015.

McLaren, Brian D. *Faith After Doubt: Why Your Beliefs Stopped Working and What to Do About It*. New York, NY: St. Martins, 2021.

ABOUT THE AUTHOR

Deena M. Lin is a lecturer in philosophy and religious studies at California State University, East Bay and San Francisco State University, where she teaches courses in comparative religion and philosophy. She received her Ph.D. in Philosophy of Religion and Theology from Claremont Graduate University, and her research interests are in philosophical theology, poststructuralist thought, mystical theology, and identity politics. She co-edited *Butler on Whitehead: On the Occasion* with Roland Faber and Michael Halewood (Lexington Books, 2012). She has also published various articles and chapters in edited volumes on Judith Butler, Alfred North Whitehead, Rosi Braidotti, and others in the areas of philosophy, philosophy of religion, and theology.

MORE FROM THE AUTHOR

Butler on Whitehead: On the Occasion
Lexington Books, 2012

Whitehead and Continental Philosophy in the Twenty-First Century
Lexington Books, 2019

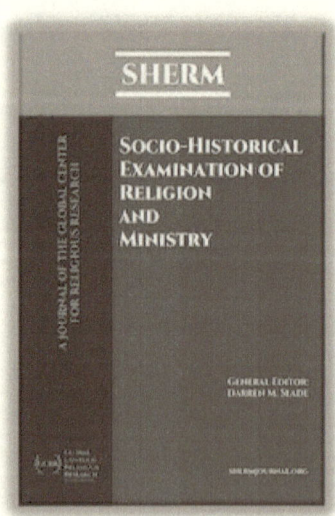

Book Review:
The Date of the Muratorian Fragment
By John F. Lingelbach

Lucy C. Bajjani,
Lebanese American University

Abstract: *This book seeks to put an end to the debate concerning the date of production of the Muratorian Fragment by applying the second phase of the Inference to the Best Explanation method. The author presents extensive research on the debates, a clear methodology, and his own conclusions on the subject. This is a book mainly about New Testament canons and church authority, but also church history and historiography.*

Keywords: Muratorian Fragment, Early Church History, New Testament Canon, Inference to the Best Explanation, Historiography

---

John Lingelbach's work is a comprehensive study on the date of composition of the Muratorian Fragment. The author presents the reader with a scholarly work, which exposes the debates around two hypotheses: The first places the Fragment's production in the late second to early third century (Early Hypothesis), and the second places it in the fourth century (Late Hypothesis).[1]

The Muratorian Fragment was discovered and first published in the eighteenth century by Ludovico Antonio Muratori. It was found in a fragmentary state, missing the beginning "and probably the end."[2] The piece includes a portion of what is believed to be the Gospel of Mark, the Gospels of Luke and John, the Acts of the Apostles, the Wisdom of Solomon, and the Shepherd of Hermas. It bears no indication of authorship or place of composition and, since its finding, was generally accepted to be a late second or early third century product. It was not until the second half of the twentieth century that, based on Albert Sunberg's claims that the Fragment was composed in the fourth century, the date was subject to debate. Although many scholars

---

[1] As per the definitions proposed by Lingelbach, *The Date of the Muratorian Fragment*, 22.

[2] Schnabel, *The Muratorian Fragment*, 231.

maintained that the evidence suggests a second century composition, Sundberg was joined by Geoffrey Hahneman, who "brought several new reasons to the debate,"[3] and Clare Rothschild, who "argued that the Fragment is a fictional piece, written in the fourth century in an attempt to link the standards of canonicity back to the second century by pretending to have been written then."[4] Knowing the date of composition of the Fragment is important since it "narrows the list of possible authors and thus lends to the ultimate desired outcome: that of understanding the early church's New Testament canon and theological authority."[5]

Lingelbach's work has a clear purpose: through the application of phase two of an Inference to the Best Explanation (IBE) method, the author intends to put an end to the debate. He states that scholars have, so far, engaged in abductive reasoning while attempting to determine the date, but they have not weighed all the evidence to decide which is best. If the author's purpose seems ambitious, his extensive research, detailed analysis of the Fragment, and weighing of the hypotheses are efficient in persuading the reader. In addition to this exhaustive research, Lingelbach succeeds in engaging the reader through the organization of his book: clear presentation of the research question, delimitations, and methodology. Moreover, each chapter begins with a brief review of what was exposed in the previous chapter and an introduction of what is to follow, as well as finishes with a summary of the discussion that provides a much-needed structure for such a long and detailed debate.

The first three chapters offer "a general overview of the Fragment and some of its problems, a list of the evidence which scholars cite while attempting to determine the date of its composition, and a description of each of the two hypotheses."[6] Chapter One, entitled "The Muratorian Fragment," describes the codex where the Fragment was found and the Fragment itself; it also recounts the history of its discovery. The same chapter also offers an account of the Fragment's contents and an overview on the questions of authorship, provenance, and language, all important elements for the debate. Lingelbach clearly states that such problems are dealt with in relation to the date question and that he has no intention to settle any of them. The chapter also provides a transcription of the original Latin text, a "restored" version, and an English translation (by Bruce Metzger). These appear as appendices at the end of the book. Additionally, Lingelbach writes about the intentions of the Fragmentist,

---

[3] Lingelbach, *The Date of the Muratorian Fragment*, 3.
[4] Lingelbach, *The Date of the Muratorian Fragment*, 4.
[5] Lingelbach, *The Date of the Muratorian Fragment*, 39.
[6] Lingelbach, *The Date of the Muratorian Fragment*, 97.

who "appears primarily interested in demonstrating [the Gospels] historical value," and in emphasizing the Epistles' universal applicability.[7]

Chapters Two ("A Date: The Evidence") and Three ("A Date: The Hypotheses") are extensive exposés of historiography and the different source critics. Lingelbach presents and analyzes all the evidence of the Fragment: the accepted and rejected texts, their order of presentation, possible context of production, and a discussion on the possibility of determining the date through the expressions found in the Fragment.

Having introduced the reader to the Fragment, debates, and arguments, Lingelbach, in Chapter Four, meticulously weighs the hypotheses based on the five Harman-McCullagh criteria of *plausibility, explanatory scope, explanatory power, credibility,* and *simplicity*. This method has not been applied before, according to the author: "To date, no scholar has weighed the merits of the two hypotheses regarding the Fragment's date in a deliberately and rigorously conducted 'Lipton Stage Two scenario.'"[8] Finally, in Chapter Five ("Chronological Fiction Argument"), he records and refutes the possibility that "writing in the fourth century, [the Fragmentist] deliberately made his manuscript appear to have been written early."[9]

The Date of the Muratorian Fragment is an important contribution to the history of the church, canon, and authority. It places itself in the intersection between historiography, source criticism, patristics, and history of the New Testament. It is a must-read for academics, as well as members of the general public interested in the history and developments of early Christianity.

---

[7] Lingelbach, *The Date of the Muratorian Fragment*, 37.
[8] Lingelbach, *The Date of the Muratorian Fragment*, 24.
[9] Lingelbach, *The Date of the Muratorian Fragment*, 122.

BIBLIOGRAPHY

Lingelbach, John. *The Date of the Muratorian Fragment.* Denver, CO: GCRR Press, 2020.

Schnabel, Echkard. "The Muratorian Fragment: The State of Research." *Journal of the Evangelical Theological Society* 57, no. 2 (2014): 231-64.

ABOUT THE AUTHOR

Lucy Bajjani is currently a lecturer at the Lebanese American University and has a PhD from the University of São Paulo. Bajjani specializes in the relationship between Eastern Romans, Carolingians, and the papacy through their debates on holy images. Her main areas of research are church history, the iconoclastic struggles of the eight century, and the history of religions.

The World's Premier Research Institute and Publishing House

JOIN THE GCRR ACADEMIC SOCIETY

And be part of tens of thousands of scholars, educators and students researching religion from around the globe.

SIGNIFICANTLY LOWER MEMBERSHIP COSTS

PRIORITY PEER-REVIEW AND PUBLISHING

FREE DIGITAL SUBSCRIPTION TO SHERM ACADEMIC JOURNAL

PAID "RESIDENT SCHOLAR" POSITIONS AVAILABLE

GCRR — GLOBAL CENTER for RELIGIOUS RESEARCH
ACADEMIC INSTITUTE

WHERE RELIGIOUS STUDENTS, SCHOLARS AND SPECIALISTS FLOURISH

GCRR.ORG/JOINGCRR

www.ingramcontent.com/pod-product-compliance
Lightning Source LLC
Chambersburg PA
CBHW020905080526
44589CB00011B/459